THE LIFE CYCLE OF GROUPS

Group Developmental Stage Theory

Roy B. Lacoursiere, M.D.

*Veterans Administration Medical Center,
Washburn University Law School,
Menninger School of Psychiatry,
Topeka, Kansas*

HUMAN SCIENCES PRESS
72 Fifth Avenue   3 Henrietta Street
NEW YORK, NY 10011 ● LONDON, WC2E 8LU

Printed in the United States of America
012345678   987654321

Library of Congress Cataloging in Publication Data

Lacoursiere, Roy B
    The life cycle of groups.

    Includes index.   1. Small groups.   2. Social groups.   3. Morale.
I. Title.
HM133.I28   302.3'4   LC79-27112
ISBN 0-87705-469-X

This book is dedicated to each of us who struggles with developmental stages and the related morale in groups and other experiences, whether as a leader, participant, or student of these phenomena. Keep up your spirits!

CONTENTS

LIST OF TABLES

11

LIST OF FIGURES

PREFACE

Have you noticed at the beginning of a new experience—a job, for example, or a learning or group experience—that you have been looking forward to the experience and are eager and pleased to be starting? And then have you later noticed that the same experience may seem unstimulating, or worse, almost intolerable? Perhaps you have also noted that when certain such experiences are about to stop, you feel that you will miss something, that there will be an empty place in your life. Additionally, it may seem that if the experience is shared by several people, many, or all, have reactions similar to yours.

These reactions occur so frequently that one can easily conclude that individuals and groups often go through an orderly sequence of feelings, reactions, hopes, and frustrations during the course of their experience. These changes are described as the developmental stages of orientation, dissatisfaction, resolution, production, and termination. These developmental stages can also be used to describe the systematic fluctuations in morale during the experience, and these changes in morale describe a morale curve.

The material to support these ideas comes from a wide data base, most particularly group studies. In groups these stages are both facilitated and appear in concentrated form in several individuals, and so they are more noticeable. These studies include reports on training or "T" groups, problem-solving groups, psychotherapy groups, and encounter groups, but they also include many types of groups in more natural settings, such as learning groups, committees, and work teams. Data are also used from miscellaneous studies dealing with such behavior as moving one's residence and rebellions. In turn, applications of this material are considered for group settings, but also for individual, organizational, and sociopolitical contexts.

This book should therefore hold interest for students of any of these areas, and it may well have something to offer to all who are participants in such settings. This includes most people, for few are free of experiences governed by these developmental stages and the associated changes in morale. Is "being in love" an example? How about Carter's presidency?

These developmental stages and the relationship between stages will be described first, then the concept of morale and its relationship to the developmental stages will be discussed. The hard data for these group and general developmental stages (GDSs for short) will be considered, especially in one chapter examining research questions and issues that face workers in this field, and in another chapter reviewing relevant research. A GDS theory will be proposed, and a psychological understanding of GDSs will be offered. A chapter will look at how this information can be used to help groups and individuals throughout these stages of orientation, dissatisfaction, resolution, production, and termination. A final chapter will take up some loose ends.

THANKS

I am very thankful for the help of various kinds that I received in writing this book. My teachers and colleagues at the Veterans Administration Medical Center, Menninger Foundation, and Washburn University Law School helped seed the soil from which this writing grew. P. Jeannie Kleinhammer, PhD, provided needed and appreciated moral (really "morale") support and assistance in numerous discussions. She and other friends kindly read all or parts of the manuscript. These readers were Howard Baumgartel, PhD, of the University of Kansas; Robert Cancro, MD, DMS, of New York University; Tom Dolgoff, MSE, of the Menninger Foundation; and Donald B. Rinsley, MD, primarily of the Topeka Veterans Administration Medical Center. Of course, the responsibility for the final product is my own.

Nancy Vaughn and other librarians at the Topeka Veterans Administration and Menninger Foundation libraries were repeatedly and graciously helpful in tracking down references, and Bernie Schmidt was equally helpful in making hundreds of trips to the VA library to pick up and return materials. My thanks to several typists, most particularly Genny Nyman and Patty Delaney, who completed the final typescript. Lastly, a special thanks to Human Sciences Press and Norma Fox, their editor-in-chief, for publishing my work.

Chapter 1

INTRODUCTION:

Group and General Developmental Stages (GDSs)

What feelings and reactions do the following people have in common? Executives in a one-week seminar on understanding human behavior, law students during a semester of legal internship, participants in a training group experience, psychiatric residents in a three-year training program, undergraduate students going through college, members of a government advisory committee, members of a psychotherapy group, and maybe people "in love"? Studying people in these situations reveals strikingly that they go through considerably similar stages or phases.

People in each of these situations generally start with a period of assessment or *orientation* to the experience, with some concerns over what it is all about but with positive expectations that something good will come of it. Almost invariably, after some period of time, the realities of the situation—the difficulties of learning and applying learning to actual external situations, the degree of acceptance of the committee's advice, the difficulties of psychotherapy, the foibles of the loved one—force themselves upon a person, and reality almost never lives up to the person's hopes and fantasies. This "encounter with reality" is usually a disappointing confrontation bringing about frustration, *dissatisfaction,* often anger, and sometimes a sense of discouragement or depression. The person's enthusiasm and morale fall, sometime precipitously.

If the individual or group is to persevere in the situation and profit from it—learn what one is trying to learn, present appropriate advice in an acceptable form, improve one's mental distress, grow in the love relationship—there must be a *resolution* of this stage or phase of frustration and dissatisfaction. Then the individual will reach a more productive period or stage of *production,* in which he or she achieves what is considered a decent level of return—in learning, work, or mutuality —and in which greater enthusiasm and morale are restored. This improved stage of learning and working with less frustration and dissatisfaction can then continue, often with milder fluctuations, until the end of the experience is approached.

As this end is approached, and reached, the person has certain feelings about *termination.* Usually there is some sense of loss, and possibly sadness, over the end or anticipated end of a favorable experience. Often there is also a positive feeling from having accomplished something worthwhile, but sometimes the positive feeling of accomplishment covers up experiencing what is being lost. For example, the elation of completing college may cover up the loss of college friends, a certain carefree life, and so on. Instead of a visible sense of loss there may be one of denial and of otherwise covering up the sadness. The denial may go all the way to pseudoeuphoria, and this or more subtle denial may alternate with a sense of loss and sadness.

Most of the more rigorous data to substantiate the above stages comes from research on the stages of development of groups during their life cycle. Several of these studies will be examined here, some in detail. Data will also be cited from more anecdotal and descriptive reports on the development of groups and from various other areas. Psychotherapy groups, training or T groups, and other types of groups provide a context in which these stages can be observed in a concentrated way. In fact, group settings enhance the development of these stages by decreasing defensiveness and fostering the expressing of feelings, hopes, and so on.

Although isolated individuals can show these stages, it is often only when the stages have been seen repeatedly in many individuals in the same or in a similar context that they are apt to be noticed, for example, by someone repeatedly observing new teachers or new mental health or alcoholism counselors. And observing these stages in a group context makes it easier to see them in individuals, particularly when one considers where a person is in the sequence of his or her experience, that is, near the beginning or middle or end of the life cycle of a therapy group, job, or educational program.

From the initial examples (executives in a seminar, members in a training group, legal interns, psychiatric residents, college students, committee members, group psychotherapy participants, people "in love"), it can be seen that the word "group" is used in different ways, from its usual sense of a collection of individuals together for a common purpose, to a sense approximating a class of individuals, for example, the class of individuals who are college students or who are "in love." More will be said about this in later chapters, but the use of the word *group* will usually be clear from the context, and when necessary this will be made explicit. In fact, most of the research and of the anecdotal data on developmental stages that we look at first will be on groups as usually defined, that is, as actual collections of individuals with a shared task. Accordingly, the phrase *group developmental stage or stages* will be used.

Later we will turn to situations in which the developmental stages are those of a class of individuals—a "conceptual" group —as they go through a new experience, such as moving, a new job, or psychiatric treatment. One can still think in terms of *group* developmental stages here, and this helps retain the connection with the most certain data base, but sometimes it will appear more reasonable to think in terms of *general* developmental stages. This phrase will seem particularly appropriate when the focus is largely on individual data and applications of these developmental stages.

Both the phrases *group developmental stage or stages* and *general developmental stage or stages* can be designated by the abbreviation GDS or GDSs, read as group developmental stage or stages or general developmental stage or stages, as the context requires. This abbreviation will be used to refer specifically to the concept of the developmental stages presented in this book. It is less cumbersome than repeatedly writing one or both of the longer designated phrases, and helps provide continuity to the range of contexts in which these developmental stages are found and can be used. But, to reiterate, it is in groups as they are usually considered that these developmental stages are most consistently found, and such groups provide conditions that can enhance their occurrence.

It is appropriate that much of the data base for GDSs should come from groups as usually considered since it is frequently in these settings that this material can be used to help morale and enthusiasm, and often to improve work on the task, whatever it may be. By helping with the initial enthusiasm in the orientation stage, we can help people keep their expectations from being so extravagant that they achieve few realistic goals. By helping with the sense of frustration in the dissatisfaction stage, we can help neutralize some of the negative feelings so that people can more fruitfully attend to the task. And by helping a group or individual with the termination experience, we can assist them so that the sense of loss does not get in the way of their completing the task or evaluating what has been accomplished. (There will be detailed discussion later of these applications and references thereto, but here are some preliminary ones: For the orientation stage see Wanous, 1973, regarding new jobs, and Owen, 1976(a), in foreign relations; for orientation and other stages see Gazda, 1975, and Hill, 1974, for counselling and therapy groups, and Lacoursiere, 1974, for learning groups.)

The proposed GDSs assume an "average expectable environment" (Hartmann, 1958), and when this environment does not exist the sequence of developmental stages discussed here may well not occur, or may take some considerable assistance to bring about. Much more will be said later about this "average expectable environment" for GDSs but, for example, if a task is put forth that is too vaguely specified, or almost impossible to do, and if on top of this unrealistic expectations are initially established, then a group or individual may not move beyond dissatisfaction, which may be rather exaggerated. Under these conditions, if circumstances continue to foster unrealistic expectations, and if those responsible for defining the task fail to clarify it and make it achievable, then one's personal experience may be very unsatisfying, or one's skills in GDS consultation work may be sorely tested and the dissatisfaction stage scarcely resolvable. An illustration from my work follows—a comparable example dealing with the staff and patients of wards for the terminally ill is Reynolds & Kalish (1974).

Such an almost impossible situation occurred in group consultation work with the staff of a four-ward unit for chronically and seriously ill psychiatric patients in a Veterans Administration Hospital. The previously closed building had been reopened two years earlier for patients who had not responded to treatment elsewhere. Their average hospital stay was over ten years, and many of them had organic brain syndromes besides other psychiatric diagnoses. The staff had been recruited partly on the basis of being given an opportunity to work slowly and diligently with patients in need of careful attention so that they could make therapeutic progress. These were the explicit expectations of the staff group (part of their expectations in the orientation stage), but there were many problems, and many other messages to them. In the first place, the goal in terms of treatment progress was considerably unrealistic other than in rather limited terms such as long-term nursing or foster home placement for almost all of these patients. Additionally, the wards had a lack of consistent medical and psychiatric leadership and staff, some staff began to be assigned there for apparently disciplinary reasons, and there were complaints from the hospital administration because patients were being moved out of the hospital too slowly. In this context, without clarification of the goals, and realistic ones, and without adequate means to carry out the task, such a staff group can and did remain in a stage of chronic dissatisfaction and poor morale.

Care must be exercised not to forget that there can be significant individual differences in these developmental stages; some individuals may not experience them the same way others do. In a group that otherwise follows the expected course of development, one or more members may not do so in the same way that the rest of the group does. So, in helping this group with its developmental stages, it may be necessary to assist those in the group who are exceptions to the usual developmental process.

For example, certain individuals may be frustrated and have low morale right from the start of a group experience because they do not particularly want to be there but feel forced, because they are especially uncomfortable in groups, and so on. Or conversely, certain individuals may not experience much or any of a dissatisfaction stage for a variety of reasons, such as very low expectations in the first place, or ease in acquiring the skills to succeed in the task.

There will necessarily be much about groups that will be omitted or only sampled, not because it is unimportant to the developmental stages of groups, but because it is not central to the thesis of this book. For example, more democratic as opposed to more authoritarian group leaders in discussion or work groups may make participation in the group and the task more congenial so that there is less of a dissatisfaction stage in democratically led groups of these types (Anderson, 1959; Lewin, Lippitt & White, 1939; and Rosenbaum & Rosenbaum,

1971; these references will be returned to). Similarly, when doing the task adequately requires a concerted group effort, it is obvious that conditions have to be structured to allow the group to work together. For general information on groups the reader is referred to standard references, and many of these data are necessary for adequate work with group developmental stages. (See, for example, in general group dynamics, Cartwright & Zander, 1960; in group psychotherapy, Yalom, 1975; and in industrial relations, Argyle, 1972.)

STAGES, PHASES, OR TRENDS?

Are these developmental stages, phases, or trends? Each of these terms is used by various students of this area, for example, stages by Tuckman (1965) and Runkel et al. (1971); phases by Bales and Strodtbeck (1951), Braaten (1974–1975), Dunphy (1968), and Kaplan and Roman (1963); and trends by Cooper and Mangham (1971), and Heinicke and Bales (1953). There are differences in emphasis in what some of these authors are describing, but in general they are similar enough to allow us to use a common term. The dictionary of psychological terms of English and English (1958) offers some help: A stage is "a presumably natural or nonarbitrary division of a changing process"; a phase is "a recurrent state in something that exhibits a series of changes; for example, the several phases of the moon"; and a trend is "the direction manifested in a series of events; a dynamic tendency or inclination to behave in a given way or in a certain direction" (pp. 520, 386, 564).

For our purposes *stage* seems the best choice, since the developmental process being discussed has largely natural divisions, but this is not meant to give the impression that these stages are completely separate from each other, or that, once passed, those particular aspects of the process are completely gone. The group and general developmental process is a living growth process in which vestiges of earlier stages can be seen in later stages, and hints of later stages seen earlier. This idea is illustrated in Figure 1.1.

Phase denotes too much of an idea of recurrence for our purposes, although later, when we discuss the developmental stage process in successive experiences, we will see that these stages recur under these conditions. *Trend* connotes too weak a change process. Anyone who has observed GDS processes or experienced them—and we all have—will realize that these are often strongly felt and highly visible experiences and not merely trends. So, for the sake of continuity, the word *stage* will usually be used even when referring to studies that use other terms, unless such a substitution would distort the meaning.

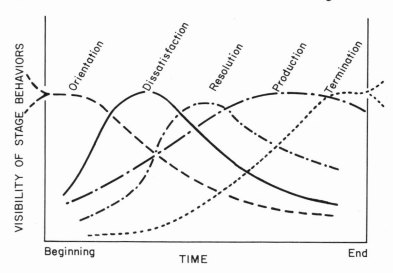

FIGURE 1.1.   SCHEMATIZATION OF THE TEMPORAL LIMITS OF EACH GDS. This figure shows the approximate limits of each GDS during the life cycle of the experience. It shows that characteristics of each stage are also seen in other stages, though less obviously, and that in the participants some of these behaviors spread beyond the formal temporal boundaries of the experience.

Group and General Developmental Stages:
An Overview

A more detailed overview of these stages will now be presented to serve as a framework with which to approach much
of the book, including the more rigorous research data, and to
see to what extent it supports such a sequence of stages. An
alternative approach would be to examine the "harder" research data first to see what emerges, but to a naive examiner
these data appear so diverse that a solid framework is required
to avoid getting lost or hopelessly entangled in details. This is
an arbitrary emphasis because, to a large extent, the framework
to be presented draws upon conclusions from considerable anecdotal data and research data in the first place. This overview
will emphasize actual group contexts (group developmental
stages), with more emphasis on conceptual groups (general
developmental stages) later. The overview will fit many group
situations under average circumstances; some variations from
the usual GDSs and the effects of different actual group types
will be discussed later.

Most groups and the individuals in them can be considered
as going through a sequence of developmental stages during the
group history or life cycle. These stages—like most psychological and social processes—blend into each other to some extent
so that where one divides one stage from the others, and how
many divisions are made, depends partly on one's purposes, on
how one views the data, and so on. If one attempts to be too
precise about where one stage stops and the next begins, or if
too many divisions are made, it will be difficult to generalize the
findings and replicate the work.

A good compromise that adequately delineates these
stages and yet is not too cumbersome for didactic and practical
purposes is to consider that there are five stages. These stages
are named according to the predominant social-emotional or
task-related behaviors in each stage, or in a way that alludes to

both the social-emotional and task areas. From the start to the end of the group experience, these stages are *orientation, dissatisfaction, resolution, production,* and *termination.* (Others may prefer different names for essentially the same phenomena. For example, Tuckman (1965) used *forming, storming, norming,* and *performing,* which can be supplemented with *mourning,* or as Tuckman and Jensen (1977) subsequently did, with *adjourning.*)

In shorter group experiences or in settings where the GDSs are less pronounced, it may be unnecessary to focus on resolution as a distinct stage. Thus only four stages need be considered, namely orientation, dissatisfaction, production, and termination (see Lacoursiere, 1974). In some applications it may be feasible to ignore termination so that only the three stages of orientation, dissatisfaction, and production are important, for example, in some short-term problem-solving and task groups.

The main characteristics of each of these stages will be described. Although these main characteristics are especially seen within each particular stage, as stated earlier, there is a considerable degree of overlap, and, in fact, hints of most stages can often be found during each of the other stages. For example, at least a certain amount of orientation continues throughout much of a group experience, and not all the dissatisfaction over the lack of accomplishment or with the leader occurs by any means in the dissatisfaction stage. This notion is illustrated in Figure 1.1, which also shows that behaviors seen in the experience are not precisely limited by the time boundaries of the group.

The description of each stage will include task and social-emotional behaviors. In less personal settings such as artificial problem-solving and some naturalistic groups these are separate areas, but in more personal, interactive groups, such as training or T groups and therapy groups, the task is in fair part the interpersonal, social-emotional behavior, so that the task and social-emotional areas are inseparable.

In describing the social-emotional behaviors, both the more individual, intrapersonal emotions and reactions will be described, such as sadness and hope, and the social or more interpersonal emotions and reactions, such as anger toward or affection for the group leader or other group members. Some of the groups are classes of people, or groups in a general conceptual sense, such as a group of new teachers. In these cases the interpersonal aspects of behavior can be less important, though the importance varies with the setting. For example, a group of college students leaving their friends after graduation can experience considerable feelings of loss in the termination stage.

The location and duration of each stage in the experience will be described now in a general way.

Orientation Stage

At the start of a group's life cycle the participants are mildly to moderately eager. They generally have positive expectations that something good will come from participation in their training or therapy group, class, or job. In fact, fantasies of highly positive expectations can be elicited in many group settings, for example, legal interns having a case that goes to the State Supreme Court, psychiatric residents curing a severely ill schizophrenic patient, or patients quickly ridding themselves of their emotional problems.

At the same time there is a certain amount of anxiety and concern as individuals try to discover why they are there, what they will get out of it, what the stated purpose of the group means in practice for them, what they will do, what the leader, teacher, or therapist will do if there is one, whether it will be worth the trouble, and so on. There will usually be some similar questions about other members of the group such as who they are, what they are like, and what they will do.

Group members at this stage are quite dependent on the situation and on whomever is in authority. The amount of work done on the task in this stage varies with the type of group and task. But generally the amount of work is moderate, since considerable energy and time are used in defining the task, how to approach it, what skills it requires, and so on.

The length of this stage will vary with the task, how clearly it is defined, and how easy it is to achieve. In a problem-solving or naturalistic group in which the task can be easily and clearly defined, orientation may be short and quite distinct so that only a small percentage of the group's history is needed, perhaps 10 to 15 minutes of a three-hour sequence. At the other extreme, in something like a therapy group in which the task is more difficult to define precisely and to achieve, the orientation stage may last a longer percentage of time and blend more into the subsequent stages. For example, aspects of orientation may still be easily discernible one-third or one-half or even more of the way into the life cycle of a therapy group that will meet weekly for one to two years.

Dissatisfaction Stage

After some time the participants learn that what they hope for or want from the experience and what they feel is actually happening do not coincide. It is rare when the reality lives up to fantasied expectations. Also, the earlier dependence on the situation is found unsatisfying. This leads to unpleasant feelings of frustration, sometimes anger against the task, and usually also against the authority figure—the leader, teacher, and so on. If the task is an interpersonal one, as in training and therapy groups, then some of the negative reaction to the task will also be to other members. Sometimes there is also a sense of sadness because people feel they cannot succeed in the task, are not competent, and so on.

Overall, this is a time of some dissatisfaction. These negative feelings usually become stronger and more prominent than the earlier positive feelings of eagerness and hope of gaining from the experience. The negative feelings may be so strong and disruptive that work on the task decreases, but this will depend on the type of experience and the specific group.

The length, intensity, and actual placement of the dissatisfaction stage within the experience depends on several variables. The start of the dissatisfaction stage will depend particularly on the difficulty of clearly ascertaining what precisely constitutes the task, how difficult it is to do, and what skills the group members possess and can acquire to accomplish it. The intensity of the dissatisfaction will depend considerably on the amount of the discrepancy between the realities of the situation on the one hand, and the participants' expectations regarding the task and their ability to acquire the skills to complete it on the other. The ending or resolving of this dissatisfaction stage (see the next stage) in turn will depend on how easy or difficult it is to resolve the sense of frustration, anger, and so on. This depends partly on gaining the skills for the task, but usually also partly on redefining the achievable task and expectations to make them more compatible.

The dissatisfaction stage constitutes a small fraction to up to a half and sometimes more of the length of the experience. Some groups, and individuals, become arrested at this stage and become so demoralized that they hardly get beyond it (see, for example, Heinicke & Bales, 1953; Stock & Thelen, 1958; and the previous psychiatric staff example). They may continue while extremely dissatisfied and work ineffectively on the task until their official termination, or the group may dissolve prematurely as members gradually come to sessions later and later and eventually not at all (see, for example, Cronin & Thomas, 1971, on government advisory committee work).

Occasionally the dissatisfaction stage will not be very prominent, and whether or not it is seen will depend on one's observational skills. Some groups may not enter such a dissatisfaction stage, but this is rare—not because most groups do not function well, but because expectations can so easily exceed the possibilities. If there were not strong positive expectations in the first place, one would usually not go through the bother of entering the experience. (An exception is when a person joins a group under some degree of coercion. This results in a "negative orientation stage," which will be discussed shortly.)

Resolution Stage

What happens between the period of maximum dissatisfaction and the beginning of the production stage can be considered part of these stages or a separate stage of resolution that falls between them. Delineating this resolution stage is somewhat arbitrary, but for some groups and situations the transformation from dissatisfaction to production will be fairly difficult and take long enough to allow us to consider this a separate stage. (There is much work on group developmental stages discussing this separate stage, such as the work of Mann, 1966, and Mann, Gibbard & Hartman, 1967; and Tuckman, 1965, in his "norming" stage.)

At other times the transition from the dissatisfaction to production stages occurs fairly easily and quickly so that it seems unnecessary and didactic to isolate a resolution stage. Under such conditions it is probably better to consider the transition as part of the production stage.

When there is a separate resolution stage its boundaries can be considered to start with a decrease in dissatisfaction at one end, and to extend to neutral or clearly positive feelings at the other end, with perhaps an associated increase in work on the task. (These two alternatives of GDSs with and without a separate resolution stage are illustrated in Figures 1.2 and 1.3.)

What happens in this stage is some rapprochement between expectations and the realities (task, leader, abilities, other members, and so on), and also some increase in skills to complete the task, either as originally construed or as redefined. Sufficient mastery of the situation, and perhaps new skills, allow positive feelings of increased self-esteem, pleasure in accomplishment, and so on, to exceed the earlier negative feelings of

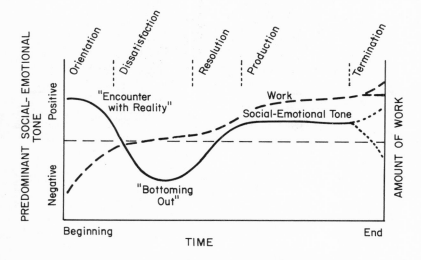

FIGURE 1.2.   GDS SCHEMATIZATION OF EACH OF THE FIVE STAGES. This figure shows the location of each of the five stages and the fluctuations in social-emotional reactions and work on the task during the life cycle of the group or other experience.

frustration and anger. Or these latter feelings may be worked through or resolved.

Important interpersonal aspects of resolution may entail decreasing animosity between group members and between members and the leader, often partly by implied or explicit agreement about what is appropriate interpersonal behavior. These aspects will be most noticeable in interpersonally oriented groups, such as training and therapy groups. Also, group cohesion may first be noticed at this stage. Throughout the resolution stage there may be a gradual increase in work on the task, which continues into the production stage.

The length of the resolution stage may range from being very short to being a significant percentage of the experience. This will depend, as mentioned earlier, on the ease of resolving

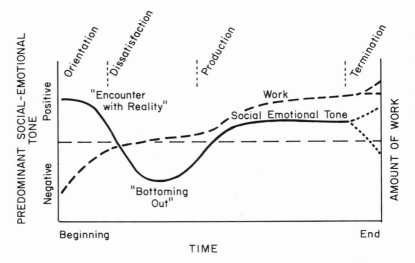

FIGURE 1.3. GDS SCHEMATIZATION OF EACH STAGE WHEN RESOLUTION IS EXCLUDED. This figure shows the location of the four stages of orientation, dissatisfaction, production, and termination when a separate resolution stage need not be considered, for example, in short group life cycles, or when the dissatisfaction stage is not strongly negative.

feelings of dissatisfaction, the ease of learning new skills, the quality of interpersonal relations, and so on. When these conditions are unfavorable the group may dissolve even as attempts at resolution are still underway.

Production Stage

The production stage is characterized by the positive feelings of eagerness to be part of the experience; hope for a good outcome exceeding the negative feelings of discouragement, frustration, anger, and so on, of the earlier dissatisfaction stage; and by a good level of work on the task, whatever it is. If it is a group-oriented activity, members are working well together with satisfactory agreement—implicit or explicit—about the nature of their relationships. Also, a group that was initially quite dependent on the leader and situation will now have more autonomy.

If one considers a separate resolution stage, then the transition from it to the production stage occurs when the growth in positive feelings in the resolution stage has leveled off on the positive side of a neutral baseline (see Figure 1.2). If a separate resolution stage is not considered, then the production stage starts when the negative feelings of the dissatisfaction stage significantly lessen, and the rate of work perhaps begins to increase. In either case the production stage is brought about by a rapprochement between the initial expectations and what the situation actually delivers, along with a progressive increase in the skills needed to accomplish the task, which allows it to be done more easily and more successfully. Success in the task helps to increase positive feelings about being in the group. This all leads to more efficient use of time, with less time spent in struggling against the leader, the other group members, or the task itself.

This stage of production will then continue, with more moderate fluctuations in feelings of pleasantness and unpleasantness, until the final stage of termination. The proportion of time spent in the production stage will vary with such factors as the ease of defining the task clearly, the ease of acquiring the requisite skills, the discrepancy between expectations and realities, and the difficulties of the task.

When the task is fairly easy to define clearly and the skills easy to acquire, most time may well be spent in a production stage, such as in work groups of bricklayers on a new job or in a task force organizing graduation ceremonies. When the task is more difficult to define and the skills harder to acquire, such as in a training or therapy group, a distinct production stage with a high level of work and predominantly positive emotions about being in the group may make up only a small percentage of the group's history, perhaps one-quarter or less.

This is not to say that work on the task is not going on at other times, even throughout the full life cycle of the group, because it usually is. Even a training group that spends much time or even most of its time in the orientation and dissatisfaction stages is learning about groups in general and their group in particular throughout this experience. In other words, they are constantly working on their task, but the actual production stage—marked by a high level of work and positive feelings about it—may be a relatively small part of their group life cycle. Some groups never reach this production stage (see, for example, Cronin & Thomas, 1971; and Stock & Thelen, 1958).

Termination Stage

As the end of the experience approaches, the participants begin to concern themselves with what they have accomplished and with the impending dissolution of the group or other experience. There is often a sense of loss or mourning for the experience in general, for other group members, and maybe especially for the leader. Sometimes the feelings of loss or anticipated loss are largely denied or covered up in some way, such as by joking (sometimes about death), missing the final meeting or meetings, and so on. In some settings in which the sense of accomplishment is strong, the positive feelings may be stronger than the negative ones of loss.

The work on the task during the termination stage generally decreases, but sometimes it may increase to cover up the sense of loss or sadness, or it may have to be increased to complete the task on time. If the experience of termination is part of the task, as in training and therapy groups, then group members should be examining these feelings, but if they are intense and predominately negative, that may be very difficult to do.

The signal for the end of the group experience will often be clear enough from an approaching time boundary and/or indications that the task is nearly completed or soon will be. Occasionally, in groups in which the experience has not been satisfactory, termination may result from disintegration of the group as members come later and later or don't come at all. This sometimes happens when an adequate production stage has never been entered because of a particularly difficult dissatisfaction stage.

The termination stage can occupy anywhere from part of the last meeting of a group to the last several meetings, depending on the duration of the group; the personal meaningfulness of the task; the closeness of ties between members; the closeness of ties to the leader; and so on. When strong group ties develop between members and between members and the leader, the earliest indications of termination may clearly begin when as much as one-quarter or more of the group experience is still left. At the other extreme, such as in a problem-solving or task group of a few hours, termination may take only a few minutes at the end of the last meeting.

Table 1.1 summarizes the preceding description of GDSs. In the social-emotional area, the table emphasizes actual group experiences rather than more general experiences in which the social behavior may be much less important.

Negative Orientation Stage

Sometimes the GDS sequence begins with various kinds of resistance and perhaps hostility instead of the usually more positive and eager beginning. The degree of initial work on the task under these resistive conditions is apt to be rather low. This more negative beginning seems to occur particularly when participation is not completely voluntary, such as in therapy groups with delinquents or alcohol or drug abuse patients, or in training and learning groups with required participation.

This negative, resistive, beginning stage is called the negative orientation stage. It usually will blend into the dissatisfaction stage so that the whole first part of the GDS sequence tends to be negative. The resolution stage then resolves not only the usual dissatisfaction with the task, unrealistic expectations, and so on, but also the resistance about being in the group in the

Table 1.1. GDS tabular overview

	Stage				
	Orientation	*Dissatisfaction*	*Resolution*	*Production*	*Termination*
	Learn nature of task	Complete learning nature of task	Reconcile real and expected task	Add additional goals if appropriate	Complete task
Nature of Task	Early skills acquisition	Begin to get skills for task when necessary	Increase in skills	Application of skills to task	Review or check task accomplished
Work Area	Early work on task	Work at task	Increase in application of skills		
Work Area — Degree of Work	Medium	Low to medium	Medium to high	Medium to high	Medium to low

Table 1.1. GDS tabular overview (Cont'd)

Stage

	Orientation	Dissatisfaction	Resolution	Production	Termination
Social-Emotional Area Positive	Eagerness to be there	Some liking of skill	Slowly growing satisfaction	Increase in close feelings toward others	Saying good-bye
	Like task or expected task and/or other aspects of situation	Growing positive feelings toward other participants	Growing group feeling and cohesion	More autonomy in relation to leader	Increase in self-esteem with satisfactory task completion
	Early positive feelings toward other participants and leader, maybe especially latter		Some increase of positive feelings toward leader, more as teacher or consultant than as "feeder"	Increase in self-esteem with increasing task accomplishment	
	Dependent on situation			Helpful competition between participants, and between participants and leader	

Table 1.1. GDS tabular overview (Cont'd)

| | | Stage | | | | |
		Orientation	Dissatisfaction	Resolution	Production	Termination
		Mild anxiety and apprehension	Frustration, anger at task, maybe at whole situation	Persistence of prior negative feelings, but lessened	Fatigue with work	Sadness of parting, loss
		Mild anger if partici-pation is forced	Dissatisfaction			Loss of self-esteem with failure to complete task satisfactorily
			Perhaps depressed because task is difficult			
Social-Emotional Area	Negative		Decrease in self-esteem			
			Anger toward leader, perhaps with less dependency			
			Aggressive nonproductive competition between participants, and participants and leader			

first place. After resolution, the sequence continues with production and termination stages.

Sometimes a negative orientation stage will be followed by all of the usual stages—negative orientation, (positive) orientation, dissatisfaction, resolution, production, and termination—but this is not what usually happens under these conditions. (Further material on and examples of studies with a negative orientation stage will be cited later, particularly in the section reviewing GDSs of therapy groups, but also in the section on naturalistic groups.)

The dichotomy between positive and negative orientation stage beginnings is supported in the published studies, as Chapter 4 will show. Nonetheless, what exists in practice is a continuum of beginnings with fully voluntary, highly eager participants on the one extreme, and strongly coerced, highly resistant participants on the other. Any group will contain a mixture of participants along this continuum, but they will often cluster toward one end or the other so that the resultant orientation stage of the group is either the usual positive orientation or a negative orientation.

Examples of actual groups with predominantly voluntary, eager participants are learning groups, encounter groups, many outpatient psychotherapy groups, and generally training groups. And, as stated above, examples of actual groups with predominantly coerced, resistant participants are therapy groups for delinquents and alcohol and drug abuse patients.

Chapter 2

MORALE AND GROUP AND GENERAL DEVELOPMENTAL STAGES

Morale has been mentioned in the previous pages without particular attention to its specific meaning, which will now be examined, along with ways to measure morale. Morale is an elusive term with a range of definitions. It was popular in the behavioral and social science literature around the time of World War II and into the early 1950s, but it now appears in the literature only in circumscribed areas.*

*In the psychologically oriented behavioral science indices, there were many entries under *morale* in the 1940s since many respected workers in psychiatry, psychoanalysis, and psychology were interested in the subject (for example, Child, 1941; K. A. Menninger, 1941). But then the use of the term becomes rarer. In the "Cumulative Subject Index" to *Psychological Abstracts* for 1929–1960, there are three columns of entries, but the entries decrease to a half column in the indexes for 1961–1965 and 1966–1968, and disappear completely in the 1969–1971 volume. In the individual volumes of *Psychological Abstracts, morale* is no longer an index item by 1969; the reader is referred instead to *job satisfaction, attitude,* and *emotion.* However, the term returned in 1978. In the occasionally issued *Index of Psychoanalytic Writings,* there are 24 entries for 1960, 17 for 1966—most of these in one book (Galdston, 1958)

Such areas include industrial psychology and sociology (Argyle, 1972; Benoit-Guilbot, 1968; Dubin, 1968; Gellerman, 1953; Guion, 1958; Martin, 1969; Sayles, 1968; and Viteles, 1953); personnel work (Wnuk, 1966); education (Blocker & Richardson, 1963; Connaughton, 1971); and, interestingly, gerontology (Ross, 1962; Lawton, 1975; Morris & Sherwood, 1975) and rehabilitation medicine (Akehurst, 1972; a brief overview of several of these areas can be found in Prasannarao, 1969). Recent incidental uses of the term in the professional literature appeared in a paper on morale in clinical medicine (Richardson, 1972) and in work with Peace Corps volunteers (W. W. Menninger, 1975).

The space taken by *morale* gradually dwindled in the behavioral science index *Psychological Abstracts* until it vanished altogether in 1969; it was reinstated in 1978. Conversely, the term has persisted in *Sociological Abstracts,* and in the more lay-oriented *Readers Guide to Periodical Literature. Morale,* or its negative counterpart, *demoralization,* are regularly heard in conversations or read in newspapers or other lay literature. For example, a book about Americans by John Gardner, founder of the consumer advocate group Common Cause, is entitled *Morale* (1978).

THE DEFINITION OF MORALE

Morale has been defined in a variety of ways by workers in different areas. At times, it has been defined narrowly as synonomous with group cohesion or job satisfaction (Guion, 1958), but it is often given a broader meaning. Galdston's (1958) report of a conference on morale spent several pages on

---

—and only three entries for 1975. One can still find a few entries per year in *Index Medicus,* particularly in the fields of gerontology and rehabilitation medicine. Although *morale* appeared in the third edition of Hinsie and Campbell's *Psychiatric Dictionary* in 1960, it was missing from the fourth in 1970.

the definition, and other publications have done likewise (Viteles, 1953; Whitlock, 1960, found some 30 definitions that applied to work situations).

For our purposes it will be easy enough to define the term adequately. *Morale* can refer to the morale of a single individual, the morale of an individual in relation to various groups in which he or she participates, the morale of an individual within a particular group, or the morale of the whole group. Examples of each of these definitions will be given.

Individual morale:

The healthy mental attitude of the resolute and energetic individual in connection with goals to be achieved (Sterba, 1943 p. 69).

A zestful, energetic, well-integrated positive mental attitude toward the business of living (Ross, 1962 p. 54).

The ability to maintain a high degree of optimistic and purposeful activity in the face of adversity (Alexander, 1958 p. 105).

Individuals relative to groups or within a group:

A condition of physical and emotional well being in the individual that makes it possible for him to work and live hopefully and effectively, feeling that he shares the basic purposes of the groups of which he is member; and that makes it possible for him to perform his tasks with energy, enthusiasm and self-discipline sustained by a conviction that in spite of obstacles and conflict his personal and social ideals are worth pursuing (Child, 1941 p. 393-4).

A prevailing temper or spirit, in individuals forming a group, which is marked by confidence in the group, self-confidence with respect to one's role in the group, group loyalty, and readiness to strive for group goals (English & English, 1958 p. 328).

Group morale:

The above definition except for group morale it is the composite morale of the individuals in the group (English & English, 1958 p. 328).

> [High group morale exists in] a group where there are clear
> and fixed group goals that are felt to be important and integrated
> with individual goals; where there is confidence in the attainment
> of these goals; and subordinately, confidence is the means of
> attainment, in the leader, associates, and finally oneself; where
> the group's actions are integrated and cooperative; and where
> aggression and hostility are expressed against the forces frustrat-
> ing the group rather than towards other individuals within the
> group. (Child, 1941 p. 394).

Morale exists over a span of time, usually a duration measured in terms of a significant part of an experience. In practice
this usually means the morale of an individual or group over
days or weeks, or even months, depending on the experience in
question. There would be little value in speaking of the morale
of our armed forces over only a matter of a few days, but morale
defined by these limits might be meaningful in reference to a
combat unit. Similarly, with a group scheduled to meet for a
week, it would be meaningful to consider the morale over a
half-day or so but not over a few minutes. A minimum practical
time unit might be the few minutes that mark the turning point
of an athletic contest.

There has been a suggestion (modified from Galdston,
1958, p. 77) that the types of morale fall along a continuum.
The lowest level of morale on such a continuum would be that
of a solitary individual, the next level that of a group that allows
gratification of pre-existing individual needs (for example, an
individually oriented learning group), the next level that of a
group that provides gratification of existing individual needs
and new individual needs that emerge on a higher level (for
example, interpersonal relations in a training group), and the
highest level that achieved in a group that not only permits
gratification of existing individual needs, but in which membership is essential for the emergence of new, higher goals that
cannot be achieved by isolated individuals (for example, social
projects and battles).

Another dimension to the broad use of the term *morale* has

been added by Grinker (in Galdston, 1958, p. 130): "Morale, which to me is an integrative component appearing in greater or lesser strength under certain conditions, is a concept which is applicable whether it be in relation to coordinated systemic functions, the development of integrative personality or social cohesiveness, or even, I think, one could imagine a world order. They are all of the same nature of events." (See below our discussion of the work of Davies, 1969, and Feierabend, Feierabend & Nesvold, 1969, regarding revolutions and rebellions.)

High or positive morale, then, is an integrative, moderately enduring condition in individuals, in individuals within or in relation to a group or groups, or in whole groups in which there are hope, optimism, enthusiasm, self-confidence, and energetic, purposeful movement toward goals, even in the face of obstacles. Morale is a dynamic, changing characteristic, but individuals and groups do have certain predispositions to more or less morale. For example, persons with (mentally and physically) healthier upbringings may have a greater potential for positive morale than those with less healthy upbringings (compare Meerloo, 1957), even though these things are not easy to predict, and even though some individuals from considerably deprived backgrounds have generally good morale.

There are some analogous considerations regarding groups of various kinds. For example, a group such as a business group or conglomerate that has successfully overcome obstacles may well face a new obstacle with higher morale than a group that has not come through such difficulties. Occasionally this rule does not hold, and the next obstacle is the straw that breaks the camel's back (Meerloo, 1957).

An individual whose morale in an isolated situation is not particularly good may have better morale in other isolated situations, or in certain group situations. This phenomenon may pull individuals into group situations looking for something about which they can feel positive and optimistic. (Does this have anything to do with the current popularity of the "group movement," the growth, encounter, and EST groups?) Likewise, a group may have high morale while handling one task but not another, such as an athletic team that rises to the occasion against some foes but not others (compare Galdston, 1958). Also, of course, the degree of a person's morale in a group depends in good part on the morale of other individuals, and of the group as a whole. But a group can have generally high morale even though some members have low morale, and vice versa.

SOME RELATIONSHIPS OF MORALE

Morale has also been used in other ways or confused with other terms, so it will be helpful to look at how our use of the word compares or contrasts with these various other uses.

MORALE AND GROUP COHESION.   Some workers in the group area have equated morale with group cohesion. This is a very group-oriented definition of morale and a rather restrictive one. Cohesion in groups does contribute to morale, but other things do also, for example, task success. What is more, a cohesive group that is not successful in its task may well have difficulty maintaining a good level of morale. And whether group cohesion contributes to work on the task depends, among other things, on the task itself. If the task requires little teamwork, as in some industrial jobs, then energy spent on group cohesion may actually detract from work on the task.

In terms of our use of morale during GDSs, it is often quite high at the beginning of the group. Yet significant cohesion may not be noticeable until the resolution stage or sometimes until the production stage, especially if a clear resolution stage cannot be distinguished.

MORALE AND JOB SATISFACTION.   Some people equate morale with job satisfaction, but this is again a restricted use of the term. Even on the job, morale entails more than satisfaction. Two studies that give data on this issue (Mahoney, 1956, and Baehr & Renck, 1958) will soon be discussed.

Conversely, job satisfaction itself involves a variety of factors, and the types of factors associated with job satisfaction are likely to be different from those associated with job dissatisfaction. This suggests that even if one wants to define morale restrictively by equating it with job satisfaction, the defining characteristics associated with demoralization (job dissatisfaction) will be different from those associated with positive morale. This line of reasoning leads to the two-factor theory of work motivation of Herzberg (Herzberg, Mausner & Snyderman, 1959), but this is too tangential for our purposes. (The interested reader is referred to Herzberg et al., 1959; and Argyle, 1972.)

Our position, consistent with a broader definition of morale, is that job satisfaction is only one part of morale, just as satisfaction with the task in a group is only one part of what contributes to group morale. The many other contributing factors include the group leader (immediate supervisor), other group members (fellow employees), and the individual members' predispositions.

(Many empirical questions remain in this area of morale and job satisfaction, yet the usage explained here seems generally consistent with other uses and definitions of morale, and not excessively arbitrary.)

MORALE AND PRODUCTIVITY.   It is probably already clear that there is no simple relationship between morale and productivity, that is, the rate and amount of work on a task. For example, a review of the literature by Martin (1969) led to the conclusion that "there is no positive correlation between morale, job satisfaction, and productivity" (p. 44). Similarly, in encounter groups there was no simple relationship between productivity measured as personal change and morale considered as enthusiasm or "being turned on" (Lieberman, Yalom & Miles, 1973, p. 259).

Some of the factors contributing to positive morale also help productivity, for example, a certain amount of group cohesion on some tasks, increasing skill, and a lack of preoccupation with various negative feelings. But other factors contributing to positive morale may detract from productivity, for example, excessive group cohesion on some tasks, excessive enthusiasm that interferes with careful attention to complex tasks, and stimuli from outside the group that contribute to an individual's positive morale but detract from group morale. Nonetheless, the correlation between morale and productivity is generally positive, although it may be small. But there are other gains from good morale, such as decreased voluntary absenteeism and reduced job turnover (Argyle, 1972, p. 241).

THE RELATIONSHIP BETWEEN MORALE AND ADJUSTMENT.   The terms *morale* and *adjustment* overlap somewhat. *Adjustment* refers to a relatively more static relationship between a person and a particular setting (compare English & English, 1958), and by extension between a group and a particular setting. Morale, on the other hand, is a more dynamic term with more implications about duration and the ability to adjust now and in the future.

The type of adjustment achieved and the degree of morale reverberate with each other; good morale is apt to help with better adjustment, which in turn fosters good morale, and conversely, poor morale is apt to hinder good adjustment, and so on. Also, previously good morale can be decreased by poor adjustment. A person or group with good morale may or may not be well adjusted in a particular setting at a particular time; good adjustment in a particular setting at a particular time may be associated with good or poor morale.

THE RELATIONSHIP BETWEEN MORALE AND DEPRESSION.   Morale and its explicit absence, demoralization, tend to describe general conditions of living and not to denote clinical conditions. *Depression* is a more clinical term usually implying psychopathology. The Beck Depression Inventory (Beck, 1967) has 21 items, each scaled over a range of four or five units, and only seven of these 21 (pessimism, dissatisfaction, irritability, social withdrawal, indecisiveness, work retardation, and fatigability) would usually be considered measures of the degree of morale or its absence, and only in their mildest degrees. The other items would generally be considered beyond the range of morale and demoralization, though this might vary somewhat with one's definition. (These 14 others are sadness, sense of failure, guilt, expectation of punishment, self-dislike, self-accusations, suicidal ideas, crying, body image change, insomnia, anorexia, weight loss, somatic preoccupation, and loss of libido.) A depressed person may have low individual morale, but in certain group settings the same person may have high morale, which may or may not be in some sense compensatory. Also, a lack of depression may not particularly mean very positive or high morale.

Further elaboration of the differences between morale and depression can be found in a factor analytic study looking for common themes in a 22-item geriatric morale scale (the Philadelphia Geriatric Center Morale Scale) and two depression inventories (the Gardner-Hetznecker Sign and Symptom Checklist, and the Zung Self-Rating Depression Scale; Morris, Wolf & Klerman, 1975). These three instruments were administered to long-term mental hospital patients. Although this particular morale scale has many items that are very depression-oriented, for example, "I have a lot to be sad about," and although there was a common "clinical depression element" found in the scales, it included only three items from the morale scale.

PSEUDO-MORALE.   Pseudo-morale is a fragile veneer of morale covering deep-lying and pervasive feelings and attitudes. It is often fairly easily penetrated by the deeper dispositions. Pseudo-morale is frequently seen tandem with the defense mechanism of denial in persons with serious physical or emotional illness such as cancer or depression. It is also often associated with anger, to provide a superficial cover.

MEASURING MORALE

One can attempt to measure morale directly, with a morale scale, for example, or indirectly by its effects, such as promptness in turning in work, quality of work, rate of nonillness job absenteeism, and job turnover. Most work on measuring morale either directly or indirectly has been done in industrial settings or in the armed forces, but some of the results are applicable to other settings. The studies of Mahoney (1956) and Baehr and Renck (1958) are representative.

Mahoney (1956) discussed the development of scales to measure morale and their correlations and multiple correlations with absenteeism and the supervisors' ratings of "the degree of enthusiasm, eagerness, and energy with which a man goes about the work he is called upon to do." These scales are (1) feelings of status at work, (2) feelings of status outside of work, (3) attitudes toward leadership at the immediate level, (4) at the intermediate level, and (5) at the top level, (6) evaluation of past successes and failures, (7) outlook for the future, (8) feelings of belonging, and (9) feelings of the extent of sacrifice. The first four of these scales were most highly correlated with absenteeism and supervisors' ratings.

Baehr and Renck (1958) took a different approach. They sought to measure morale via employees' ratings on a wide range of items relative to their work, all of which were considered to have a bearing on employee morale according to prior research work. Factor analyses of three separate studies on thousands of employees using their Employee Inventory Questionnaire found high consistency in identifying the same five factors describing the work situation. These factors are (1) the employee's relation to management and the organization, (2) attitudes toward the immediate supervisor, (3) material rewards, (4) relationships with fellow employees, and (5) extrinsic job satisfaction.

Although both of these studies worked on measuring devices that could have some applicability in nonindustrial, nonwork situations, methods directly developed for these other areas are very limited. For example, there is very little to find in various Buros' editions cataloging and evaluating psychological tests (1949, 1970, 1972). Similarly, other sources such as *The Source Book for Mental Health Measures* (Comrey, Backer

& Glaser, 1973) contain little on measuring morale; it does have a few items such as the previously mentioned Philadelphia Geriatric Morale Scale, and items to measure self-esteem.

The available morale measures seem adequate only for particular applications, and even then one can take issue with some of the tests within the limited areas. For example, one can argue that the Philadelphia Geriatric Morale Scale is too depression-oriented to be only a measure of morale. One is rather forced to define as well as possible what is important for morale in a particular context, and then to decide how to measure it. This is what several studies have done in work settings, and what many studies have done with the elderly (for example, Pierce & Clark, 1973).

Other specific morale measures that have been developed are the Purdue Teacher Opinionarie for teacher morale (see Greenwood & Soar, 1973); the Student Attitude Survey for high school student morale (Hendrickson, 1973); the Robinson and Seligman (1969) scale for campus morale; and the Index of Emotional Stress, which contains a measure of personal morale (see Estes, 1973). This all seems reminiscent of Katzell's (1958) comment some 20 years ago that "no single measure or type of measure now known to exist is by itself an adequate measure of morale" (p. 76).

Measuring Morale During Group and General Developmental Stages

The measurement of morale in various individual or group settings must reflect the contingencies of each situation. For example, with a work group one would have to consider absenteeism, job turnover, lateness, and so on, and with an individual student study, one would consider quality of assignments, when they were turned in, and so on.

Besides these specific measures in various situations, a more general measure of morale that can be used under conditions in which GDSs can be determined might be explained thus: The measurement of morale is the repeated algebraic summation of the positive and negative emotions, reactions, and attitudes related to the task and to the social-emotional goals of the experience, including relations to both the leader and other members when these are part of the experience. Measuring morale, then, consists of measuring an adequate sampling of these positive (for example, hope, pleasure, self-esteem, and attraction) and negative (for example, pessimism, anger, fear, depression, self-derogation, and dislike) emotions, reactions, and attitudes, taking an algebraic summation, and doing this repeatedly during the experience in question.

A *morale curve* will result from plotting such repeated algebraic summations during the experience, preferably many times throughout the full life cycle of the experience. In a research approach to this measurement, comparable scales would be required for the positive and negative emotions, reactions, and attitudes; this would not be easy to achieve, though it could be done, for example, by having point-referenced rating scales on which multiple raters achieve satisfactory agreement. In a practical approach to such measurement, approximations of such comparability are adequate. In many settings where GDS ideas can be applied, an experienced observer can make useful assessments of morale without special measuring devices.

In the orientation stage we have particularly the liking of the task and group participation, and the hope for positive gains. There is usually also a certain degree of anxiety or apprehension about participation. In milder forms this is generally a positive motivating factor, but in stronger forms it is more disruptive and negative (compare Malmo's activation theory, 1962). Overall morale in the usual orientation stage is usually moderately positive, and it may be considerably so.

In the dissatisfaction stage the desire to do the task, the hope for gain, the enjoyment of the group, and so on, are more than outweighed by the negative feelings of frustration, discouragement, anger, growing dislike for the task, negative feelings toward the leader and other group members, and perhaps some sense of sadness because of one's inability to adequately achieve. The overall result here is usually a fall in morale, and in situations with difficult problems, significant personal involvement, and extended participation, the result is a fall below the neutral baseline into negative morale or demoralization.

The morale at each stage can be looked at in the same way, but it is easier to describe the stages graphically. The reader's indulgence is asked, because this graph represents an attempt to portray—in a single graph for various types of groups and experiences—something that varies with the type of group and experience and with the specific groups and experiences in question. Such morale curve was, in fact, presented earlier (Figures 1.2 and 1.3), labeled as the curve of the predominant "social-emotional tone." This curve is now shown in Figure 2.1, "GDSs

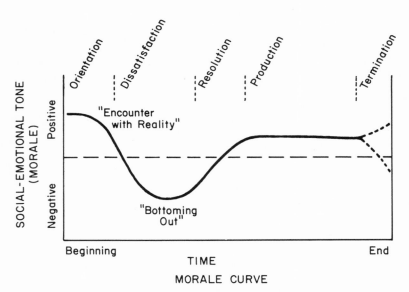

FIGURE 2.1. GDSs AS A MORALE CURVE. This figure shows the predominant social-emotional tone of GDSs as a morale curve. (This curve is conceptually related to and adapted from the work of W. W. Menninger, 1975, as well as my own work.)

as a Morale Curve." Examples of morale curves using data from specific studies will also be found later (Figures 4.1, 4.2, and 4.4).

DEMORALIZATION DURING GDSs

Demoralization (negative or low morale) can occur during any stage during GDSs. But under average conditions for an experience, negative or low morale is expected during the dissatisfaction stage, and often also during the termination stage, depending on the type of experience, its personal significance, and so on. Negative or low morale is also the expected state during a GDS sequence that begins with a negative orientation stage, that is, when the participants are reluctant to be part of the experience in the first place.

Demoralization can also occur during the production stage when the task is difficult and tends to wear people down, such as work with chronic and/or severely ill medical or psychiatric patients, or work that one has done for such a long time that it has lost its interest. Demoralization can also occur at this stage when the task is inherently boring, such as some repetitive factory work. These various types of demoralization will be returned to later.

WHY ATTEND TO MORALE IN GDSs?

As suggested earlier, several practical advantages can be expected from attending to morale in group experiences and various general experiences during GDSs. If morale can be kept as favorable as possible, more work on the task and more satisfaction with the task can usually be expected. Greater task satisfaction will contribute to more persistence in doing the task, including less voluntary absenteeism and less dropping out of the experience. In actual groups better morale will usually enhance group cohesion. When the experience is over, more favorable reports about the experience can subsequently be expected.

It may help to emphasize some related points. The optimal state of GDS affairs is not to try to keep morale highly positive or even moderately positive throughout the experience; this would be unnatural, for example, if during the ostensible dissatisfaction stage everything was "just fine" and morale was very high. Under rare circumstances this might be appropriate, but it is not the expected course. Also, high morale should not usually be bought at the price of work on the task, which could happen if the high morale were largely the result of excessive enthusiasm or cohesion that interfered with task performance.

A major focus of this book is how to facilitate GDSs so that they are minimally disruptive and so that morale is kept as favorable as practical. This will help to insure optimal work on the task and satisfaction among participants. This subject will be returned to several times, notably in a chapter devoted to applications of GDS material.

Chapter 3

DEFINITIONS AND RESEARCH QUESTIONS CONCERNING GROUP AND GENERAL DEVELOPMENTAL STAGES

Various questions of definition and some of the specific research requirements for establishing developmental stages will now be discussed without focusing much on the broader questions of general research methodology and statistical analysis. The emphasis will be primarily on actual group settings in which the developmental stage data rest on firmer ground. The expert in the area of group research and group developmental stages may find this chapter too elementary, or at most a quick overview, but for the less expert this chapter will convey some of the research questions that must be addressed by a careful worker on these developmental stages.

Here are some of the questions that will be considered: What is meant in this book by a group? What exactly is group development? Does group development have to do with changing relationships toward the leader, with how the group gets organized to work on the task at hand, or with both these and other things? Are there different ways to conceptualize theories of group development?

What Is a Group?

For many purposes in this book, the usual concept of a group will suffice. But to facilitate mutual understanding, two definitions from the literature will be given.

Merton (1957) defines a group as a collection of people who spend certain periods of *time together,* who *see themselves as members,* and/or are *identified as members* by outsiders. This definition stresses *time together* and the idea of group *membership.* A definition by Cartwright and Zander (1960) stresses goals and interrelationships: "A group is a collection of individuals sharing a *common goal* who have relationships to one another that make them *interdependent* to some significant degree" (p. 46, italics added).

Most of the groups to be discussed will meet the qualifications of both of these definitions—time together, identified membership, common, shared goals, and interdependence. For example, problem-solving groups, committees, athletic teams, work groups, and so on can be considered *actual groups.* Some "groups" will not fit these definitions. At times the "goal" or "task" will involve a *similar* goal or task rather than a common, shared one, and in such cases the interdependence is usually less or even negligible. All such "groups" will be called *conceptual groups.*

These conceptual groups span a range covering those that spend some time together under their usual conditions to those that do not usually do this. Examples of the former conceptual groups are college classes, work groups in which the workers are involved in a similar area but each on their own nonshared task, and people hospitalized for psychiatric treatment. Such conceptual groups approach actual groups, but they do not have a common, shared task, and they are minimally interdependent.

Examples of conceptual groups that usually spend little or no time together are people with terminal illnesses and those in individual new jobs. These conceptual groups are further removed from actual groups not only because they lack a common task and are negligibly or for practical purposes not interdependent, but also because they will not usually spend time with other members of the conceptual group. This second type of conceptual group is on a continuum with the first type of conceptual group and with actual groups. At this point it is not necessary to distinguish the two types of conceptual groups any further, but practical GDS applications are usually easier with the former conceptual groups whose members are together at certain times.

At times members of both types of conceptual groups will meet in actual groups in which they then share the common task of that group. This happens, for example, when legal interns meet in learning groups; when they do so they are not only members of the conceptual group of legal interns with individual goals and tasks, but also members of the actual (learning) group brought together with the shared goal or task of fostering their learning as legal interns and whatever else this learning group is doing (Lacoursiere, 1980). Similarly, when people with terminal illnesses are brought together in a supportive therapy group, the members are not only members of the conceptual group of people with the individual tasks of dealing with their own terminal illness, they are also members of the actual (therapy) group with the shared task of helping each other with terminal illness (Spiegel & Yalom, 1978).

The developmental stages of conceptual groups can be considered the general developmental stages discussed earlier, if one keeps in mind the primarily actual (non-"conceptual") group data on which these stages are based. Alternatively, conceptual group developmental stages might sometimes be considered individual developmental stages, if one accepts that they are similar for many of the individuals involved. But this could be confused with individual personality developmental stages (the psychoanalytic oral, anal, and so on, or with other conceptualizations) and would not underscore the relationship of the group and general developmental stages to a particular new experience, or to the large body of material on actual group developmental stages.

In most instances the sense of the word *group* as used in this book will be clear from the context. In fact, *group* will be used almost exclusively in the traditional sense for most of this chapter and the next, until we discuss some of the "naturalistic" groups. The literature on groups is primarily a literature on actual groups, that is, collections of individuals meeting together with a shared purpose requiring their cooperation; this also applies to the literature on development in groups. As research issues and questions are examined, the focus will be mostly on actual groups, since it is here that more material, and more rigorous material, are available. Analogous issues and questions apply to conceptual groups, and a few specific comments will be made about conceptual groups.

What Is Group Development?

What is group development? What are group developmental stages? Development of what? For group development this might mean everything from the growth of group solidarity or cohesiveness, changes in the relationship toward the leader, changes in task orientation and output, intrapsychic changes, questions of why the group came together initially and why it ceased being a group, and so on.

The word *development* has been used in the literature on groups in at least five different ways; the first three are on a continuum from the particular to the more general or universal, and the last two are somewhat different uses of the term. First, there is a considerable body of literature dealing with specific aspects of the group during the course of its life, for example, the changing relationships to the leader during the group's history, the amount of cohesion at the beginning of the group as compared to the end, the types of inter-member relationships throughout the group's history, the development of acceptance of new members, and so on. (See, for example, Arsenian, Semrad & Shapiro, 1962; Bion, 1961; and some of the work reported in Cartwright & Zander, 1960, and in Hare, 1962 and 1976.) Although this literature describes specific aspects of a group's development, it makes no attempt at an overall picture of that development.

Second, the word *development* is used with an eye toward a more comprehensive picture of group development. Sometimes in this work researchers will examine the patterns of significant changes or stages or phases or trends that occur over the course of the group's life cycle. Here the emphasis is on qualitatively different stages of development of a particular group, whatever might comprise such stages for that group, such as the relationship to the leader, task productivity, and so on. According to this concept, if the relationship to the leader is examined it is because it is thought to be part of a broader picture of stages of development in *this* group. There is no special implication that these stages apply to other groups of a similar or different kind.

This type of study has been called work on "group development" in a wider sense than the first type, insofar as overall development is studied. Kaplan and Roman's paper, "Phases of Development in Adult Therapy Groups" (1963), is largely this type of study, with only a minimal attempt to tie their group's development to that of other groups. Stock and Thelen's work (1958), an example of earlier work that will be discussed later in some detail, tends also to be of this type. They stated that "there is no indication that the particular developmental characteristics of this group would necessarily be found in other groups" (p. 206); when a second group was studied they found that it had a different development.

The third major developmental focus of group studies, and the one that is the main focus of this book, can be called work on group developmental stages (compare Cooper & Mangham, 1971; and Lubin & Zuckerman, 1967). Here the attempt is to discern whether or not any similar group developmental stages occur during the lifetimes of different groups. Although they prefer the term *trend* rather than *stage,* Lubin and Zuckerman's (1967) definition is appropriate; they used the term "group developmental trends" "to refer to predictable sequences of events which appear at similar points in time in various groups. In this definition the emphasis is on similarity of trends across groups" (p. 366). This type of work requires the study of more than one group's life cycle because it is looking for general rather than unique developmental patterns.

The approach may be moderately narrow, however, in that it looks for group developmental stages in only one type of group, for example, problem-solving groups (see Bales & Strodtbeck, 1951), or it may be very broad and look for group developmental stages that seem applicable to most types of groups. Tuckman's (1965) work, which examined particularly therapy and training groups, but also some other group types, is this broad-based type of study. As the scope becomes broader, specificity may be lost, but it is precisely this breadth of approach that is being pursued in this book so that similarities might be found in a wide range of group contexts. (Of course, it is possible to look at the overall development of several groups and still be unable to conclude that widely applicable developmental stages exist; the bias here has already been revealed.)

These distinctions on specific aspects of the development of groups, group development of a single, specific group, and more general group developmental stages are not mutually exclusive, but they proceed from the more particular to the more general so that a worker on group developmental stages may incorporate material from the other areas. For example, in looking at some aspect of a group's history, such as the development of relationships to the leader, or the orientation to the task, certain behaviors may be found that can be generalized to or included in a conceptualization of overall, general group developmental stages. Or a researcher may look at several studies on the group development of single groups and find that there are similarities, that is, that there are general group developmental stages. This was largely the approach with therapy groups taken by Tuckman (1965). Conversely, any material on specific aspects of a group's development, such as the relationship to the leader or to the task, should not be inconsistent with group developmental stage work, though there may be differences in emphasis under different conditions with different leaders, or a particular group may proceed in an atypical way for various reasons.

The sequence of these uses of the word *development* from specific aspects of development, to group development of a specific group, to general group developmental stages is partly a historical sequence in that as knowledge about groups has grown it has become feasible to broaden the scope of study. For example, a worker today who wants to study the development of a particular, single group would have the advantage of the general group developmental stage literature already at his disposal. With it he could see if the group under study shows general group developmental stages, and, if not, how it differs from other, similar groups that have been studied, and so on.

For completeness, and to avoid confusion in looking at the group literature, two other uses of the word *development* must be mentioned. One of these is the use of *development* in group work in which the focus is on what occurs in groups of people facing life's "developmental" problems. Possible examples are groups of youngsters dealing with their age-related developmental problems, such as groups of latency-aged children or adolescents (Button, 1974; Gazda, 1975; Smith, 1960), or groups of adults dealing with such developmental issues as effective parenting or the death of a spouse (Drum & Knott, 1977).

There will be little further mention of such developmental groups, but the reader can see that such groups can also be studied in terms of all of the preceding points of view on *development,* although there may be a lower age limit for some of these phenomena, such as significant group developmental stages. Gazda (1975 and 1976) explicitly makes use of group developmental stages in working with such "developmental groups," particularly in school counseling.

Finally, *development* is used in reference to groups that are part of and operate parallel to group-oriented training or treatment programs. These development or "D groups" are used to follow and work on the developing training or treatment that members are undergoing. For example, in the Topeka VA Medical Center human relations alcohol-drug treatment module, patients are divided into D groups whose task is largely to follow and work on the course of development of their overall treatment.

The answer to the question "the development of what?" or "group developmental stages of what?" is whatever is significant in the patterns or sequences of development across different groups at comparable points in time. Many of the specifics of the answer have already been addressed in the introductory chapter, which is a distillation of experience with group developmental stages and the relevant literature.

Group developmental stage variables will be considered in relation to the task—defining it, learning how to accomplish it, determining how well the task is achieved, and so on—and the social and emotional reactions of the group members—including the affects of individual members, the interactions between members, and the interactions between members and the leader. The focus will be on the members and on the group as a whole when it is an actual group, which will usually be the case.

One could also study the developmental stages of group leaders, but that is not the task here, and there is little data in this area. It may not be surprising to suggest that when there is a group leader he or she experiences developmental stages analogous to those of the members, that is, orientation, dissatisfaction, resolution, production, and termination. Winter, (1976) has written an anecdotal paper on this topic for leaders of training groups.

Types of Group Developmental Stage Models

Various types of group developmental stage models have been pursued (Mann, Gibbard & Hartman, 1967; Gibbard, Hartman & Mann, 1974, pp. 83–93; and compare Banet, 1976); one of these is the recurrent cycle model, which can be contrasted with the successive stage model. In the recurrent cycle model, various issues or problems or approaches to problems are viewed as recurring within a group's life cycle—for example, concerns with dependency, usually with improved ability to handle these concerns when they recur.

An example of this model is the work of Bradford (1964), who looks at the development of T groups and sees it

> ... as a cyclic process in which learning recurs in increasing depth. The T group approaches and reapproaches the same basic problems of relationships to authority, of interpersonal distance and relationships, of goal formation, of decision making, of norm setting, of communication. Growth lies not in ultimate "solutions" but in the readiness to face up to basic problems and in the improvement of methods by which the group approaches them (p. 205).

(See also the recent similar summary by Bradford, 1978.) This recurrent cycle model makes the discovery of group developmental stages more difficult in that it requires discovering not only the characteristics of the cycle, but also the number of recurrences in different groups and group types if possible, and then some way of deciding whether those are similar enough across groups to talk of generalized group developmental stages.

Sometimes the recurrent cycle approach focuses not so much on overall group development or group developmental stages as on underlying concerns or dynamics of groups. Bion's (1961) theoretical speculations tend to be of this type. In Bion's model there is a recurrence of such things as concern with dependency, but since there is no clear specification of when these concerns occur and recur, his work tends to deal more with underlying group concerns (compare Braaten, 1974–1975) or group preoccupations, rather than with group developmental stages.

Others have put Bion's theory into a group developmental stage format with successive stages, for example, Babad and Amir, 1978; Kingdom, 1973, pp. 80–81; Slater, 1966; and here in Chapter 5. Also see Hare, 1973, pp. 301–302 concerning Slater. Levine (1971) obtained largely negative results in a research attempt at this issue, but Babad and Amir (1978) obtained positive results. Some of these studies will be returned to later.

The recurrent cycle model contrasts with the successive stage model, which postulates more of a progression with the solving of certain issues, which are then somewhat resolved, moving on to other issues, which are resolved, then to other issues, and so on. For example, one of the earliest issues will be clarifying why the group is together and what its goals are, reaching a fairly thorough answer to these questions, and then moving on to something else. Tuckman's (1965) group developmental stage model is an example of this work.

The difference between the recurrent and successive stage models is sometimes a question of emphasis. In the recurrent cycle model it is usually acknowledged that there is progress in the handling of an issue, even though the same issue may recur —for example, the ability to work on the problem of dependency should improve each time it is approached. In fact, the previously mentioned Bradford work (1964, pp. 207–208) tends toward a successive stage model in that when barriers are faced there is dissatisfaction, but the first such episode of dissatisfaction is particularly pronounced ("failure shock"), making a first cycle that is quite different from subsequent ones. Similarly, in the successive stage model such issues as dependency or why the group is together, which are examined early in the group's history, are apt to be reexamined to some extent later when the group is predominately within a different developmental stage.

The distinction between the recurrent cycle and successive stage models can break down, as will be explained later, in that in the successive stage model there may be partial cycles that recur within the group developmental stages. For example, in groups with a long history, such as therapy groups, there may be repetitive episodes within the production stage that resemble the earlier dissatisfaction and resolution stages but are less intense.

Another set of contrasting approaches to the development of groups is a partial history versus a full history or full life cycle model (Mann et al., 1967, p. 192; Gibbard et al., 1974, p. 85). Many studies on the development of groups stop at the point where the group is working well or adequately with the implication—probably at least partly inadvertent—that that is all there is to group developmental stages. Tuckman's model and review (1965) is an example of this approach, as is apparently the work of Ottaway (1966).

The alternative is to study the full history or life cycle of the group until its official ending. This is the approach followed here and in many studies on group developmental stages. A failure to study the full group life cycle can only give an incomplete picture, though some studies that stopped before a group's ending have excellent data on the earlier group developmental stages (Lubin & Zuckerman, 1967; and Tuckman, 1965).

In some sense "group developmental stage" phenomena continue after a group's official termination, for example, in the fantasy recall of the individual members or their occasional chance meetings, or arranged meetings in various alumni reunions. There is little in the literature in this area, and not much will be said about it. Rodgers (1970) alludes to this post-group behavior in talking about members of encounter groups helping each other outside the group sessions, which can of course be after the group experience formally terminates. Libo (1977), in a book entitled *Is there Life After Group?*, makes at least tangential comments on the subject.

The model proposed here is a full life cycle, successive

stage model with the acknowledgment that some of the problems, such as the purpose of the group, may to some extent continue throughout the group's history. (See Figure 1.1)

SOME RESEARCH PROBLEMS IN GROUP DEVELOPMENTAL STAGE WORK

Good research work on group developmental stages must, of course, follow accepted research principles and practices, including appropriate nonbiased observations, controls when possible, appropriate tests of statistical significance, and so on. Little will be said about most of these areas except when it seems necessary to comment on a particular study, and except for an occasional general comment, such as the tendency of group developmental stage work to be more anecdotal than strongly research oriented.

What we will briefly discuss here are some of the specific research problems in the group developmental stage area, and how these have been handled. (Additional general material on group developmental stage research is provided by Hare, 1973 and 1976, and by Gibbard et al., 1974, pp. 83–93.)

Once there is a clear understanding of what constitutes a group, and the type of development we are considering (group developmental stages), the next questions ask what data does one look for, how are these data collected and handled, and in what group contexts? These topics will be considered under the following headings: (1) data collection and measurement; (2) data analysis; and (3) group characteristics: type and size of group, length and number of meetings.

These areas will be briefly discussed before we look at the available literature and the degree to which it meets these and the requirements discussed earlier. No attempt will be made to suggest an ideal group developmental stage research project, which is yet to be undertaken. This section will be more concerned with discussing the questions that a researcher in this area has to consider, realizing that if he doesn't, the research will be somewhat the worse for it. Only a few studies achieve praiseworthy standards in these regards. This discussion will also help in testing the strength of the foundation of the GDSs and the GDS theory developed here.

Data Collection and Measurement

The student of group developmental stages must learn whether different groups show some similarity or consistency of changes (stages) during the group's life cycle. To do this, one must decide what to look for in the group and its members. This partly depends on each researcher's orientation, but there is considerable agreement that there must be an adequate sampling of variables relating to the task and to the social-emotional behavior in the group if the researcher is to characterize adequately the important events and behaviors throughout the group's history.

For example, Bales' (1950) categories classify the group's behavior into attempted answers and questions (the task) and positive and negative reactions. Stock and Thelen (1958), Lubin and Zuckerman (1967), and many others sample task and affect variables, and this is the organizing structure Tuckman followed in his review (1965). This allows each stage of the development to be characterized by its emotional tone or tones, often including social-emotional interactions, and the degree and/or kind of attention to the task. Similarly, this book will focus mainly on the predominate emotions experienced and usually shown by the members of the group, on the social interaction, and on the attention to and success with the task.

Related to the question of *what* to measure is the question of how *deeply* one measures. If an angry comment is made from one group member to another, is it taken at face value only? Is it also considered that the real target of the comment may be the group leader, and further, that the anger may be not real anger, but a thinly veiled plea for help? And how does one decide these questions? Do you let one rater do so? Or do you use two and try to obtain consensus? Do you ask the group members after the meeting what they "really" meant? Will they know, or will the significance of some of their behavior be beyond the reach of their awareness?

Might the more knowledgeable group leader be asked? Will the group leader recall or know what particular members were experiencing at a certain time? Will the leader's evaluations be too biased because of knowledge of the research, so that the group will be led down particular developmental paths in the first place? It can be easily seen that as one proceeds from the more superficial, face-value level, the possibilities for disagreement and bias increase considerably. There are no simple answers to these questions, and, as we shall see, many solutions have been tried.

Having decided to assess task and social-emotional behaviors, does one try to assess all the behavior in the group and consider it from task and social-emotional perspectives? Or does one assess only the easy-to-rate explicit verbal behavior? But even when confined to only verbal behavior, the amount of data from a single meeting can be massive. In Bales' problem-solving groups, where nearly only verbal behavior is assessed, the number of acts or statements per problem-unit is usually several hundred (Bales & Strodtbeck, 1951), or about 1000 per hour (Hare, 1973, p. 295). Mann and colleagues (1967) rate units in which the expressed feelings are uniform, and they record about 200 units per hour (pp. 60–61).

For practical purposes, with groups meeting for a number of meetings one is usually forced to examine only a sample of the data, and one hopes a representative sample. If only certain meetings are sampled, which ones? If the first and last meetings are not examined, it will not be possible to say anything about these meetings. (For example, Lubin and Zuckerman [1967], omitted data on the last two meetings of a 12-meeting sequence, and thus excluded data on termination stage behavior.)

How safely can one assume that what happens in the meetings between sampled meetings is consonant with what is sampled and is not quite different behavior? Might one miss an entire stage? And if one samples only parts of meetings, which parts? What parts of a group meeting are typical—the beginnings, middles, ends? And does one examine all the members of the group or only a sample?

In most actual groups that have been studied it has been feasible to sample all members at whatever times data collecting is done, and this method is usually preferred to examining only a sample of the members on a greater number of occasions. One important advantage of gathering data from all members is that it allows an examination of overall group phenomena; that would be much more difficult, or even impossible, if only some members were studied at each data gathering point.

As the size of actual groups becomes very large, for example, sociopolitical groups, it becomes necessary to study only some members of the group. This is also true with most conceptual groups, unless the size of the conceptual group is delimited by definition. For example, a conceptual group of new teachers might include only those under a particular school board.

These questions on what and how to measure and sample will be answered in only a limited way with material from the literature. Some of this material will be presented here, and some in a more detailed discussion of various pieces of research presented in the next chapter. The reader who is more interested in these questions will have to turn to standard reference materials on research methodology and observational methods, such as Hare, 1962 and 1976; Heyns and Zander, 1953; Mills, 1967; Selltiz et al., 1959 and 1976; Stock and Lieberman, 1962; Weick, 1968; and the journal, *Small Group Behavior,* Volume 7, No. 1, February 1976.

The most frequent solution to the above observational problems has been to try for an adequate sampling of group behavior over the course of the group's life cycle, and to have observers assess the behavior and either categorize or rate it. These are two overlapping ways of taking the raw data and making it manageable by grouping it in certain ways. A category system places the behavior in certain categories and examines how much behavior falls into each category devised. A rating scale assesses the degree to which behavior belongs to a certain type, for example, aggressiveness between members can be rated on a seven-point scale.

The number of categories or rating devices used will depend on what one is looking for, what is practical, and so on. In either case, few to many categories or ratings can be used. However one classifies the data, if particular behaviors have not been separated into a category or rating scale, it will be difficult to say much or anything about these behaviors. And if a sufficient range of behavior is not categorized or rated, too much data will be lost.

Some of the best developed and most widely used category systems and ratings scales are Bales' Interaction Process Analysis category system (Bales, 1950 and 1970), Hill's Interaction Matrix for statement-by-statement assessment and the related rating scales, for example, Hill Interaction Matrix-G or HIM-G, which reduces the assessor's job to 72 rating scales (Hill, 1977; Hill & Gruner, 1973), and the scales developed by Mann and colleagues (Mann et al., 1967).

Details of these scales will not be discussed here since examples of the use of each will be given in the next chapter, where the measuring devices will also be briefly described. Suffice it to say that each of these systems is capable of assessing a wide range of group behavior, including task and social-emotional behavior, and with considerable reliability when the raters are trained. (Bales has achieved reliability coefficients of 0.75 to 0.95, and the Hill and Mann scales approximate similar reliabilities; the reliability coefficients vary with the study, the type of reliability, and other factors, but the levels achieved are well within the useful range.) In general, these three sets of devices tend to go from more directly observable behavior to more in-depth, inferential assessments.

Many other approaches to data collection and assessment

can be and have been used, and there is no magic answer in any of these. It is important for the researcher to be aware of the strengths and weaknesses of whatever devices are used. There are many measuring instruments available to assess anxiety, hostility, depression, group interaction, and so on, and several different instruments can be used together with attention to what data one is gathering, what is being lost, and so on. Such instruments should sample a range of behaviors, and should not be too highly intercorrelated. (This is what happened with Lubin and Zuckerman's work [1967]; their affect measures of *anxiety, hostility,* and *depression* had Pearson intercorrelations of 0.81 to 0.92 in their subjects.) An approach to data collection and handling that allows the examining of large amounts of data is a computer system called the "General Inquirer," a method of content analysis for written material from meetings (Stone et al., 1962, 1966).

In addition, use should be made of whatever natural data are available. These data that need no special rating or measuring devices include whether members show up for meetings early or late, or not at all, whether work to be done between meetings is done well and on time, and when these things happen in the sequence of meetings. Also, such phenomena as lingering after meetings can be recorded.

These data tell something about the members' eagerness or lack of eagerness to be there, their diligence on the task, and so forth. Although the literature contains many remarks about these natural observations, they are often not incorporated into the data for group developmental stages, or they are incorporated with reluctance, supposedly because they are "soft" data. (For literature on unobtrusive measures, see Palmer and McGuire [1973] and Webb et al., [1966].)

There are many other sources of difficulty in data collection. For example, if the group is led by a leader who conducts a group in accordance with particular group developmental stage ideas, or if observers have such a bias, then that can distort the neutrality of the data and observations (see the discussion of Bennis, [1964]). In one interesting study (Runkel et al., 1971) that attempted to confirm Tuckman's ideas (1965) for group developmental stages the observers were informed about Tuckman's hypotheses ahead of time. Then the researchers did not attempt to record all data that might impinge on group development, but only that related to the hypotheses in question.

If the observations of meetings are not rated or otherwise evaluated while they are occurring, or immediately after an observed meeting, then there must be some way to record the group meeting data for later evaluation. One can choose here on the basis of how stringent one wants to be, and what is available, practical, and so on. Many things are possible, from handwritten notes during the meetings to audio and videotape recordings. If only an audio recording is used, much of the social-emotional behavior is lost. One practical method is to have an observer or two record the nonverbal material, either at the meeting itself or from a videotape, and then to place these observations in the appropriate place on a transcript of the verbal portion of the meeting (Psathas, 1960).

Data Analysis

After one decides what data to collect, and actually collects it, it is necessary to see if it can be divided into stages. Does one arbitrarily decide that there are five stages and divide the total number of group meetings into fifths and see if these fifths differ from each other? Or does one divide by quarters or thirds? Are these fractions figured on a temporal basis, or a quantitative basis of the amount of group interaction, which is not especially equally distributed over time? Or does one look for other organizing principles and divide the group meetings on this basis without attention to whether the stages are equal in length or amount of behavior? Or does one do this by other means, whatever these might be?

The literature reveals a considerable number of different methods of dividing data from group meetings, including breakdowns into equal time, quantity of interaction, and other organizing principles. If the emphasis is more on the degree of work or task output, then that can lead to dividing one way; if it is more on the interaction between members, it can lead to dividing another way; and if it is more on the interaction between the members and leader, yet another way (see Mann et al., 1967). (The method of dividing into stages used here is primarily based on a conceptual schema emphasizing task and social-emotional group behavior.)

The number of stages or trends or phases one finds will also depend on how "coarse" or "fine" one wants the distinctions to be. The coarser distinctions will be easier to find and replicate in more settings, whereas the finer distinctions are apt to be more difficult to replicate in many group settings. For example, it is easy to find behaviors of the two stages of orientation and termination in many experiences. We will soon see that there are many mutually supporting research and anecdotal papers that find three or four or five discernible group developmental stages. Some of the studies that found three of four stages failed to find a fourth or a fifth stage because they neglected the ending or termination stage of the group. Occasionally studies may have found more stages than other studies because they subdivided a division by focusing more on certain problems or areas than other studies.

The next question of when each stage occurs in the history of the group is very much related to what stages one sees, how one looks for them, how the stages are characterized, and so on. It is also often difficult to be very precise about a stage's location because the stages blend into each other, and each group is somewhat idiosyncratic in spite of a focus on similarities across groups. More important than the number of a particular meeting, whether it is the third or tenth, and so on, will be whether a meeting is at or near the start, middle, or end of the group's life cycle. If the tenth meeting is one of an anticipated hundred or so meetings, that will be very different than if it is the last meeting of a ten-meeting sequence.

Some final cautions are necessary in this area regarding the naming, numbering, and placing of stages within the group's life cycle. Because two writers call a stage by the same name does not necessarily mean that they refer to the same behaviors and, conversely, when different names are used writers may be referring to basically the same behaviors. Also, one worker may describe a group developmental stage that is not located at quite the same place in development by another writer describing a similar stage. Not many studies are so precise in this regard that this is often a significant problem.

Data on group developmental stages have not usually been subjected to vigorous statistical analysis, though there are several exceptions; these include the work of Bales (for example, Bales & Strodtbeck, 1951), Levine (1971), Lubin & Zuckerman (1967), Mann (1966), Psathas (1960), and Tindall (1971). The interested reader is referred to their publications for the various statistical analyses they employed.

Leik and Mathews (1968) have developed a scale and statistical methods for handling developmental processes, and this might be useful in work with group developmental stages. Following their suggestions, it may be possible to do cross-sectional studies of different, similar groups at different developmental times, and to look for group developmental stages. One of the questions about such an approach is whether the "cross-sections" are representative of a continuous process, for example, whether the later cross-sectional data come from groups that had earlier experiences similar to those of the groups from which there is earlier cross-sectional data. These crucial methodological questions are addressed but left unanswered by Krain (1975), in a communications-focused study of "stages" of dating behavior. The study did not find different general developmental stages, but a linear progression in the development of communication.

One must be cautious in assessing the actual as opposed to

the statistical significance of any study, since many studies have examined only one group or one type of group, and under limited conditions. More definitive work in this area will eventually require the study of different types of groups by a similar methodology.

Group Characteristics: Type and Size of Group, Length and Number of Meetings

If we grant that developmental stages can be found in groups, in what types of groups can they be found? Are the stages similar regardless of the type of group, or do they differ in different group settings and, if so, in what ways? Is this material applicable only to actual groups, or does it apply also to conceptual groups?

A comprehensive theory of group developmental stages should be applicable to as wide a range of group types as possible and not only to one type of group, or not only to groups that have a long or short history, and so on. Of course, differences are to be expected, but the emphasis will be on seeing whether there are enough similarities to deduce the existence of general group developmental stages. The available literature has looked at several types of groups, considered largely according to their task. These group types and whether they are actual or conceptual groups are:

1. Problem-solving or laboratory groups (actual groups)
2. Training or T groups (actual groups)
3. Encounter groups (actual groups)
4. Therapy groups (actual groups)
5. "Naturalistic" groups (The tasks in this heterogeneous collection of groups vary widely, but these groups include committees, learning groups of various kinds, several types of work teams, and some sociopolitical groups. This category includes both actual and conceptual groups.)

There is some overlap between these group types, but they are usually distinct enough to be considered separately. Generally, from the top to the bottom of this list, the quality of the group study goes from more to less rigorous in terms of experimental conditions, methodology, quality and reliability of observations, and preference for controlled rather than more anecdotal observations. On the other hand, the closer a group is to the bottom of the list, usually the more directly applicable it is to usual life situations.

Group developmental stages should be seen within actual groups varying widely in size, length of meetings, and number of meetings. The groups examined as the literature is reviewed will usually vary in size from three to 20 members. Occasional problem-solving groups may have only two members, and some encounter groups and occasionally training groups exceed 20 members. Some of the naturalistic groups will be much larger than this, particularly the conceptual groups consisting of a class of individuals and loosely formed actual groups (see, for example, the sociopolitical studies of Davies, 1969, and Feierabend, Feierabend & Nesvold, 1969). A dyad can be considered a group, but except when we consider "being in love," dyads will be largely excluded.

Group meetings of actual groups usually range from one to two hours in length, but encounter groups usually exceed this. Some actual naturalistic groups may also be longer, for example, long committee meetings and longer work groups. Conceptual groups may or may not have meetings in which the members are together.

The number of group meetings in the actual groups reviewed will vary from one to 100 or more. But this factor will not usually be crucial, as long as the number of meetings constitutes the full history of the group and the group is not abruptly and artificially terminated. It is important in this regard that there be a definite start and end to the group's history, and generally that members have some awareness of when the end will come.

Shorter group histories, especially in groups that have only one or two meetings, can make group developmental stage phenomena more difficult, but not impossible, to observe. These shorter groups often call forth the observer's skills more than groups with longer histories. We will soon see that in Bales' work (Bales & Strodtbeck, 1951), meetings of a single hour can be long enough to provide identifiable group developmental stage data.

RESEARCH ON GENERAL DEVELOPMENTAL STAGES IN CONCEPTUAL GROUPS

There will be no detailed discussion of research require-ments for studying GDSs in conceptual groups that have simi-lar but not shared tasks and whose participants may or may not spend time together. Much of what is required here follows from what has been said already. There should be an evaluation of social-emotional and task behaviors throughout the experi-ence, and the experience should be one that elicits adequate personal involvement from the participants. There should be a definite starting point and usually an ending point, although the latter may be clearly established only as the experience devel-ops.

There is little information on the minimum length of time for the experience, but this will depend on the personal signifi-cance of the task as well as on other factors. These temporal considerations apply not only to calendar days, but also time per day, and an experience of only a few minutes per day even for months may or may not be adequate to show GDSs. There may also be a practical length of time beyond which other factors, such as other significant experiences, obscure the rela-tively simple GDSs.

Questions of conceptual group size are partly questions of the number of individuals required to show these general devel-opmental stage phenomena in spite of individual differences.

This will vary with the context and the specific individuals, but if the sample size is too small, individual differences may obscure the GDSs that might be present.

There are not many conceptual group studies available, but examples will be seen in the next chapter, particularly in the naturalistic group section—for example, Mitchell's (1975) study of people moving their residences. Also, there are GDS conceptual group studies beginning with a negative orientation stage, such as those of Masterson (1972) and Rinsley (1974).

CONCLUSIONS

To complete rigorous studies in this developmental stage area is a difficult sociopsychological research task, and to do this and end up with data that are sufficiently useful in practical settings is an even more formidable job. There are only a few studies with high research standards, and several of these will be discussed later. Even when good scientific methods are used, we have to accept that different groups have some significant differences between them in terms of members, leaders, and so on. And as we cross from one group type to another, for example, from problem-solving to training to naturalistic groups, there are even more differences. So the job of finding group developmental stages in a variety of settings becomes progressively more difficult. In spite of these problems, a considerable degree of consistency can be found in the wealth of material that is available.

Chapter 4

THE DATA BASE:

Group and General Developmental Stage Studies

What do the studies of group developmental stages show? If we accept that studies with exemplary methodological rigor are few and far between, what data are available? Do the studies sufficiently substantiate the summary of stages presented in Chapter one—orientation, dissatisfaction, resolution, production, and termination—or its shorter variation—orientation, dissatisfaction, production, and termination? Some literature reviews are available (for example, Braaten, 1974–1975; Cooper & Mangham, 1971; Hare, 1963 and 1973; and Tuckman, 1965), but a more extensive review will be undertaken here.

The literature will be reviewed under the previously mentioned categories of training or T groups, problem-solving or laboratory groups, therapy groups, encounter groups, and "naturalistic" groups. We begin with training groups since they represent a feasible compromise between the rigor of the studies and "naturalness" and general applicability. Subsequently, the more rigorous but more artificial problem-solving or laboratory group work will be examined, then therapy groups, encounter groups, and finally "naturalistic" groups, the group type most seen in everyday experience. These are primarily actual group studies.

Studies were included only if they were written in English, were recent and/or significant, and concentrated on the development of more than one group or at least on a comparison between the development of the group under consideration and that of other groups (group developmental stage studies). Citations of essentially the same material in multiple sources have generally not been included. Only a few dissertations are included.

Within these limits the review is extensive, excluding by design only some of the older, primarily single-group studies, many of which were included in Tuckman's review published in 1965.

TRAINING GROUPS

Training groups are those that meet so that the members can examine how groups function and how the participants behave in them; they are usually composed of 10 to 15 members. These groups are often known as T groups, or sometimes as laboratory or laboratory training groups, but the term *laboratory* applies even more to the problem-solving groups considered later, so its use will be restricted to them.

In recent years training groups have been called sensitivity or sensitivity training groups, to emphasize the goal of increasing sensitivity to one's own and to others' feelings and reactions in a group context. When these groups began about 30 years ago they were primarily to teach and train about groups, and sometimes for academic credit. Then, as part of the recent "group movement" with encounter groups, Gestalt groups, and so on, there was sometimes an additional goal of personal growth—something that is often (always?) part of the members' fantasies anyway.

All of this makes it difficult to delimit training groups precisely, although most of the group studies discussed in this section will be at the more traditional, nonpersonal growth end of the continuum of these groups; even here there is still a continuum of approaches. Among the differences are the degree to which the leadership is authoritarian and is perceived as such, and the degree of leader confrontation in the dissatisfaction stage. Especially some of the earlier nonpersonal growth approaches with training groups were engineered, probably somewhat inadvertently, to have a high degree of confrontation of the leader (for example, Bennis & Shepard, 1956). More recent training groups do not, and cannot, avoid this altogether. But it is less deliberately created and less marked, partly because of what has been learned over the years about these and other groups (see Mann, 1975).

(For additional discussion of training group approaches, see Klein & Astrachan, 1971, and Crowfoot, 1971; some more explicitly personal growth and encounter group data will be reviewed in another section of this chapter.)

It is also necessary to distinguish training groups from learning groups; these latter groups utilize group processes and phenomena to facilitate learning and training primarily about something other than the group itself, for example, about psychiatric nursing or practicing law (Lacoursiere, 1974 and 1980). Several examples of learning group developmental stage studies will be reviewed later in this chapter.

Training group meetings usually last one to two hours, and they may meet for anywhere from about 10 to 50 meetings. The number of meetings is usually spelled out ahead of time. The goal of these groups requires considerable cooperation among group members so that the task or group goal is largely a shared goal. Even without group cooperation there are group data to study, including the lack of cooperation, but it is very difficult to function under these conditions. This cooperative group goal can be contrasted with the goals of other groups in which less cooperation is required for an individual member to achieve his or her goals, for example, many learning groups, some therapy groups such as transactional analysis and Gestalt groups, or a member of a sales force.

Training groups generally have a group leader who may be called a trainer, facilitator, or consultant rather than a leader. The leader of the types of training groups discussed here would rarely, if ever, consider himself or herself a therapist, although members may often consider them such, explicitly or implicitly. The leader usually provides only a minimum amount of guidance to the group, allowing intragroup and intergroup and intrapsychic experiences and fantasies to develop to a considerable extent. Such groups get their members very involved, and the experience can be quite stressful—in extreme cases to the point of provoking or precipitating significant psychiatric problems.

There is an additional point about training groups that will sometimes also apply to other types of group experiences. Training groups as considered here are sometimes conducted as part of a program on training groups and related group phenomena. In such programs, besides the training group itself, there are larger group experiences, sometimes intergroup exercises with other training groups, and sometimes interspersed didactic sessions. Often there are some differences in leadership in the different experiences. What this means is that there are a variety of group experiences going on in the same program, and this obscures GDSs and makes their discovery more difficult.

Most of the studies described here do not emanate from such programs, but the reader should be alerted to these possibilities in examining for GDSs. (The reader interested in more general information on training groups can see Bales, 1970; Cooper, 1975; Cooper & Mangham, 1971; Dyer, 1972; or Kissen, 1976. Kissen's work is a collection of articles, several of which are referred to here in their original published source, especially in the chapter on theory.)

Some of the better studies in this area will be discussed in some detail to show the type of group developmental stage material that is available, how it was gathered, and so on. This will also help the reader understand that the generalization from particulars required for a full picture in this area depends on a broad view and on an examination of many studies under many conditions. These same comments will apply to studies of other group types.

Stock and Thelen

One of the significant, early pieces of research on training groups was done by Stock and Thelen (1958). (Also see Stock, 1964; Thelen & Dickerman, 1949; and Whitaker & Thelen, 1975.) They studied a training group of 16 members, including a trainer and an associate trainer, during each of its 13 two-hour meetings over a two-week period. There was no set agenda other than that the goals of the group " . . . were to provide experiences for the members that could help each of them grow towards a greater understanding of the character of group operations and their own behaviors and feelings in a group situation" (Stock & Thelen, 1958, p. 192).

Two nonparticipating observers, the authors, independently rated every statement made during a "natural" sample averaging 60 minutes per group meeting. The statements were rated according to the quality of work on a four-point scale, and the emotional character of the statement was categorized if there was any detectable affect (detected in 41% of statements). The emotionality was categorized according to Bion's ideas (1961; see also Rioch, 1970) that groups frequently function as if there were certain basic assumptions regarding the emotional and interpersonal character of the group at that particular time.

These "basic assumptions," with Stock and Thelen's interpretations in parentheses, are fight (hostility and aggression), flight (avoidance, withdrawal), pairing (warmth, intimacy, supportiveness), and dependency (depending or relying on a person or thing external to the group members). Besides these four emotional categories (fight, flight, pairing, and dependency), a fifth miscellaneous category was used when the affect did not clearly belong in one of the other categories. Disagreements between the raters were reconciled via discussions between them.

They identified what they considered natural units of group interaction, which ranged from 4 to 20 units per meeting; the average amount of emotionality of all types and the average work level on the task of studying the group were calculated for each statement in these units. Then for each meeting the overall average amount of emotionality per statement and the overall average amount of work per statement for all units were calculated.

They defined stages in the group's development by putting a meeting's statements, rated according to the amount of work and emotionality, into each of four quadrants according to high and low work and high and low emotionality for each statement. (Note here that they distinguished only the amount of emotionality, not the type.) In this way they found that their group moved through four stages.

The first stage was a period of exploration and included attempts to define a task. This lasted for three meetings and took place in the quadrants with low work and either high or low amounts of emotionality. Their brief description of emotions in this stage includes a statement that the feeling tone was " . . . one of aimlessness and increasing frustration" (p. 199).

The second stage, which lasted for two meetings, showed some movement toward more organized discussion of the issues, but when this occurred it tended to be accompanied by decreased emotionality, that is, there was either low work and high emotionality, or high work and low emotionality.

In the third and longest stage (six of 13 meetings), there was more work on the task, and feelings were at a high level and were integrated with and supportive of the task.

In the final stage (in the last two meetings), they found members still working hard, but withdrawing their affect from the situation (decreased emotionality). "In general, then, this group increased its ability to work effectively as a unit. Personal expressions of feelings were more relevantly introduced as time went on. The [overall amount of] expression of affect did not decrease (except in the last two meetings), but the way affect was expressed and used did change" (p. 232). That is, the affect or emotionality became more relevant to the task. They noted parenthetically that the decreased emotionality in the last two meetings " . . . may be an effect of anticipating the breakup of the group" (p. 197).

Can this study reasonably be interpreted according to the GDS terms proposed here? The first exploratory stage of three meetings—which included attempts to define the task, a low work level, and increasing frustration—seems to include the orientation and dissatisfaction stages. The second stage of two meetings was an attempt at more organized discussion of the issues, but there was difficulty integrating the discussion with the affect expressed. This stage corresponds to the proposed resolution stage. In the next stage of six meetings, work and affect are better integrated; this can be considered the production stage. The final stage of two meetings, with continued hard work but with a withdrawal of affect from the group, is the termination stage.

From their work Stock and Thelen felt that "there is no indication that the particular developmental characteristics of this group would necessarily be found in other groups" (p. 206). They did study another group and felt that it largely stayed within their stage one (p. 233). Nonetheless, they felt that examining a group in terms of work and emotionality was a profitable way of looking at group development, and that any attempt to study only one of these areas would be inadequate. "In general," they added later, "we do not expect the particular sequence of work-emotionality cultures to be constant from group to group, but to depend on such factors as the particular valency characteristics of the members, the leader's personal needs and leadership approach, and the task demands to which the group is subject" (Whitaker & Thelen, 1975, p. 76). The term *valency characteristics* refers to Bion's (1961) idea of the tendency of an individual to respond particularly in one of the basic assumption ways—pairing, dependency, fight, or flight— with these latter two often being the opposite sides of the same coin.

This study is a good example of early work in this field, at a time when it was not yet clearly realized that general group developmental stages might be found. It would have been helpful if Stock and Thelen had given more details on the types of emotionality in each stage, rather than primarily only the amount of emotionality. Nonetheless, the reader can see how later group developmental stage work owes considerable credit to this study, which strictly speaking is more a study of group development than of group developmental stages, since they did not find general developmental stages in different groups.

Mann, Gibbard, and Hartman

Mann and his associates, Gibbard and Hartman (1967; Mann, 1966; and see also Hare, 1973), studied group developmental stages primarily from the perspective of the member-to-leader relationship in four groups of students in a course in the Social Relations Department at Harvard University. The purpose of the course was "to improve the student's ability to observe, analyze, and understand behavior in interpersonal relations."

Each group met for a one-hour meeting five times per week for 32 meetings. The researchers made verbatim transcripts from tape recordings. They then created a scoring system based on units consisting of a single speech or sentence group within which the expressed feelings toward the leader were uniform; there were about 200 such units per hour. The statements of the leader himself were considered reflections of the feelings of the group members. The researchers restricted themselves to units of feelings toward the leader to make it easier to assess the mass of data generated by any communication that simultaneously includes direct and indirect, and explicit and implicit messages to several people in the group (Mann et al., 1967, p. 66).

The units were divided into four levels ranging from direct to inferential expressions toward the leader. They were also divided into 16 social-emotional categories (Table 4.1). These categories were grouped according to hostile and affectionate impulses toward the leader, dependent and competitive authority relations, and an ego-state area reflecting expressed self-esteem and expressed and denied anxiety and depression.

They then factor analyzed the data and derived six basic factors (Table 4.2). The first factor, "relations with the leader as analyst," varied from (positive) enactment to (negative) dependent complaining. There were comparable peaks of positive enactment and valleys of negative dependent complaining for this factor for each of the four groups. This factor, most particularly its positive side, is central to the task of the group, that is, using data from the leader to help understand the group. Accordingly, the other factors were compared with this first factor.

These other factors dealt with loyalty versus rebellion, counterdependent flight versus resistant complaining, the leader as a colleague versus concern with inner distress, anxiety versus depression, and emotional involvement versus emotional neutrality toward the leader. There was a significant one-way analysis of variance for these five factors arranged to correspond in time with the fluctuations of factor I—that is, group developmental stages were statistically confirmed.

This work contains a wealth of data on group developmental stages, but for our purposes only some of the more relevant highlights will be pointed out. (The stages are organized differently in the two studies; although the 1967 work is emphasized.) The following description combines the two presentations.

During the first two stages, which are an *appraisal,* counterdependent flight and anxiety are at their peaks, and high

Table 4.1. Member-To-Leader scoring system categories

Area	Subarea	Category
Impulse	Hostility	1. Moving against
		2. Resisting
		3. Withdrawing
		4. Guilt inducing
	Affection	5. Making reparation
		6. Identifying
		7. Accepting
		8. Moving toward
Authority relations		9. Showing dependency
		10. Showing independence
		11. Showing counterdependence
Ego state	Anxiety	12. Expressing anxiety
		13. Denying anxiety
		14. Expressing self-esteem
	Depression	15. Expressing depression
		16. Denying depression

Adapted from Mann et al., 1967. Used with permission.

Table 4.2. Factors identified in Mann's 1967 Study

Factor I	Relations with the leader as analyst
	I + : Enactment
	I − : Dependent complaining
Factor II	Relations with the leader as authority figure
	II + : Rebellion
	II − : Loyalty
Factor III	Relations with the leader as manipulator
	III + : Counterdependent flight
	III − : Resistant complaining
Factor IV	Relations with the leader as audience
	IV + : Relating to the leader as colleague
	IV − : Concern with inner distress
Factor V	The effect of the leader on the ego state of the member
	V + : Anxiety
	V − : Depression
Factor VI	Commitment to the member–leader relationship
	VI + : Emotional involvement
	VI − : Emotional neutrality

Used with permission.

initial loyalty and involvement quickly decrease. In the next stage of *confrontation,* there is much rebellion, resistant complaining, and emotional neutrality with decreased anxiety. In the following stage of *internalization,* rebellion disappears, anxiety and depression are fairly low, and involvement increases. The last two stages, a *separation,* are marked by high loyalty and involvement, maximum depression, and a renewal of resistant complaining. Table 4.3 lists the stages as named by Mann (Mann, 1966; Mann et al., 1967), compared with the GDS names proposed here; there is considerable consistency between these two systems.

Table 4.3. A comparison of GDSs and the Mann stages

GDSs	Orientation	Dissatisfaction	Resolution	Production	Termination
Mann, 1966	Appraisal	Confrontation	Re-evaluation	Internalization	Separation
Mann et al., 1967	Initial complaining	Confrontation		Internalization	Separation
	Premature enactment				Terminal review

Mann's Stages as a Morale Curve

To illustrate viewing group developmental stages as a morale curve, the Mann work has been translated into a morale curve by algebraically summing the factor scores for each stage. Although this grossly oversimplifies Mann's work, it may still give a useful schematic view.

Enactment, loyalty, leader as colleague, and involvement have been considered positive scores, the others all negative. Some scores that were on the positive end of the factor continua, namely rebellion, counterdependent flight, and anxiety, have not been considered positive here since they are largely negative emotions or attitudes from the point of view of group morale.* Since the raw data were not published, approximate values have been read from the factor groupings (Mann et al., 1967, p. 151). These data are a summary of four separate training groups, but of course what we are looking for are general group developmental stages and not individual group particulars.

Figure 4.1, shows that when so plotted, the data describe a curve similar to the morale curve proposed earlier. The major discrepancy is that the orientation portion is below the baseline, possibly because the whole curve is low since the measuring instruments primarily assessed feelings toward the leader. Also, data for the first of the 32 meetings were not recorded in three of the four groups, and there might have been more positive morale data in those meetings—more data contributing to the factors considered positive, such as loyalty and involvement.

Since much of these initial data are missing, our conclusion is only speculative, but it appears that this group developmental stage sequence began with a negative orientation stage. In other words, with students in such an academic course there is less overall positive morale, or less positive morale initially: The students may have wanted or needed the academic credit, but they may not have been particularly eager to be in a class requiring such personal involvement. The naming of the stages in the 1967 report (Mann et al., 1967) begins with an "initial complaining" stage, which may be a negative orientation stage.

Levine (1971) also found that most of his training groups studied under similar academic conditions started negatively. This type of course is quite unlike other academic classes in that one's personal experience in, and reaction to, the class make up a large part of the data studied. We will have more to say later on negative orientation stages.

*If this regrouping is not done, the resultant curve is similar except for a highly positive orientation; much of this comes from a high counterdependent flight reinterpreted above as a "negative" score.

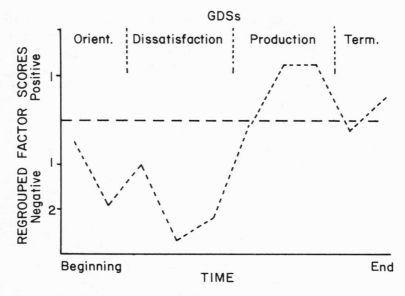

FIGURE 4.1.   MANN'S STAGES AS A MORALE CURVE.
This figure shows the results of dividing Mann's factors (Mann et al., 1967) into positive and negative sets, and then plotting the algebraic difference over the life of the groups to form a morale curve. The groups have been arranged along the time axis to correspond in their fluctuations in factor I—relations with the leader as analyst—which is the crucial aspect of the groups' task.

Hartman and Gibbard

A recent outgrowth of Mann's work was a study by two of his collaborators, Hartman and Gibbard (1974), who evaluated two training groups of 40 sessions each. They used a rating methodology similar to that of the earlier work, except that it was expanded to include member-to-member interactions and two additional categories for expressing guilt and denying guilt. By a statistical assessment of the degree of association between one session and the next, they delineated four group developmental stages, which can be related to their earlier work and to the stages we have proposed. Their stages are compared below to the GDSs:

	Hartman and Gibbard	GDSs
Stage 1	Group reaction to a leader who does not lead in the usual way, with revolt against the leader and the course	Orientation Dissatisfaction
Stage 2	Attempt to create a "utopian group"	Resolution
Stage 3	Competition, rivalry, sexuality, and emerging disappointment at the breakdown of a new order. (This stage has the least ego-state distress.)	Production (These two stages are less distinct than usual.)
Stage 4	Concern with the end of the group, evaluation of previous performance, and sadness associated with termination.	Termination

Hartman and Gibbard then determined the amount of ego-state distress (anxiety, depression, guilt) across these stages. This represents aspects of the negative side of morale, so that when there is low distress one can think partly in terms of higher morale. (This is somewhat of a unidimensional and negative approach to morale, though it is similar to the previously mentioned Philadelphia Geriatric Center Morale Scale, which includes many "negative" items such as those concerning depression.)

One can describe a curve (Figure 4.2) that is the inverse of their ego distress curve (Hartman & Gibbard, 1974, p. 165). This morale curve starts above the baseline (orientation, in their

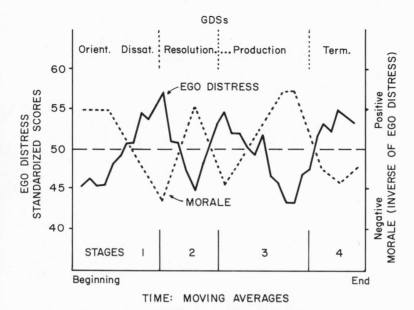

TIME: MOVING AVERAGES

FIGURE 4.2.   HARTMAN AND GIBBARD'S EGO-STATE
DISTRESS DATA AS A MORALE CURVE. This figure, modified from Hartman and Gibbard (1974, p. 165), shows the moving averages of the two groups for the expression of distress by
stage. It also shows the inverse of this curve considered as a
morale curve. Their stages were identified statistically on the
basis of data other than those on the expression of ego-state
distress. (The ego distress curve has a mean of 50 and a standard
deviation of 10.)

stage one), descends in a few meetings (dissatisfaction, also in
their stage one), ascends, descends, and reascends again (all
part of resolution), goes above the baseline (production, in their
combined stages two and three), until it finally descends below
the baseline in termination (their stage four).

There is an extra hill and valley in this curve that is difficult
to reconcile easily with concepts of GDSs and the morale curve.
One possible explanation is that dissatisfaction, resolution, and
production, especially the latter two (their stages two and three)
were more intermixed than usual in the two groups they stud-

ied, and that resolution and production were more indistinct; the result is that there is extra fluctuation in this part of the morale curve. (Farrell [1967] found similar fluctuations in this portion of the group developmental stages in training groups.)

This examination barely samples the wealth of data in the Hartman and Gibbard work (1974, and elsewhere; see the references in their work), some of which is also discussed in the subsequent chapter on theory. But it does show that their work is quite consistent with the ideas proposed here.

Lubin and Zuckerman

One final article on training groups will be examined briefly, that by Lubin and Zuckerman (1967). They studied four training groups with 45 total members who met for 12 sessions during the course of a one-week group training program. They collected data on the participants' responses to a 132-item Multiple Affect Adjective Check List, which yields scores for the three affect states of anxiety, hostility, and depression, and they also rated the participants on five perceptual-cognitive nine-point scales that particularly addressed the task aspects of the group. These five scales were the worth of the session, their activity in the session, the degree of sharing of feelings, the level of conflict, and the relevance of content to what was going on in the group.

The Check List was administered before the first session, and the Check List and rating scales were administered at the end of eight of the sessions.

> Analysis of variance indicated significant session meeting differences on all eight variables. Some similarity of group trends over sessions, therefore, is present. However, group by session interactions were significant for six of the eight variables, which implies some degree of dissimilarity of the group trends over sessions [for the different groups]. Thus the hypothesis of consistency of trends from one group to another is not supported (p. 365).

In other words, when the above variables are compared from meeting to meeting there are significant differences that indicate a developmental pattern, but when one tries to look for a similar developmental pattern (group developmental stages) in these four groups, such stages were not statistically substantiated in these data. In spite of this, when the variables are looked at individually, as Lubin and Zuckerman did, there is some tendency toward group developmental stages, at times broken by one or two groups at only certain meetings.

One wonders what would have happened if they had added additional data, such as those of nonparticipant observers and affect variables that were not all for "negative" emotions and were not so highly intercorrelated (the Pearson intercorrelations between anxiety, hostility, and depression were 0.81 to 0.92; p. 374). In addition, they failed to collect data in the last two sessions, which might have revealed a termination stage. (Many older studies are consistent in ignoring termination phenomena.)

Summary of Training Group Developmental Stage Studies

To give a broader picture of training group developmental stages, the above studies and several others are summarized in Table 4.4. Most of these studies are either in general agreement with the proposed GDSs (Braaten, 1974–1975; Dunphy, 1968; Mann, 1966; Mann et al., 1967; Mills, 1964; Tuckman, 1965; and Zenger, 1970) or can be made to agree without doing injustice to them (Bennis, 1964; Bennis & Shepard, 1956; Bradford, 1964; Cohen, 1971; Flack, 1971; Gibb, 1964; Kaplan, 1967; Shepard & Bennis, 1956; Stock & Thelen, 1958; Thelen & Dickerman, 1949; and Whitaker & Thelen, 1975).

Two of the studies (Lakin & Carson, 1964; Theodorson, 1953) report the general developmental characteristics of decreasing animosity or competition and increasing cooperation with group maturity, which seems particularly to describe aspects of the dissatisfaction to production phases. Also, Brad-

Table 4.4. Group developmental

Author and Year	Method	Number of Groups	Comments
Bennis & Shepard, 1956; Shepard & Bennis, 1956; Bennis, 1964	Anecdotal	Several	Grouped as two main phases with three subphases each. (Phase I: Dependence-power relations; Phase II: Interdependence-interpersonal relations)
Bradford, 1964, 1978	Anecdotal	Several	See text; group development "a cyclic process in which learning recurs in increasing depth" (p. 205, 1964), with improvement in facing basic problems
Charrier, 1972	Anecdotal	Several	Apparently various types of groups; polite stage often short or absent
Cohen, 1971	Anecdotal	Several	Discusses 7 phases, here regrouped
Culbert, 1970, 1972	Anecdotal	1 + others	Interesting example with wives of group trainers
Day, 1967	Anecdotal	Several	

stages in training groups — 1

Orientation	Dissatisfaction	Resolution	Production	Termination
Dependence	Counterdependence	Resolution	Enchantment, Disenchantment, Consensual validation	Not discussed
Loose cohesion	"Failure shock" caused by first major barrier	Reorganizing	Satisfaction (to dissatisfaction to satisfaction, etc.) with growth in skill	Not discussed
"Why we're here" or polite stage	Bid for power stage	Constructive stage	Esprit stage	Not discussed
Encounter anxiety; Data processing or diagnosis	Confrontation	Working out; Confrontation analysis; Search for alternatives	Gratification and pleasure	Not discussed
Developing trust climate	Expose individual differences	Exchanging perceptions of others	Individual then group problem solving	Reconnaissance and evaluation of learning
Fantasied closeness	Victimization	Exaggerated unity	Individualization	Not discussed

Table 4.4. Group developmental

Author and Year	Method	Number of Groups	Comments
Dunphy, 1966, 1968	Research	2	Used the ''General Inquirer'' computer methodology; arbitrarily made 6 ''phases''; consistent with GDSs
Farrell, 1976	Research	3	Somewhat arbitrary division into 7 phases, here regrouped
Flack, 1971	Anecdotal	Several	Medical student participants; stages drawn from study
Gibb, 1964	Research	Several	Does not describe set stages, but the progression shown
Hare, 1973	Research	Several	Developed from T. Parsons' (e.g., 1953) work; meant to apply to various group types

Orientation	Dissatisfaction	Resolution	Production	Termination
External normative standards	Rivalry and aggression	Negative affect but concerns with communication	Emotional concerns, especially affection, high	Present
I Anomie over lack of leadership	II, III, IV Fluctuating conflicts between emphasis on authority and intimacy	V Consensus over realistic goals, consolidation of group culture	VI Work	VII Separation; breakdown of group, evaluation
Present	Present	Present	Present	Present
Loosely organized		Proceeds to	coalescence to	dissolution
Latent pattern maintenance (group purpose defined)	Adaptation (new skills acquired)	Integration (group reorganizes to try skills)	Goal attainment (work on task)	Latent pattern maintenance (terminal phase in which members redefine relationships in the group as it disbands)

Table 4.4. Group developmental

Author and Year	Method	Number of Groups	Comments
Hartman & Gibbard, 1974	Research	2	See text; 4 phases described
Horwitz, 1967	Anecdotal	Several	Discusses typical events in training group without specifying stages, but considerable consistency with GDSs
Kaplan, 1967	Anecdotal	1	Training group members also observed a therapy group; training and therapy group processes compared; discusses major themes in each phase of development
King, 1975	Anecdotal	Several	Groups with histories as short as 2 1/2 hours
Knight, 1974	Research	20	Seen as 3 stages; can be interpreted as 5

Orientation	*Dissatisfaction*	*Resolution*	*Production*	*Termination*
I Group reaction to leader leads to	Revolt against the authority of leader	II Attempts to create "Utopian group" III Breakdown of "Utopia" (More realistic work?)		IV Concern with end of group, evaluation of performance, sadness about termination
Anxious over agenda, leader preoccupation, resent being observed, wish for therapeutic experience	Anger and dissatisfaction with leader	Resolution of authority problem, agreement between external vs. internal resources, intimacy vs. distance		Reluctant to disband, angry that they did not learn more, realistic appraisal of benefits
Dependency theme	Power theme		Intimacy theme	Implied
Birth, Infancy, Latency	Adolescent rebellion	Young adulthood	Continued maturation	Death

Preparation for work .....Work ...... Preparation for separation

(Most negative time)

Table 4.4.   Group developmental

Author and Year	Method	Number of Groups	Comments
Lakin & Carson, 1964	Research	4	Did not substantiate developmental stages but general trends
Lubin & Zuckerman, 1967	Research	4	See text; tendency toward group developmental stages but not statistically substantiated
Lundgren, 1977	Research	5	Hypothesizes stages which data only partly support
Mann, 1966; Mann, Gibbard, Hartman, 1967	Research	4	See text; two related studies with some differences in stage naming.
Mills, 1964	Research	1	
Slater, 1966	Review	Several	Discusses group processes and development; although Slater disclaims looking for developmental stages, they are there
Stock & Thelen, 1958 (Thelen & Dickerman, 1949; Whitaker & Thelen, 1975)	Research	2	See text; they felt that most groups do not reach advanced "stages of maturity"

Orientation	Dissatisfaction	Resolution	Production	Termination
Competitiveness decreases and cooperation increases with group maturity				Not found or discussed
Present	Present	Present	Present	Few data collected
Initial encounter	Intermember conflict and confrontation of trainer	Group solidarity	Exchange of interpersonal feedback	Termination and separation
Present	Confrontation	Re-evaluation	Internalization	Separation, Terminal review
Encounter	Testing boundaries and modeling roles	Negotiating indigenous norms	Production	Separation
Present ("Deification" of leader, etc.)	Present ("Attack on leader")	Present	Present ("The New Order")	Present
Individually centered, exploration	Frustration and conflict among stereotypes	Attempted group harmony, feeling and work not integrated	Productivity and flexibility, integration of feeling and work	Good work with withdrawal of feelings

Table 4.4. Group developmental

Author and Year	Method	Number of Groups	Comments
Theodorson, 1953	Anecdotal	8	Found only general trends
Tuckman, 1965; Tuckman & Jensen, 1977 (See Jones, 1973)	Review	11 studies	Found work and/or social-emotional behavior in most studies
Tucker, 1973	Research	6	Attempt to relate individual and group developmental levels
Yalom & Moos, 1965	Anecdotal	10	Research data collected, but not on developmental stages
Zenger, 1970	Anecdotal	?	Comparisons of individual and group development

In this and subsequent similar tables, the following conventions have been used. An *anecdotal* method generally refers to a descriptive study in which few objective data have been gathered. In many of these instances the study is based on the "overall group experience" of the writer or writers, and the number of groups is not specified, so the term *several* is used. A *research* method means at least systematic and objective data collecting; several of these studies have been reported in more detail in the body of the book where the reader can find additional details. Research studies were usually based on a specified small number of groups, but occasionally data from various studies contributed to the model and not an easily specified number of groups, so again the term *several* is used. *Present* is used to identify a group developmental stage when the stage is described in the study but not specifically designated; *present* is also occasionally used when the author's, or authors', designation of a similar stage is too complex or cumbersome to be summarized in such a table. *Implied* is used when a stage is not described but is implied, for example, the stage between a dissatisfaction stage with much anger and a production stage with more congenial work on the task.

stages in training groups — 5

Orientation	Dissatisfaction	Resolution	Production	Termination
With maturity get decreasing animosity and increasing harmony.				Not discussed
Forming	Storming	Norming	Performing	Adjourning (1977)
Present	Present for more developed individuals	Present	(Data dropped)	Not discussed
Orientation, anxiety over lack of structure	Demands for structure	Resolution to go deeper, backing off	Meaningful interaction	"Disengagement and testimonials"
Infant, Child	Adolescent	Young adult	Adult	Not discussed

ford (1964) discusses recurrent cycles of satisfaction to dissatisfaction in facing the groups' problems, but he emphasizes the first episode of dissatisfaction as a major episode or "failure shock" (dissatisfaction). It takes considerable work (resolution) to overcome this failure shock and return to satisfaction (production), and get the group on the cyclical road toward increasing growth through periods of satisfaction to dissatisfaction to satisfaction to dissatisfaction and so on.

Most of the above studies find an initial *orientation* stage in which there is some inquiry and testing of what is required, with a certain dependence on the group situation. The task for training groups in this stage is precisely this orientation behavior—to discover why they are there, what they are doing, what is expected of them, how to deal with the leader and other members, and so on. Members may be somewhat apprehensive about what they are doing there, but there is usually some sense of hope that it will be a positive experience.

Several studies then describe a stage in which there is conflict within the group over what to do, what is expected of each of them, and what is expected of the leader, and a sense of frustration and anger with decreased morale. This can be called the *dissatisfaction* stage. Task behavior (studying the functioning of the group) may, and often does, decrease. The task at this time is to study this period of frustration, conflict, and so on, and as long as members attend to this behavior, they are doing their work.

Unfortunately some groups are so conflicted and demoralized at this stage that they do not progress beyond it, but seem to continue in this stage until the group experience stops (for example, see Stock & Thelen, 1958, p. 233). It is frequently during this dissatisfaction stage that members drop out, especially if they can easily do so; but if the group experience is a required course it may be difficult to do so.

Several studies discuss the transition between dissatisfaction and the stage of production as a separate stage that can be called *resolution*. Whether to see this stage as distinct or to incorporate it into the production stage depends on one's purposes, the length of the group experience, and so on. In the resolution stage, the problems, conflicts, and demoralization of the dissatisfaction stage are resolved through some consensus about goals and some agreement about acceptable member roles and leader roles. Group anger and frustration lessen, and enthusiasm begins to pick up. Work on the task may increase as skills for the task increase and group members are better able to reflect on what they are doing.

In the next stage of *production,* the social-emotional relationships are moderately congenial, the amount of anger and frustration is not remarkable, and when expressed it is generally less aggressive and hostile. Work on studying the group (the task) is progressing satisfactorily. Morale in this stage has improved. (Tuckman [1965] identified the social-emotional aspect of this stage in most training group studies he reviewed, but the work aspect was seldom mentioned; for example, it is found in Stock and Thelen [1958], but not in Bradford [1964] or Bennis and Shepard [1956]).

A final *termination* stage is only occasionally referred to in training group work. It is mentioned explicitly only in a few works, for example, Braaten, 1974–1975; Hartman and Gibbard, 1974; Mann, 1966; Mann et al., 1967; Mills, 1964; Slater, 1966; and by inference in the work of Flack, 1971; Gibb, 1964; Kaplan, 1967; and Stock and Thelen, 1958. In this stage there is a sense of loss and sadness over the anticipated, and then actual, breaking up of the group. The group work at this time in a training group is the need to discuss and experience this termination, and often also to review the training group experience and what has been learned.

PROBLEM-SOLVING GROUPS

There are many types of problem-solving groups whose group developmental stages have been studied, from artificial laboratory groups set up specifically to study group problem solving, to more naturalistic groups that meet to address a real-life problem. The laboratory-type groups are usually susceptible to better experimental control and are the main types of groups that will be considered here; groups dealing with real-life problems will be examined later in a section on naturalistic groups.

The problem-solving groups to be discussed here have addressed a wide range of problems, usually without a particularly easy or clear-cut solution, in order to involve group members and keep them involved. Examples are small groups solving chess problems or contrived human relations problems such as how to approach an irascible employer for a raise. One of the studies presented in the accompanying table (Hare, 1967) had a real-life problem concerning the quantity of production in a manufacturing context. This study is placed in this section because the high degree of experimental manipulation made it a rather artificial situation.

These problem-solving groups are usually fairly small, ranging from three to six members. They can be larger, but they should not exceed the number of people who can work face to face, that is, about 20 members at most. Such groups are often without a formal leader, though they may have one. Sessions are usually about an hour long, but may be shorter.

Bales and collaborators have been among the foremost students in this area (for example, Bales & Strodtbeck, 1951; Heinicke & Bales, 1953; and see also Hare, 1973), and an example of their work will be presented in some detail. Besides the intrinsic value of this research with problem-solving groups, their methodology and rationale in group developmental stage work has some application to other group types, including therapy groups, and has been so used. (For other applications and extensions of their work see Theodorson [1953] on training groups, above; Psathas [1960] on psychotherapy groups, below; Philp and Dunphy [1958–1959] on naturalistic groups, below; and the modifications by Hill, for example, Hill and Gruner [1973] reported below.)

Bales and Strodtbeck

This work used Bales' Interaction Process Analysis (IPA) category system, a method for organizing observed behaviors into 12 categories on the basis of individual statements or acts. It is intended primarily for verbal behavior, but can be used with nonverbal behavior. The categories can then be grouped according to the task (problems of orientation, evaluation, and control or solutions) and to social-emotional areas of behavior (positive and negative reactions) (Table 4.5). Each task area of orientation, evaluation, and control includes one of each of the areas of attempted answers and questions.

In one of their reports, Bales and Strodtbeck (1951) examined several groups in 22 different problem-solving sessions in which they looked for "phases" ("qualitatively different subperiods within a total continuous period of interaction in which a group proceeds from initiation to completion of a problem involving group decision" [p. 485]). They hypothesized that " ... groups tend to move in their interaction from a relative emphasis upon problems of *orientation,* to problems of *evaluation* and subsequently to problems of *control* [solutions], and that concurrent with these transitions, the relative frequencies

Table 4.5.   Bales' interaction process analysis
(IPA) categories

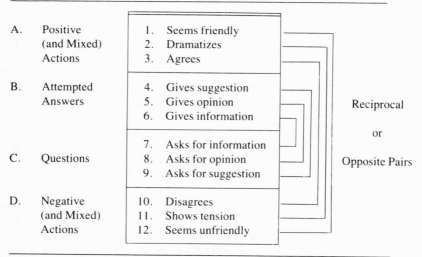

This table shows the categories and their grouping by types. A and D are the social-emotional area, B and C the task area, and within the task area problems of orientation are represented in categories 6 and 7, problems of evaluation in categories 5 and 8, and problems of control in categories 4 and 9. (This table is adapted from Bales and Strodtbeck, 1951, p. 486. Copyright 1951 by the American Psychological Association. Reprinted by permission.)

of both negative reactions and positive reactions tend to increase." They did " . . . not mean that the absolute magnitude for the selected [task] activity [of orientation, evaluation, or control] is greater than all others in that phase—we mean, rather, that the rate of the selected activity is at its own high point in the designated phase" (Bales & Strodtbeck, 1951, p. 488) (Figure 4.3).

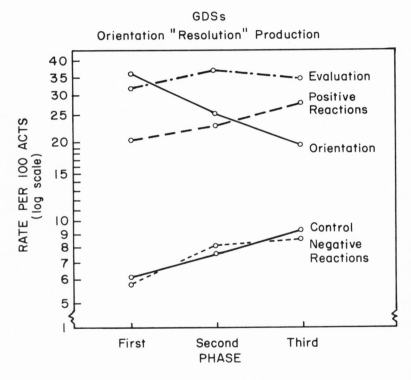

FIGURE 4.3.   BALES AND STRODTBECK'S PHASES IN PROBLEM-SOLVING GROUPS. The relative frequency of acts is expressed according to types of acts and phases, based on 22 separate problem-solving sessions. The comparable GDSs are shown. (From Bales and Strodtbeck, 1951, p. 488. Copyright 1951 by the American Psychological Association. Reprinted by permission.)

Most of the problem-solving group sessions that met their criteria of a clear problem and full cycle of work on the problem also supported their phase development hypothesis. The other problem-solving group sessions did not meet statistical requirements when taken individually, but when the 22 studies were taken as a whole they were largely consistent with the hypothesis. (The interested reader is referred to the original article for their statistical handling of the data.)

Within the limits of groups requiring only a single session to do their task, this study substantiated a group developmental stage model with three stages (phases). The number of stages was set at three by dividing the total number of acts into thirds for examination and analysis. This gives an initial stage with high orientation and considerable evaluation and positive reactions, and low control (solutions) and negative reactions; this can be considered the orientation stage. The last stage (phase) had control (solutions) at its maximum, orientation its minimum, positive reactions high and at their maximum, and negative reactions at their high but still fairly low. This last phase can be considered the production stage, with positive reactions high and well exceeding negative reactions, and solutions at their peak.

There is a phase between these in which evaluation is high and at its peak, orientation is decreasing, and positive and negative reactions are between the lows and highs of their first and last sessions. This phase, with decreasing orientation behaviors and an emphasis on clarifying the task, seems closest to the proposed resolution stage.

No clear dissatisfaction stage marked by anger and similar feelings was seen in this study, probably because the groups' histories were short and the problems were defined with relative clarity (solving chess problems or composing projective stories). Partial substantiation for this interpretation comes from a related problem-solving study using the IPA categories (Heinicke & Bales, 1953). In this work the researchers studied ten groups that were given a more indefinite and probably more ego-involving human relations problem for each of four to six sessions (for example, the question of whether a man should tell his wife about an affair). Under these conditions the task stages were not the same; here the rates of task-oriented behaviors generally decreased over the sessions. At the same time there was an increase in the social-emotional categories, but a sharp rise in the negative reaction category in the second session and then a fall. Here session two was, on the average, the one with the greatest conflict, and it seemed to be a time of crisis for the group. With these problem-solving conditions and a longer group history, there does appear to be an initial orientation stage followed by a dissatisfaction stage, then resolution and production stages.

In neither of these studies is a termination stage explicitly labeled. Nonetheless, Bales and Strodtbeck (1951) comment on termination-type behaviors: "We note joking and laughter so frequently at the end of meetings that they might almost be taken as a signal that the group has completed what it considers to be a task effort, and is ready for disbandment or a new problem" (p. 489). Also, although it is not shown in the previous graph, the negative reactions decrease in the last minutes of these meetings (Bales, 1952, p. 158); this is probably a termination stage phenomenon.

Summary of Problem-Solving Group Developmental Stage Studies

The number of published studies of group developmental stages in problem-solving groups is not large (Table 4.6). In Tuckman's 1965 review he placed a handful of studies in a combined problem-solving and natural group category, including the Bales and Strodtbeck work above, and other studies that in this work have been put elsewhere—for example, Modlin and Faris (1956) with naturalistic groups; Theodorson (1953) with training groups; and Schutz (1958) with encounter groups because of his later (1967) emphasis on these groups.

It should be clear from the previous discussion and Table 4.6 that these problem-solving groups have stages consistent with GDS categories—an orientation stage, a dissatisfaction stage if the group lasts more than one session, then resolution and production stages. In addition, termination stage behaviors can be found in problem-solving group studies with only a one-session history (Bales & Strodtbeck, 1951), but conditions in most of these studies did not generally lead to the identification of a termination stage by the author(s).

Although there are few data available on the issue, it would not be unusual to expect at least mild dissatisfaction stages, even in one-session problem-solving groups, if the problems led to high ego involvement and the sessions were long enough, probably at least about an hour.

THERAPY GROUPS

The types of therapy groups that will be considered here are traditional psychotherapy and counseling groups as opposed to those of more recent years such as transactional analysis groups, Gestalt groups, and so on. Some group developmental stage data for growth-oriented as opposed to therapy-oriented groups are included in the section on encounter groups. There were no reports found on group developmental stages for therapy groups that base their treatment on a medium other than talking, such as occupational therapy or music therapy groups, but of course such groups would also have group developmental stages if they met the requisite conditions for such development, such as time boundaries, membership, and so on. (These requisite conditions will be discussed in detail in the subsequent chapter.)

Almost all of the group developmental stage work on traditional therapy groups is anecdotal; there has been little attempt to test theories or to gather careful data. In spite of this shortcoming, they are rather remarkable for their consistency.

Table 4.6.   Group developmental

Author and Year	Method	Number of Groups	Comments
Bales & Strodtbeck, 1951; Bales 1952	Research	22	See discussion above
Hare, 1967	Anecdotal-research	1	Interesting study looking at group developmental stages in the classic Western Electric-Hawthorne study of 1927 – 1929
Heinicke & Bales, 1953	Research	10	Some groups stopped early so that terminati n data were not clearly seen; studied for 4 to 6 sessions
Jordan et al., 1963	Research	5	Three member crews in a study of information processing; studied for up to 6 sessions

See footnote to Table 4.4.

First we will look at two studies that did collect data under fairly careful conditions—the works of Hill and Gruner (1973) and Psathas (1960).

Hill and Gruner

These workers (Hill & Gruner, 1973; see also Hill, 1977, and references therein) studied therapy groups of seriously de-linquent 15- to 17-year-old boys. They classified the group data using the Hill Interaction Matrix (HIM) category system (Hill, 1965, 1977) and attempted to test a theory of group development derived from the work of Bales, such as that in the Bales

stages in problem-solving groups

Orientation	Dissatisfaction	Resolution	Production	Termination
Present	Not seen	Present	Present	Present in brief form
Present	Present	Present	Present	Group did not terminate
Present	Present	Implied	Present	Not clear
Formulating an individual model	Formulating an homologous model (opposition between members)	Emergence of trust	Learning to cooperate	Not looked for

and Strodtbeck (1951) work discussed above. The Hill version states that a group passes through the three phases (stages) of orientation, exploration, and production. (Referring to the task portion only, Bales' three phases emphasize behavior called "orientation," "evaluation," and "control" or "solutions" respectively; see the previous discussion of this work.)

The HIM category system rating scales were derived from the study of therapy groups and led to two basic dimensions, one dealing with content areas on a continuum considered from least to most important for group therapy, and one dealing with differences in the level of work. The content areas go from general topics of discussion, to general talk about the group, to talk about oneself, to eventual talk about relationships in the group (called respectively Topic, Group, Personal, and Relationship). Similarly, the levels of work become progressively more personally and interpersonally relevant (these are called Conventional, Assertive, Speculative, and Confrontive levels).

These dimensions are arranged perpendicular to each other so that a matrix or grid is formed. Each statement can then be placed in the appropriate part of the matrix for the type of content and level of work. The matrix is then divided into quadrants (Table 4.7), with quadrant one focusing on orienting data (searching for structure or testing the situation), quadrant four focusing on production data (concern with process problems and their resolution, and enough group awareness to insure that individual and group goals are met), and quadrants two and three focusing on exploration data (a great deal of interpersonal exploration, and developing awareness of individual differences).

If the tested developmental theory is applicable, behaviors (statements) in quadrant one should be at their maximum at the beginning of the group and lowest at the end. The reverse should be true of quadrant four, and the combined quadrants two and three should reach their peaks in the middle exploration stage and then decline.

Because the groups met 50 or more times and there were many statements to categorize for each meeting, they rated a sample of 15% of the meetings. There were two initial groups, and when members were doing well enough they left the group treatment and new members were added to the nucleus that remained. This happened several times, so Hill and Gruner actually studied the initial groups and eight additional groups composed of combinations of old members and new ones. This meant that only the initial two groups had a distinct beginning, and a less distinct ending, and that all the other groups had their beginnings contaminated by the combination of old and new members. Also, only the final two groups had a full group termination.

Table 4.7. The Hill Interaction Matrix and the quadrants used in examining group developmental stages.

Content

		Topic	Group	Personal	Relationship
Work	Conventional	Quadrant I Orienting Data: Searching for structure or testing the situation.		Quadrant II Exploration Data: Much interpersonal exploration and a developing awareness of individual differences	
	Assertive				
	Speculative	Quadrant III Exploration Data: Much interpersonal exploration and a developing awareness of individual differences.		Quadrant IV Production Data: Concerns with group process problems and their resolution, and enough group awareness to insure that individual and group goals are met.	
	Confrontive				

This table shows the content and work categories used in the Hill Interaction Matrix, the quadrants used for examining group developmental stages, and a general description of the behavior in each quadrant. (This table has been adapted from one in "A Study of Development in Open and Closed groups" by Wm. Fawcett Hill and LeRoy Gruner in Small Group Behavior, vol. 4, No. 3, Aug. 1973, p. 360 and is reprinted by permission of the publisher, Sage Publications, Inc., and the senior author. See also Hill [1974].)

Under these conditions the predictions for quadrant one (orientation) behavior and quadrant four (production) behavior held up. The same was true to a lesser extent for the predictions for quadrants two and three (exploration) behaviors, but only for the two initial groups, which they called the "closed" groups. This need not be surprising since the subsequent groups did not have the same type of beginning, nor a typical beginning for a new therapy group.* How does this study compare with the proposed GDS model of orientation, dissatisfaction, resolution, production, and termination? Hill and Gruner's "orientation" was a negative stage marked by "considerable resistance and testing" (p. 363), which would not be unexpected from members who were more or less forced into treatment. This means that there was no initial period of positive orientation characterized by considerable eagerness to be in the group, but rather that their orientation was a negative orientation stage with some of the characteristics of the dissatisfaction stage.

This then led into a resolution stage marked by working through of this resistance and testing in what they called exploration. A production stage then followed in Hill and Gruner's work, as it does with the proposed GDSs. No termination stage was found in Bales' theory, and Hill and Gruner did not address themselves to one. Also, since neither of these initial groups actually terminated, it would have been difficult to see termina-

---

*However, Hoch and Kaufer (1955) studied two open-ended therapy groups on psychiatric wards and found that each time new patients were added, there was a group developmental stage sequence similar to the GDS model, except for a termination stage, which was not discussed and may not have been observable. They called their stages climate-setting (orientation), approach-avoidance (dissatisfaction), establishment of patterns of interaction (resolution), and protection of the group's existence (production). Gendlin and Beebe (1968) made some brief comments on the developmental stages of open "experiential" groups, noting that old members can get tired of the process of repeatedly adding new members and having to repeat former stages. Neither of these studies will be returned to since their settings are not close enough to the usual optimal conditions for group developmental stages. The interested reader is referred to the original reports.

tion phenomena. (There are "termination" data for the final groups, but it does not lend itself to easy interpretation.) Hill and Gruner's (1973) conclusions seem apropos:

> Under properly controlled conditions—where a group meets for a sufficiently long time—then a theory of group development might well be approximated in the behavior pattern of such a group. If the conditions do not approach the ideal that is postulated for the theory, then the effects may be masked, distorted, or absent.
>
> Thus, this theory of group development (and this is probably true of others) may be considered at best a theory depending on pure states, and these ideal conditions rarely obtain. Thus, these theories might well have limited validity but are not necessarily without validity (p. 380).

Psathas

An experiment of Psathas (1960) exemplifies a more direct application of Bales' (1950) categories to a therapy group; the approach is based on a group developmental stage recurrent cycle theory in which the cycles are looked for in individual meetings. The direct application of the Bales system itself is interesting since therapy groups do not meet some of the basic conditions Bales (Bales & Strodtbeck, 1951) thought were necessary. For example, two of their conditions are that groups be composed of "normal" people and that they work on rather isolated units or problems until reaching a solution. Therapy groups, on the contrary, usually work on many problems without reaching definite solutions before leaving them, often to return to the same or similar problems later.

Psathas sampled nine of about 90 sessions over the course of two four-patient psychotherapy groups led by the same therapist. An observer noted categorizable nonverbal acts, and these were appropriately inserted in the transcript from the audiotape of the meetings. (Recall that Bales' 12 categories cover positive and negative reactions, questions, and attempted answers; see Table 4.5.) The therapist's acts were also categorized and, in fact, he was the highest initiator of acts.

For analysis of the stage or phase sequences, the total number of acts for each meeting was divided into thirds ("phases"), and for each third the number of acts for each of the five areas of orientation ("what is it"), evaluation ("how do we feel about it"), control ("what shall we do about it"), positive reactions, and negative reactions were counted. Then the overall totals of each of these acts for each third over the nine sessions were added together. This test seeks group developmental phases within each meeting and not stages that extend across meetings and over the whole life cycle of the psychotherapy groups.

A χ^2 test for deviation from random distribution for these acts was significant for both groups combined, and for one of the groups singly, but not for the other. Based on Bales' method of statistical analysis, in which each of the five areas was ranked for each phase (third) relative to theoretical expectations, each group separately and the groups combined statistically confirmed the phase sequence hypothesis. Psathas (1960) appropriately adds:

> However, the pattern observed over a series of meetings is not necessarily the modal or typical pattern when meetings are analyzed separately. Single meetings were examined and it was found that only two [of 18] conformed to the phase sequence described by Bales and Strodtbeck using their method of ranking frequencies [for each area of orientation, evaluation and control] (p. 186).

Note also that this significant finding of orientation to evaluation to control within meetings held true only when the therapist's acts were included with those of the patients.

> The data . . . are not sufficient to permit generalization concerning the interaction process in psychotherapy groups. They nevertheless provide some evidence in support of Bales' and others'

findings concerning certain system tendencies emerging in problem-solving discussions. To observe such similarities in groups which differ greatly from laboratory groups provides some indication of the generality of the interaction process (p. 193).

It would have been more relevant for our purposes if Psathas had tried to substantiate the phase sequence hypothesis—orientation to evaluation to control—as a single sequence, for example, by seeing if orientation acts progressively decreased and control acts progressively increased over all the meetings; these possibilities, of course, were not examined. One might argue that this was not a study on group developmental stages because of the narrow focus, but its research approach and relationship to other studies reported here seem to warrant its inclusion. (There is no discussion of termination phenomena in the Psathas experiment.)

Philp and Dunphy (1958–1959) used Bales' category system with discussion groups and examined not only the changes within sessions, but also across sessions. Under these conditions they found group developmental stage data largely consistent with those proposed here. This study is discussed in more detail in the section on naturalistic groups.

Summary of Therapy Group Developmental Stage Studies

Table 4.8 summarizes several studies on developmental stages in therapy groups, especially the more recent studies. The table includes group psychotherapy and group counseling studies. As with most group therapy group developmental stage studies, they are primarily anecdotal reports, but unlike many earlier studies, most of these reports are based on the authors' experience with many groups, not with single ones. The work of Psathas (1960) is excluded here since its group developmental stage focus is a narrow one limited to intrameeting stages.

An earlier overview of group developmental stages in therapy groups can be gained from Tuckman's (1965) review,

Table 4.8. Group developmental

Author and Year	Method	Number of Groups	Comments
Bonney, 1969,1974,1976; Foley & Bonney, 1966	Anecdotal	Several	School counseling groups
Foulkes & Anthony, 1957; Anthony, 1967	Anecdotal	Several	Analytic group psychotherapy
Garland, Jones & Koloday, 1965; Garland & Frey, 1970 (Also Whittaker, 1970)	Anecdotal	Several	Child and adolescent social work groups
Gazda, 1975	Anecdotal	Several	Counseling groups
Hill & Gruner, 1973	Research	2 (+ 8)	Therapy with juvenile delinquents; see text
Johnson, 1963	Anecdotal	Several	
Kaplan & Roman, 1963	Anecdotal	1	
Mahler, 1969	Anecdotal	Several	School counseling groups

stages in therapy groups — 1

Orientation	Dissatisfaction	Resolution	Production	Termination
Establishment	Transition	Experimentation	Operational; Creative	Not discussed
Present; "therapeutic honeymoon"	Leader-centered; envy and jealousy of others	Implied	Group-centered	Termination, Reindividuation
Pre-affiliation	Power and control	Intimacy	Differentiation (reality-based relations)	Separation
Exploratory	Transition		Action (Work or productive stage)	Termination
Negative orientation		Exploration	Production	Method obscured
Stage I Formation of a working relationship	Stage II Authority hostility and group identity	Implied	Stage III Mutual analysis	Termination
Loosely organized		Coalescence of psychological group	More individual psychological work	Not discussed
Involvement stage	Transition stage		Working stage	Ending stage

Table 4.8.   Group developmental

Author and Year	Method	Number of Groups	Comments
Sarri & Galinsky, 1967	Review	Several	Found 7 phases in counseling groups; reorganized in GDS framework with some difficulty
Shambaugh & Kanter, 1969	Anecdotal	1	Spouses of hemodialysis patients, supportive group
Tuckman, 1965; Tuckman & Jensen, 1977	Review	26+	
Whitaker & Lieberman, 1964	Anecdotal	Several	
Yalom, 1970, 1975	Anecdotal	Several	

See footnote to Table 4.4.

which included material on the development of therapy groups from 26 reports published between 1946 and 1961. Most of these dealt with a single group. (Included are several items found in this bibliography, for example, Bion, 1961; Abrahams, 1949; and Martin and Hill, 1957.) Reasoning inductively, Tuckman arrived at a four-stage model of forming, storming, norming, and performing, each stage having both task and social-emotional (group structure or interpersonal) components. Only one of the studies (Abrahams, 1949) reported information on both task and social-emotional components in each of the four stages, but 14 of the 26 studies reported material on at least one component in each of the four stages, and the

stages in therapy groups — 2

Orientation	Dissatisfaction	Resolution	Production	Termination
Origin phase, Formative phase	Intermediate phase I, Revision phase	Intermedi-ate phase II	Maturation phase	Termination phase
Present	Present	Present	Present	Present
Forming	Storming	Norming	Performing	Adjourning (added 1977)
Formative phase	Close of formative phase		Establish-ment phase	Not discussed
Present	Present	Development of cohesiveness	Present	Termination

average was data on five of the eight components in the four stages.

Although minor issue might be taken with Tuckman's analysis of some of these studies, the overall degree of consistency with his suggested group developmental stages is quite good. Tuckman made no attempt to comment on termination ("mourning") phenomena, but most studies, especially earlier ones, ignore this aspect of group developmental stages. Some exceptions in therapy groups are noted in Table 4.8, for example, Foulkes and Anthony, 1957; Gazda, 1975; Johnson, 1963; and Yalom, 1970 and 1975. In a subsequent, brief review Tuckman and Jensen (1977) added a termination stage, "adjourning," to the Tuckman model. (For additional material on termination stage phenomena only, see Kauff, 1977, and McGee et al., 1972.)

Negative Orientation Stage

In most groups the initial stage of orientation is a time of at least mildly positive morale, even though there may also be apprehension about the group. But occasionally the initial stage, especially in therapy with groups or individuals, is one of negativity, resistance, and sometimes open hostility. This seems particularly true with "acting out" or characterologic types of patients, such as delinquents and alcohol or other drug abusers, but also with borderline and more seriously disturbed adolescents and adults. These are all settings in which patients are not in therapy entirely on their own initiative. For example, the alcohol and other drug abusing patients I see are often in treatment under legal, medical, occupational, or familial pressure. A number of such studies are summarized in Table 4.9.

Related to the work of Hill and Gruner (1973), above and in the table, is the earlier work of Martin and Hill (1957). In a largely theoretical paper they proposed a complex group developmental stage process with an initial stage of social isolation somewhat similar to the negative orientation stage. The subsequent research work of Hill and Gruner with delinquents disclosed a more explicit negative orientation stage as part of a less complex group developmental stage sequence.

The work of Masterson (1972), and Rinsley (1974, and references therein; see also J. M. Lewis, 1970), warrant additional comment for several reasons, not the least of which is the consistency within this work and the wealth of clinical data on which it is based. This material is an example of individual therapy developmental stages viewed collectively, that is, a conceptual group, but the material has been gathered under highly structured residential conditions where a number of such individuals are viewed simultaneously by the same clinician ("the group leader"), approaching the conditions of open actual groups as in Hill and Gruner (1973).

The Masterson and Rinsley studies are concerned with the developmental process in intensive, long-term, residential treatment of seriously disturbed adolescents, usually with borderline or schizophrenic conditions. In the following description Masterson's and then Rinsley's terms are given respectively for each stage.

This developmental sequence usually begins with a stage of "testing" or "resistance" in which there is often considerable acting out and rebelliousness. Then there is a "working through" or "definitive" stage, which extends from the control of the acting out and rebelliousness until separation from the pathological real and fantasied aspects of the relationship with the parents, or parental surrogates. This is a time of considerable depression as the adolescent loses the fantasied and unhealthy aspects of himself or herself (for example, omnipotence, overidealized parents), has his or her externalizing defenses cut off, and must look within and begin to structure a more realistic self and family complex.

The final stage is one of "separation" or "resolution," which generally includes normalizing of the depression, and individuation, and extends until the termination of hospitalization and frequently the start of outpatient treatment (a new experience with its own GDS sequence). Each of the three stages may last six to 12 months, and sometimes longer.

These stages are compared with GDS stages in Table 4.10. Under the usual conditions of intensive, residential treatment of seriously disturbed adolescents, the initial resistive stage is like the previously encountered negative orientation stage, and here it seems clearly to be continuous with the usual (negative) dissatisfaction stage. Unlike the usual GDS production stage, production in these settings often has negative characteristics of depression and low morale. This can likely best be accounted for by the fact that the task involves dealing with loss and depression, real loss of significant others, loss of fantasied ideal-

Table 4.9. Negative orientation stage

Author and Year	Type of Study	Number of Groups	Comments
Austin, 1957	Anecdotal	Several	Counseling group with "street youth"
Hill & Gruner, 1973	Research	2 main groups	Institutionalized delinquents
Johnson (p. 69), 1963	Anecdotal	Several	Briefly mentions delinquent groups
Masterson, 1972	Anecdotal	Individual process — many	Primarily hospitalized borderline adolescents
Northen, 1958	Anecdotal	Several	Sometimes initial "honeymoon"; outpatient counseling with "acting-out" adolescents
Osberg & Berliner, 1956	Anecdotal	5	Hospitalized narcotic addict groups; individuals terminated but not groups
Page, 1979	Anecdotal	Several	Counseling groups with female prisoners; mentions similar male groups with more negative beginnings

therapy studies — 1

Negative Orientation	(Positive) Orientation	Dissatisfaction	Resolution	Production	Termination
Testing			Contract	Mutual interaction	Termination
(Negative) Orientation			Exploration	Production	Not discussed
Present	?Stage I Formation of a working relationship	?Stage II Authority hostility and group identity	Implied	Stage III Mutual analysis	Termination
Testing			Working	through	Separation
Present			Present	Present	Present
Present			Present	Present	Not discussed for groups
Support of current lifestyles		Anger at authority	Self-revelation	Working through problems, new ways of relating	Ending

Table 4.9.   Negative orientation stage

Author and Year	Type of Study	Number of Groups	Comments
Powles, 1959	Anecdotal	1	Changing composition — hospitalized adolescents
Rinsley, 1974	Anecdotal	Individual process — many	Hospitalized seriously disturbed adolescents ("honeymoon" sometimes observed)
Shellow, Ward & Rubenfeld, 1958	Anecdotal	5	Institutionalized delinquents
Standish & Semrad, 1951	Anecdotal	12	Hospitalized "psychotics"
Stewart & Poetter, 1976	Anecdotal	Individual and group process — many	Residential treatment of boys 7-18; "reactive characterological" and other problems
Thorpe & Smith, 1953	Anecdotal	Several — 5?	Hospitalized drug addicts
Trecker, 1955	Anecdotal	Several — general discussion	Especially counseling groups with "street youth"

See footnote to Table 4.4.

Negative Orientation	(Positive) Orientation	Dissatisfaction	Resolution	Production	Termination
I Formative		Unclear	II Structure established to (with regressions with changing members)	VIII Peak maturity	Not discussed for group
Resistance			Definitive or work	introject	Resolution (of severe pathology and hospitalization)
Present		Unclear	Present	Intermittently reached	Not discussed
Present			Present	Present	Present
Present			Development of self-control	Stages of self-discipline and basic identity	Stage of integrated identification with termination
Present		Brief mention	Present	Present	Not discussed
Stage I — Pregroup			Stages 2 and 3	Stage 4	Stage 5 and 6

Table 4.10.   GDSs and the stages of treatment
of seriously disturbed adolescents

GDSs	Negative Orientation to Dissatifaction	Resolution to Production	Termination
Masterson	Testing	Working through	Separation
Rinsley	Resistance	Definitive or introject work	Resolution

izations of self and parental figures, and depression related to these and to damaged self-esteem. (Stated conversely, it would be incongruous to be elated or to have particularly good morale while dealing with one's losses and depression. Nonetheless, this could be true if "manic-like" denial defenses were operative [Rinsley, 1979].)

A similar (negative) production stage might well be expected in individual intensive psychotherapy of seriously depressed or otherwise disturbed adults, and this is what frequently happens in clinical practice. The usual production stage in adult psychotherapy groups as reported above may not be particularly negative, insofar as morale is concerned, because the members are not usually as seriously disturbed and the treatment process is not as intensive as the process reported here with seriously disturbed adolescents.

This material on a resistant, negative, beginning of the group developmental stage sequence—a negative orientation stage—is initially perplexing from a morale curve perspective which implies that if members were more negative than positive about an experience they would not be part of it. This dilemma is resolved when it is considered that these patients are coerced in some way and that their participation can be viewed as the wish to avoid something worse—jail, divorce, the pain of ill health, and so on.

The negative orientation stage is not followed by the usual (positive) orientation stage (see Table 4.9) since in this negative orientation stage the participants are carrying out orienting behavior, even though they are rather resistant and hostile about their participation. Also, a distinct dissatisfaction stage is usually not seen since it is in good part a result of the frustration of initial positive but inaccurate expectations. Instead, the initial stage is a pronounced and sometimes protracted negative one that gets worked through in the resolution stage, where reasonable goals are set, work begins on them, and working group cohesion begins in actual groups. Then the usual stages of production and termination can follow. The Johnson (1963) study in the table may be an exception to these comments, but since he provides only a minimum of information on these resistant groups, it is difficult to judge.

Sometimes the GDS sequence for these types of patients and groups will begin with a positive "honeymoon" period (Northen, 1958; and my own experience with such patients) instead of a resistant, negative orientation stage. This honeymoon is usually affectively superficial and often short-lived, and lacks the authenticity of a true (positive) orientation stage. Nonetheless, when there is a honeymoon beginning to such a group developmental stage sequence, the sequence may appear similar to the usual GDS sequence, with (positive) orientation, dissatisfaction, resolution, production, and termination.

A study by Dell and associates (1977) found a negative orientation stage, and then the full GDS sequence from (positive) orientation to production in family therapy seminars for students. They commented that this is similar to the stages they observe in family therapy itself. The negative orientation stage in such therapy groups (a family is a special type of group) and seminars might be understood on the basis of the participants' initial resistance to accepting that the family—and not just one "sick" member—needs treatment. Why a positive orientation usually follows is unclear, but may be related to the participants' fairly rapid acceptance of positive expectations for themselves for learning and treatment. Then, when what this requires becomes clearer, there is a dissatisfaction stage, then resolution and production. Termination was not discussed.

Another study (Speck & Attneave, 1973) dealing with a special form of family therapy did not find such an initial negative orientation stage. This work will be returned to in the naturalistic group section of this chapter.

There is little reported information on such a negative orientation stage in nontherapy groups. The Dell et al. (1977) study with a learning seminar is one of these, and Berger (1976), working with learning groups on surgical wards, is another. This latter study is similar to the others in the table in that it goes from the initial negative orientation stage to resolution. Both of these studies are discussed later in the section on naturalistic groups.

The Mann et al. (1967) work with training groups may be a study with a negative orientation stage. Algebraically summing the regrouped positive and negative factor scores of Mann's scoring system to get a morale curve, one finds that the orientation stage is on the negative morale side. This finding is based on a liberal use of these data, so too much should not be made of it. (See the previously described morale curve derived from Mann et al., [1967].)

When students are pulled into taking part in a training group experience to get academic credit, there may be initial resistance to revealing oneself, taking active part in the group, and so on, and this first stage of negative orientation has to be overcome before it can blend into the dissatisfaction stage, as appeared to happen in the Mann et al. study (1967). Levine (1971) found that most of his training groups, which were studied under similar conditions, began negatively, although he did not conclude that there were general group developmental stages.

An additional training group report beginning with an apparent negative orientation stage focused on two groups composed of middle-level management personnel (Lundgren, 1971). After the first of six sessions these groups had high "intermember conflict," low "member attitudes toward trainers," and seemingly no favorable other measures. This appeared to be a negative orientation stage, but since it was a short experience of only six sessions, and since assessments were made after the first session, earlier positive orientation might have been missed. The negative orientation could be attributed to the participants having moderate ambivalence about the experience after being sent by their supervisors.

The two groups continued their early sessions with high to moderate "intermember conflict" and low but increasing "group solidarity" (dissatisfaction). A resolution stage was not easily discernible in this short experience, but there subsequently was more "group solidarity," less "intermember conflict," more "openness of communication" and "productivity," more positive "member attitudes toward trainers," and in one group moderately and apparently useful "member confrontation of trainers" (production). The only information on a termination stage was mention of a "going home effect" in one of the groups. (The negative orientation stage will be discussed again in the naturalistic group section, and in the chapter on theory.)

GDSs in Individual Psychotherapy

In contrast to the group psychotherapy field, where there are a large number of studies on group developmental stages, there is a paucity of literature on developmental stages in individual psychotherapy, that is, in a conceptual group of patients in individual psychotherapy. A literature search of the last ten years found no studies identified as such in *Psychological Abstracts.* This lack is likely accounted for in good part by the earlier-mentioned fact that these developmental stages develop more consistently in actual group settings and are more observable there. Also, the large number of methods of individual psychotherapy, the usually uncertain length of the experience, and the great variability in length, among other reasons, make developmental stages in individual psychotherapy a more formidable subject of study.

Nonetheless, a GDS-like sequence is seen in individual

psychotherapy and can be found in the literature (Weiner, 1975; Wolberg, 1977; see also Anthony, 1967). This sequence starts with an "initial" or "beginning" phase or stage in which the patients' reasons for wanting psychotherapy are discussed, as is the nature of psychotherapy, and an agreement or "contract" for therapy is reached. This is the orientation stage. The major part of the therapeutic process, called the "middle phase," then follows. This includes the dissatisfaction, resolution, and production stages, but less separate and distinct than usual, and considered from a somewhat different perspective. Here the dissatisfaction stage is seen largely as "resistance" to therapy; the patient does not work diligently on the problems that brought him or her to therapy but finds it easier instead to seek love and attention, to feel that change requires too much work, and otherwise to avoid his or her problems. The origins of this resistance are primarily unconscious, for example, transference, but that is only a difference in degree from the dissatisfaction stage in actual groups where not all the goals, expectations, and roots of frustration are conscious either.

The next main process in the middle phase is called "working through." The early part of this process, which can be called the resolution stage, includes work on resistances, work on reasonable expectations for the patient from therapy, and direct work on the patient's problems. The later, usually deeper, part of this working through can be considered the production stage and usually includes work on the patient's problems as revealed in the transference. This process is discussed here in a highly schematized manner; in practice, resistances and work on them and on the patients' expectations and problems occur throughout therapy.

The middle phase is followed by the "final" or "termination phase"; this is, of course, the termination stage. It generally includes some review of the experience, feelings of separation and examination of prior separation experiences, and plans for the future. In summary then, individual psychotherapy has a developmental stage process similar to the GDS sequence, starting with the orientation stage and ending with the termination stage.

In the usual outpatient settings where patients voluntarily present themselves for individual psychotherapy, this begins with a positive orientation stage. As Masterson (1972) and Rinsley (1974) showed, with resistant, less voluntary, generally more highly disturbed patients the individual psychotherapeutic-residential treatment developmental stage sequence begins with a negative orientation stage which largely obscures the dissatisfaction stage, and then proceeds with resolution, production, and termination stages. In practice, beginnings are found all along this continuum of positive to negative orientation.

ENCOUNTER GROUPS

Group developmental stages in encounter group settings will now be briefly examined. These groups include a wide range of theoretical persuasions and methods of working that usually have as their goal personal growth rather than learning about group functioning on the one hand or more explicit counseling or treatment on the other. It includes such orientations as Gestalt, "growth," human potential, body awareness, and many others, and they may or may not meet in a marathon format. (For a brief overview of marathon types, see Dinges and Weigel, 1971; for a more thorough discussion see Lieberman et al., 1973, and Appelbaum, 1979.)

Training groups emphasizing personal growth as opposed to group knowledge might also be included here, but training groups with a group learning focus have been emphasized in the group developmental stage literature, and they were discussed in the previous section on training groups; similarly, more explicitly counseling or therapy-oriented groups with defined patients were included in the section on therapy groups.

Encounter groups generally last a total of 10 to 30 hours,

which is in the range of most training groups, but considerably less than the 50 to 100 or more hours for many therapy groups. When the encounter group is meeting in a marathon format, all these hours may be grouped in one to three sessions. The training groups considered in the previous section generally do not use a marathon format; occasionally therapy groups will intersperse marathon-type meetings among their regular meetings.

Tindall

One research study on encounter groups will be presented. It has been selected because of its considerable methodologic sophistication compared with most other work in this area. In this study Tindall (1971) used a 72-item rating scale derived from the previously discussed Hill Interaction Matrix (HIM-Form G) to study six groups, three of which took part in an extended-time marathon encounter group of 30 hours, and three of which also met for 30 hours, but in 20 separate 1–1/2-hour sessions.

Data were collected by audiotape, and two raters blindly rated samples from the first and last hours, and from hours at each quarter division within the groups' histories (five rating periods per group). Each rating sample was 30 minutes long and included 10 minutes from the beginning, middle, and end of the sampled rating hour. The rated behavior was then categorized into 20 category cells, 16 that were discussed above in the Hill and Gruner study (1973), plus four additional, related categories. Tindall tested various hypotheses about differences between time-extended and non-time-extended encounter groups, which will not be discussed here, but he also investigated some hypotheses relative to group developmental stages, and these results will be presented.

In brief, over the life of the groups there was a statistically significant decrease in the more impersonal, external, Topic/-Conventional cell behavior, and a significant increase in Relationship/Confrontive cell behavior, indicating an increase in the quality of work. This increase in the quality of work was also shown in significantly less behavior over time in other more general cells (Group/Speculative and Group/Confrontive cells) compared with more intimate and relevant cells (Personal/Speculative, Personal/Confrontive, Relationship/Speculative, and Relationship/Confrontive). The more complex developmental changes of these groups were not significant within the limits of a low-power statistical test appropriate for a sample size of six, although most of the groups changed in the expected directions. These category changes over time are nevertheless shown below:

	Rating Period			
Start	First quarter	Second quarter	Third quarter	End
Maximum Responsive decreasing to end	Conventional decreasing to end	Maximum Assertive		Increased Confrontive compared to start
		Speculative increasing over last half		

Comparing the above material with the proposed GDSs, we see that the groups began dependent on the leader (Responsive) and with a low level of work (Conventional) in an orientation stage (start to the first quarter). The groups then became maximally Assertive (rather angry, aggressive, and hostile according to the HIM-G) in a dissatisfaction stage (second quarter), then appeared to get down to more relevant work during a resolution stage (third quarter), in which Assertive behaviors decreased and work quality increased. An apparent peak in work was reached in the production stage (the last rating period), with increased Speculative and Confrontive behaviors on the more relevant Personal and Relationship aspects of the encounter groups. (Confrontive behaviors in the HIM-G are fairly neutral discussions of behavior compared with the more negative, angry, Assertive behaviors.)

No termination was specifically discussed, but the data can be examined to see what behavior developed as the groups ended. Discussion of relationships is highest at the last rating session, and assertive negative behavior is decreased. (Five groups have their maximum Relationship scores at the last rating session, and four groups have their lowest Assertive rating then.) This high focus on Relationship and low negative, angry, behavior would lead one to wonder if there might have been a termination stage with a sense of loss and sadness. The HIM-G contains no specific ratings of sadness, loss, or depression, and these behaviors would be buried within larger, more general categories. Similarly, no data are available on the task portion of the termination stage, such as a review of the group progress made and self-knowledge gained. So, although not statistically supported, this study has considerable consistency with the proposed GDSs.

Summary of Encounter Group Developmental Stage Studies

Table 4.11 summarizes additional group developmental stage work with encounter groups. The placement of Braaten's (1974–1975) work here is arbitrary, since he talks of encounter groups but based much of his study on work with training groups. Most other available models and group developmental stage data for encounter groups tend to be discursive and less definitely organized than those presented here, or to be portions of models, that is, group development data (see, for example, Dinges and Weigel [1971]; and Long et al., [1971]). As with the previous table on therapy group developmental stage studies, the reports in this table are based primarily on anecdotal as opposed to more research-oriented studies. The table shows again that these encounter group studies are in considerable agreement with the proposed GDS model.

Naturalistic Groups

Naturalistic groups are a heterogeneous collection of groups comprised of individuals engaged in a usual or "natural" task as opposed to groups brought together for more "artificial" purposes, whether it be for therapy, for growth, for learning about groups themselves (training groups), or for researchers (problem-solving groups). The category of naturalistic groups is very large, particularly when conceptual groups are included—for example, salesmen beginning to sell vacuum cleaners, or medical students.

Several examples of studies of naturalistic groups will be presented because of their direct everyday significance and because of the transitional nature of these studies to the application of group developmental stage information in a subsequent chapter. These studies have been assembled into subsections on student groups, committees, work groups, and miscellaneous example (rebellions, for example, and people who have moved into a new housing development).

The naturalistic studies tend to be anecdotal and to be marked by minimal data measurement, poorly controlled observational conditions, and so on. Exceptions are the work of Bales, included in the work of Bales and Strodtbeck (1951), Ivancevich (1974), Mann et al. (1970), Philp and Dunphy (1958–1959, to be presented below), and to a lesser extent Mitchell (1975).

Student Groups

There are several papers on the group developmental stages of a wide range of student groups; two examples of these will be discussed in some detail, one with student-teacher groups, and the other with groups in a management and organizational behavior training program.

Table 4.11. Group developmental

Author and Year	Method	Number of Groups	Comments
Braaten, 1974-1975	Anecdotal	25-30	
Mintz, 1967	Anecdotal	24	Unclear whether there were 4 or 5 phases
Rogers, 1970	Anecdotal	Several	A complex series of occurrences in encounter groups that can be grouped according to GDS
Schutz, 1958, 1967, 1973	Research and anecdotal	Several	Earlier work (1958) is closer to the training group area; later work is in encounter area

stages in encounter groups — 1

Orientation	Dissatisfaction	Resolution	Production	Termination
Initial phase	Early phase	Mature work phase		Termination
Beginning phase	Hostile phase	Dependency phase . . .	enhanced self-acceptance	Final phase with separation anxiety
Milling, initial resistance, discussion of past feelings	Negative feelings	Beginning of more personal and group interpersonal expression of feelings	Development of healing capacity in group, self-acceptance, breaking down of facades, feedback, confrontation and feedback	Not clearly discussed
Inclusion — to belong or not	Control — who will control whom; time of confrontation	Affection — mutuality to form a bond	There may be additional cycles of inclusion to control to affection	With the termination stage there is a reversal of the cycle — affection to control to inclusion (eventual exlusion with termination)

Table 4.11.   Group developmental

Author and Year	Method	Number of Groups	Comments
Tindall, 1971	Research	6	Appears consistent with GDS formulation; see text
Winter, 1976	Anecdotal	9	

See footnote to Table 4.4.

Philp and Dunphy: Student-Teacher Groups

This study by Philp and Dunphy (1958–1959) on 11 groups of education students will be presented in detail because it is one of the studies in the naturalistic group category that is better methodologically, and also because it is related to examples previously presented (those of Bales and Strodtbeck [1951] on problem groups, and Psathas [1960] on therapy groups). Actually it is difficult to be sure if this was a naturalistic group or whether it was set up for an experiment and so viewed by the participants. It is discussed here because it has many characteristics of a naturalistic student group, such as a task directly related to a teacher education course that the students were taking.

The students were divided into 11 discussion groups of eight students each, which met for eight 40-minute discussion sessions over a 10-week period. The groups' task was stated as follows: "What would you regard as necessary elements of a general education in Australian schools at the secondary level? Outline as clearly as possible the criteria you would use in making your choice." The groups were required to try to reach stages in encounter groups — 2

Orientation	Dissatisfaction	Resolution	Production	Termination
	See above discussion in text.			
Encounter — initial uncertainty, dependency, focus on plan	Differentiation, Conflict, Norm Building — struggles between members, resentment toward leaders		Production — focus on task, looking to leaders for realistic help	Separating — evaluating experience, re-emergence of dependency

conclusions for a report that would be submitted at the end of the group meetings.

The observing and data recording utilized the previously discussed Bales' category system (Interaction Process Analysis —IPA). The researchers classified the approximately 300 to 400 distinctive acts per group session or meeting into the four Bales' areas of questions, answers, negative reactions, and positive reactions, covering task and social-emotional behaviors. They then divided each of their group sessions into "phases" of one quarter of the number of acts in each session; this practice contrasts with Bales and Strodtbeck's division of their single session groups into "phases" of one-third of the number of acts per session. (Note that "phase" here is a segment of a group meeting, a quarter of the acts in a single group meeting.)

They found that the interaction of the four category areas by phase by sessions was significant in an analysis of variance. There was " . . . a highly significant tendency in all groups to use different categories in different phases as the number of sessions increases. It matters, in terms of the relative emphasis on the [four] categories, whether a phase [quarter] is phase one in session one or phase one in session six" (p. 168).

If we take the data from the eight groups as a whole, the number of acts decreased in session two, rose to session four, and then fell slowly, with a more rapid fall in the last session, number eight. In these combined data there was relative stability in the task area of percentage of answers and questions from sessions one to eight, but there were marked changes in positive reactions, negative reactions, and number of acts per meeting. It is interesting that session two was the one of greatest conflict with the least number of acts, least positive reactions, and most negative reactions, and that in the sessions after this there was decreasing conflict and generally decreasing negative reactions, increasing positive reactions, and a greater number of acts.

These findings can be interpreted as showing an initial orientation stage (session one) with low answers and a low rate of acts with moderate positive reactions, negative reactions, and questions, followed by a dissatisfaction stage (session two) with maximum negative reactions and minimum positive reactions, a fall in the number of acts, and a rise in questions that may partly reflect negativity. The increased percentage of attempted answers at this time may reflect efforts at resolving the dissatisfaction experienced. This is followed by what can be considered a resolution stage in sessions three and four, marked by decreased negative reactions, increased positive reactions, decreased questions, and increased acts. Then a more active (increased acts) and apparently more comfortable production stage continued until the eighth session, when a termination stage may have been indicated by decreased negative reactions, which in fact reached their low point, and by a decrease in the number of acts. (Recall the decreased negativity and "assertiveness" in Tindall's [1971] data at the end of encounter groups, and the decreased negative reactions at the end of problem-solving groups in Bales and Strodtbeck's material [1951]; see the earlier discussion of problem-solving groups.)

It is not possible to make a detailed comparison of this study with the earlier study by Bales and Strodtbeck (1951) because the data were handled differently in the two studies.

Since Bales and Strodtbeck divided their sessions arbitrarily into thirds according to the number of acts, it is not possible to see the relationship between numbers of acts and other aspects of the groups' development in their study, though they do note that there is a tendency for the rate of interaction to speed up toward the end of a problem-solving episode (Bales & Strodtbeck, 1951, p. 487). Also, Bales and Strodtbeck grouped the ratings of their categories differently from Philp and Dunphy: Bales and Strodtbeck's groupings of orientation, evaluation, and control each included one category from each of the areas of "attempted answers" and "questions" (see Table 4.5).

The Philp and Dunphy study is similar to the Psathas (1960) study discussed above in the therapy group section in that both looked for cycles or phases within meetings. But the Philp and Dunphy study went further and looked for changes in the cycles or phases over the course of the groups' histories, and found them. In addition, as was seen, the Philp and Dunphy study can be interpreted as a full life cycle, successive stage, group developmental stage model.

When the Philp and Dunphy study is compared with that of Heinicke and Bales (1953), the latter study shows a similar peak of negative reactions in the second of four to six sessions, with increased positive reactions toward the end of the groups, statistically significant changes both within the positive and negative reactions themselves and when the negative reactions are compared with the positive reactions. Again, because of the method of rating and handling the data, the number of acts per session cannot be compared in the Heinicke and Bales (1953) and Philp and Dunphy studies.

As with the data from Mann et al. (1967) and Hartman and Gibbard (1974) (see Figures 4.1 and 4.2), the Philp and Dunphy data lend themselves to the construction of a morale curve. The curve is made by plotting the percentage of differences between positive reactions and negative reactions for each session (Figure 4.4). The curve is similar in shape to the GDS morale curve, although it does not get below a neutral baseline.

This could indicate that the task was not highly personal, but it might also be an artifact of a scoring system (IPA) that usually gives much higher positive than negative reactions and does not distinguish between degrees of these reactions (see Figure 4.3).

Ivancevich: Management and Organizational Behavior Training Program

This study of two groups in a five-day management and organizational behavior training program is another example of a naturalistic study with moderate research sophistication (Ivancevich, 1974). The groups were each composed of 32 matched, first-level male managers from a large manufacturing organization. Data were gathered after each of the eight training modules on an anonymously completed 50-item questionnaire on which participants noted the extent to which they agreed or disagreed with each statement. The questionnaires gathered data on "group cohesiveness," "interparticipant conflict," "openness of communication," "productivity" of the module, and favorable or unfavorable "attitudes toward the trainer." The study looked at the effects of an unstructured trainer versus a more directive trainer leading the groups, and the two groups do not coincide in their development. Yet a group developmental stage progression from orientation to termination seems evident in both of them.

The groups started with low "group cohesiveness" and "productivity," moderate "interparticipant conflict" and "openness of communication," and unfavorable "attitudes toward the trainer." These are generally orientation stage behaviors, except for the unfavorable "attitudes to the trainer," which may have reflected resistance to the administration's training program.

The middle stages of the two groups differ in the timing and magnitude of effects, and it is hard to summarize them easily. Dissatisfaction stage behavior was seen in each group

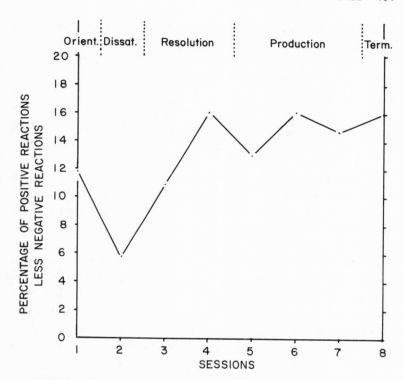

**FIGURE 4.4.   PHILP AND DUNPHY'S DATA AS A MO-
RALE CURVE.** This figure shows a morale curve constructed
from the Philp and Dunphy (1958-1959) data by plotting the
percentage of differences between the number of positive reactions and negative reactions. These differences were reported as
statistically significant from session to session between each of
the first four sessions, but not between the last four.

with a fall in "attitudes toward the trainer" in the fourth
module, after they had been improving earlier; the unstructured
group also stagnated in its "productivity" until the fourth session, and showed increasing "interparticipant conflict" peaking
in the sixth session. "Openness of communication" changed
little in the unstructured group, but it gradually increased in the
directive group.

Improvement in "attitudes toward the trainer" and increased "productivity" from the fourth to the fifth modules in both groups may be resolution stage behaviors. Then the groups' increasing "productivity," good "group cohesiveness," and sustained positive "attitudes toward the trainer" all seem parts of the production stage. (The increasing "interparticipant conflict" of the unstructured group up to the sixth module seems to be persisting dissatisfaction stage behavior, but it is somewhat counterbalanced by the increasing "group cohesiveness.")

Termination stage behaviors are suggested in both groups by a large decrease in "interparticipant conflict" at the end of the last module, with an increase in positive "attitudes toward the trainer" in the directive group and a decrease in the unstructured group.

Philp and Dunphy's and Ivancevich's studies and several others are summarized in Table 4.12. Additional comments are warranted on some of these studies. In Berger's (1976) work the groups were not composed of students in the usual sense, but primarily of nurses on a surgical unit who were in the groups to learn improved patient care. At their inception these groups had what was called a developmental stage of "ambivalence," similar, though less negative than, the negative orientation stage described for resistant therapy groups. As Berger comments, these patient-care meetings were likely resisted at first because they were "suggested" by hospital administration. These groups also had a termination-like stage called "consolidation," which was the end of one task before starting a new one. (This paper is an example of a group in which the explicit content, for example, the effect on a patient of entering into a hospital, can be an appropriate metaphor for the effect on the participants of entering into a learning group.)

Coombs (1978) collected data concentrating on medical students' reactions to patients' deaths which, with other material he reports, allows GDSs to be extracted.

Runkel et al. (1971) studied work groups associated with a course in social psychology and tested for a four-stage model of group developmental stages—Tuckman's (1965) forming, storming, norming, and performing. Although the study can be criticized methodologically because the raters looked only for group developmental stage data consistent with their hypothesis and also because they occasionally helped in the groups, some confirmatory evidence for these group developmental stages was found. The findings were complicated in that there were two cycles of each of these four stages, but this seemed to fit the fact that the groups were actually two types of groups with two tasks; first there were larger groups that had to agree on projects, and then smaller groups that had to work on the different projects.

It can be seen from these studies with a variety of student groups that there is again a high degree of correspondence with the proposed GDS sequence of stages from orientation to termination.

Committees

There are some data on the group developmental stages of committees scattered among sundry reports. Some of this information is included in the 22 problem-solving groups reported on by Bales and Strodtbeck (1951), which includes material on two committees. These were apparently single group meetings. (I will not repeat the findings of the overall study here; the reader is referred to the previous discussion.) Engs (1976) discussed the application of Tuckman's (1965) ideas on group developmental stages to citizens' committees.

Another report deals with federal government advisory committees (Cronin & Thomas, 1971). These authors talk about an initial stage of high enthusiasm leading rather invariably to frustration as their advice seems little heeded. At this time attendance at committee meetings drops, and members come late and leave early. Only subsequently, if the committee does not dissolve altogether, do they reach a more realistic and productive stage in which there is a better assessment of just

Table 4.12.   Group developmental stages

Author and Year	Method	Number of Groups	Comments
Berger, 1976	Anecdotal	"Several"	Hospital staff, especially nurses
Binder, 1976	Anecdotal	2	Psychiatric ward staff increasing patient care duties
Caple, 1978	Anecdotal	Several	Learning and other group types
Coombs, 1978	Some research data	59-62 students	Medical student conceptual group over four years; GDSs culled from material
Dell et al., 1977	Anecdotal	Several	Family therapy seminars; said to apply also to family therapy
Franck, 1972	Anecdotal	Several	Training farmers in rice growing; use of Bion's ideas
Holt, 1959	Anecdotal	238 residents	Psychiatric resident conceptual group during three years of residency
Ivancevich, 1974	Research	2	See text

Orientation	Dissatisfaction	Resolution	Production	Termination
Ambivalence, Passive receptivity	Resistance	Task orientation	Work group	Consolidation
Present	Present		Present	Groups not terminated
Orientation	Conflict	Integration	Achievement	Order (a termination stage)
Present — high idealism early in first year	Present — high stress and anxiety (5% dropout first year); first and second years	Present — improving self-image; third year	Present — less stress, more realistic anxiety, better self-image; fourth year	Present — end of fourth year (emerging "butterflies")
Battle for structure, then Naive enthusiasm	Conflictual frustration	Task orientation	Mutuality	Not discussed
Respondent	"Pairing" with anger and fighting	"Fight-flight"	Increasing morale and satisfaction	Not discussed
Present	Present	Implied	Implied	Not discussed
Present	Present	Present	Present	Present

Table 4.12. Group developmental stages

Author and Year	Method	Number of Groups	Comments
Lacoursiere, 1974	Anecdotal	3	Student nurses during a psychiatric affiliation
Lacoursiere, 1980	Anecdotal	8 +	Legal interns
Mann et al., 1970	Research	4	Lecture discussion sections of an introductory psychology class
Neilsen, 1978	Anecdotal	Not clear (several?)	Discussion classes; for example, in organizational behavior
Philp & Dunphy, 1958-1959	Research	11	See text
Rosenberg & Fuller, 1957	Anecdotal	Several	Student nurses during three years training; discusses termination, and imminent orientation as graduate nurses
Rothman & Marx, 1974	Questionnaire study	274 students	Freshman law student conceptual group; additional years not studied
Runkel et al., 1971	Research	3 that were split into 12	Social psychology students working on projects; see text

Orientation	Dissatisfaction	Resolution	Production	Termination
Orientation	Dissatisfaction	Implied	Production	Termination
Orientation	Dissatisfaction	Implied	Production	Termination
First phase	Dissatisfation and discourage-ment	Early enactment	Teacher takes control; late enactment	Separation
Safety vs. anxiety	Similarity vs. dissimilarity	Support vs. panic	Concern vs. isolation	Interdepen-dence vs. withdrawl
Present	Present	Present	Present	Present
Present	Present	Implied	Present	Present
Present	Present	Not considered	Not considered	Not considered
Forming	Storming	Norming	Performing	Not discussed

Table 4.12.   Group developmental stages

Author and Year	Method	Number of Groups	Comments
Scott & Moffett, 1977	Anecdotal	Several individuals	Development of talent in conceptual group of composers
Spitz & Sadock, 1973	Anecdotal	Several	Graduate nurses
Wogan et al., 1971	Anecdotal	5	Undergraduate students in field program about ghetto living
Zinberg et al., 1976	Anecdotal	4 +	Learning groups of teachers and students dealing with ''bigotry, drugs, sex,'' etc.

See footnote to Table 4.4.

what and how much advice will be listened to, and perhaps a better appreciation of the restrictions on the governmental bodies receiving the advice. There is no discussion of a termination stage in this report.

Among my comparable experiences is an example from the Topeka State Hospital Employees' Council, of which I was a member from its inception. Except for me and a nurse or two, it was comprised and run exclusively by rank-and-file hospital employees from all the service areas, from custodians to dieticians

in naturalistic student groups — 3

Orientation	Dissatisfaction	Resolution	Production	Termination
Possession of musical talent in child	Discouragement may ensue as talent is used	Transition from precocious youngster to adult musician	Major composi- tions by early 20s	Not discussed
Orientation	Present in attenuated form	Implied	Cohesive- ness, decreased depen- dency	Disengage- ment
Present	Crisis	Working through, increased group cohesion	Integra- tion, increased awareness about the ghetto	Present
Groups begin	Present (These stages more intermixed than usual)	Present	Home stretch	Final sessions

to nursing assistants. The council, whose purpose was an unspecific attempt to improve conditions for the "working" employees, started with much enthusiasm, hope, and sense of power about what they could accomplish (orientation). Within a few weeks this feeling was transformed into a considerable sense of hopelessness about what they could achieve; there were periods of silence in the meetings, and members, including members of the council executive, arrived late for meetings. One member expressed the mood by saying, "I've been here 21 years and been fallin' and stumblin' and I'll keep fallin' and stumblin'." This was clearly the dissatisfaction stage.

After a few more weeks of poor attendance the tenor of the group gradually picked up (resolution). We then began to see what we could do, and worked on these tasks with more realistic expectations and, incidentally, positive results (production). (The council did not terminate during my participation.)

Another interesting example of committee-like group developmental stage material is found in the discussion of the conference that led to the collection of papers on morale discussed in the earlier chapter (Galdston, 1958). There were three preliminary conferences before the final one, and the editor noted the process of these conferences. His description is worth quoting:

In each instance the dramatic progression was identical. The conferees met and at first cautiously and politely sounded each other out [orientation]. Somewhat oriented and assured, they then "attacked" the matter advanced, concentrating almost in unison and entirely on the propositions presented and on those who presented them. The concern of the specialists appeared to be to prove the propositions false and their proponents wrong, and each did this from the vantage point of his own specialist's knowledge and competence. Their authoritarian arguments at this stage seemed devastating, indeed annihilating to the entire enterprise [dissatisfaction]. But then the dynamics shifted. The specialists fell out among themselves, and their internecine disputes opened a way for the re-entry into the group's deliberations of many of the propositions originally advanced and initially rejected [early resolution].

This yielded the third stage [continuing resolution], which I cannot but label as a "guilt reaction." As if reactive to the intensity of their "hostility," the discussants seemingly discovered new meaning and significance in the matter originally presented, which made it more acceptable, that is to say, more consonant with their specialist's knowledge and ideas [production]. The meetings thus were concluded in more than fair harmony and common understanding [termination] (pp. 3–4).

Zurcher: Neighborhood Action Committees

A paper on the developmental stages of neighborhood action committees during the "war on poverty" is somewhat more complex (Zurcher, 1969). Twelve such neighborhood action committees were studied through participant observers who kept notes on each of the 174 meetings. The material was then examined for group developmental stages, of which seven were described. Only two committees reached the sixth stage, and one the seventh and last stage; the other nine committees dropped out along the way. (These seven stages are given in italics below.)

The developmental process of these somewhat atypical groups began with a need to inform (*orientation*) indigenous, and often indigent, residents about the possibility of a local Office of Economic Opportunity project, which was met with derision (*catharsis*), and only then in the committees that continued (nine of the 12) was there a specific *focus* on a definite project leading to a project grant proposal in an *action* stage. Then there was a waiting period (*limbo*) to see if the project was approved by the federal authorities. During this time there was considerable demoralization and dissatisfaction, which continued in a *testing* stage even if the project was approved. (Comments such as "It's about time!" and various concerns about whose project it really was indicated this dissatisfaction.) Only then was a *purposive* or production stage reached, which was achieved by only one of the 12 original committees.

It is a bit difficult to translate these stages into the ones proposed here. One way, suggested by Zurcher, follows Tuckman's (1965) scheme and considers the first two stages (*orientation* and *catharsis*) as "forming" and "storming" (orientation and dissatisfaction), then combines *focus, action, limbo,* and *testing* into "norming" (resolution), and considers the *purposive* stage as "performing" (production). An alternate way is to consider *orientation* and *catharsis* as a negative orientation stage before the actual (positive) orientation stage to the task (*focus* and *action*). This is analogous to the initial resistance of groups when at the outset there is a lack of trust and a need to win the group over to the task (see the earlier sections on the negative orientation stage). The *limbo* stage is a type of dissatisfaction stage, *testing* is the resolution stage, and finally, the *purposive* stage is the production stage. No termination stage was discussed. These alternative ways of looking at Zurcher's stages are summarized in Table 4.13.

Part of the complexity of this report is likely due to such things as the changing nature of the task (trusting the federal authorities, organizing a project proposal, acting on it if approved), and the definite break and near termination in the groups between the two final tasks. The negative orientation stage is probably related to the quasi-coercion experienced from the promise of a federal "carrot," and the concomitant doubt that they would ever achieve any positive results. (Anyone working with comparable groups would do well to read the original report.)

Again these examples show that the development of committees can be consistent with our GDS stages.

Work Groups

There are three anecdotal reports on work groups, two of these on mental health treatment teams, and one on Peace Corps volunteers. The reports on mental health treatment teams from various disciplines (Modlin & Faris, 1956; Berkowitz, 1974) describe an early period of functioning according to individual roles (a time of orientation), followed by unrest and rivalry (dissatisfaction), which is resolved (resolution) and eventually becomes integrated in true teamwork (production). Neither of these reports discusses an ending stage or termination.

An interesting paper on morale in Peace Corps volunteers (W. W. Menninger, 1975) described four stages of morale that

**Table 4.13.   Zurcher's stages
in neighborhood action committees**

Original Stages	Zurcher's Rearrangment	GDS	
Orientation	Forming	Orientation ⎫	Negative Orientation
Catharsis	Storming	Dissatisfaction ⎭	
Focus		⎫	(Positive) Orientation
Action	Norming	Resolution ⎬	
Limbo			Dissatisfaction
Testing			Resolution
Purposive	Performing	Production	Production

(No Termination discussed)

This table shows Zurcher's original stages and his rearrangment according to Tuckman (1965), and two ways of considering these stages as GDSs. (Zurcher, 1969).

taken together comprise a four-stage group developmental stage model. This begins with a stage of arrival (orientation) with high motivation and morale; then morale falls considerably in the stage of engagement (dissatisfaction). Next is the stage of acceptance when morale climbed again, but with the Peace Corps volunteers this was a time when the strongest feelings were anger and "activist energy." This appears to be their production stage, though perhaps also with aspects of the resolution stage. The final stage of re-entry (termination) is a period of evaluation, with some depression and concerns about the future. Morale falls to near baseline levels or below, but not as low as in the engagement stage (dissatisfaction).

Recall the Hare (1967) examination of the classic Western Electric-Hawthorne study of 1927–1929. This was placed in the section on problem-solving groups (Table 4.6) largely because of the high degree of experimental manipulation, but it was a functioning work group. Hare found stages consistent with orientation, dissatisfaction, resolution, and production. The group did not stop, so there was no termination stage. Comparable results were also found when Hare (1968) studied, without experimental manipulation, a work group consisting of a long-term government planning board.

Miscellaneous Studies

There are several miscellaneous studies of group developmental stages that do not easily fit into the previous sections or subsections. First there are two related studies of a sociopolitical nature. Davies (1969) and Feierabend and colleagues (1969) examined the relationship between expectations and their gratification, and the contribution of these factors to revolutions and rebellions. The rising expected satisfactions and the actual satisfactions can lead to a considerable gap between the two and to an insufficient and sometimes intolerable gratification level.

> Revolution is most likely to take place when a prolonged period of rising expectations and rising gratifications is followed by a short period of sharp reversal, during which the gap between expectations and gratifications quickly widens and becomes intolerable. The frustration that develops, when it is intense and widespread in society, seeks outlets in violent action (Davies, 1969, p. 547).

Feierabend and coworkers (1969, p. 531), add that gratification may actually be rising, but too slowly to keep up with more quickly rising expectations. Expectations here are relative to a wide range of human needs, including biological, psychological, and social needs, as interpreted by Maslow (1962). Davies (1969) notes that this " . . . is a psychological, not a sociological explanation. The units of analysis are individual human beings" (p. 574).

With this framework Davies examines the French Revolution of 1789, the American Civil War of 1861, the Nazi Revolution of 1933, and the American black rebellion of the 1960s. All of these occurred not when conditions were at their worst, but after they had begun to improve and then appeared to stagnate or reverse. For example, the black rebellion did not occur when the conditions for poor blacks in the United States were at their worst, but after they had steadily risen for years until, apparently, their expectations exceeded the gratifications. As an illustration, although black education increased, jobs for blacks did so at a much slower pace. At the same time there was a resurgence of violence against blacks in 1963, for example, in Birmingham, Alabama. These and related factors quickly led to an intolerable gap between the rising expectations and perceived gratifications. (A more recent example is provided by the June 1976 disturbances in Poland, when the government planned to raise food prices abruptly after not having done so for several years [Feron, 1976].)

The early part of this explanation, rising expectations, is similar to the orientation of GDSs, when there are hopes for and expectations of gratification. In both of these schemes a lack of correspondence develops between expectations and realities and leads to frustration and dissatisfaction—the dissatisfaction stage of the GDSs. In the interpretation of rebellions and revolutions, the expectations are rising and the external satisfactions may be decreasing, though at times it is less of an actual decrease than a realization of the lack of adequate gratification. In the GDS framework there may or may not be an actual decrease in external satisfactions, but there is a realization that one's expectations will not be met as anticipated.

In the usual GDS setting, expectations are not particularly rising, but undoubtedly there are times when the initial expectations in a group may rise because they are easily met. For example, early expectations in group psychotherapy may contribute to a "honeymoon" cure, or the expectations of early medical or law students may easily be satisfied because they are beginning something that is new and exciting and high in status. So, on closer examination, these formulations for GDSs and rebellions and revolutions have a considerable degree of overlap, and some of the difference is partly a matter of emphasis.

In the formulation for rebellions and revolutions some resolution (resolution stage) must follow the initial stages of the revolution or rebellion with a better alignment of expectations and reality (satisfactions), and a new feeling among the people that they are again productive members of society (production stage). Termination stage phenomena would be expected only with the termination of the sociopolitical group, for example, integration into the wider society.*

In a different type of study, Mitchell (1975) interviewed members of 121 households that voluntarily moved to a Texas community of 40,000. These moves were generally based on a well-considered examination of possible places to move, and after a change in career plans, including occasionally retirement. Fifty of the original 121 households were later reinterviewed.

> At first there was an initial period of elation; later a time period
> of introspection and generally some anxiety, depression and hesi-

*This material on revolutions and rebellions helps to show the possible scope of GDS formulations, and the possibility of broad application. For example, a government or politician that holds out unrealistic expectations for its electorate (has President Carter done this?), or lets such expectations develop irresponsibly, does so at its peril. Other GDS applications will be pursued in a subsequent chapter.

tation; and then later a period of normality and satisfaction. All persons interviewed went through the stages but the length of time in each period varied from individual to individual. One-member households, households with teenagers and households who had not [previously] moved for over eight years appeared to suffer a longer and more severe second period, although all appeared to be making a satisfactory adjustment (p. 97).

This seems to cover quite clearly the first four GDS stages—orientation, dissatisfaction, implied resolution, then production. There is no mention of termination, and of course these movers did not terminate their residences at their new homes.

Speck and Attneave (1973) give an anecdotal discussion of the developmental process in a type of family therapy called social network intervention. In this therapy as many members as possible of extended family and friends, along with the identified patient, work in large group sessions. The "phases of the network effect," as they are called, consist of "retribalization," "polarization," "mobilization," "depression," "breakthrough," and "exhaustion-elation."

Retribalization is the initial socializing and resocializing of people who have not seen each other for some time; their concerns about why they are there and what they will do are similar to concerns in the GDS orientation stage. Polarization is a period of disgruntlement and anger between opposing factions and subgroups, and it is similar to the dissatisfaction stage. Mobilization, an attempt to resolve the polarization, is comparable to the resolution stage. Depression ("the confrontation with a difficult task [resolving polarization] will meet with initial resistance, despair, and even desperation" p. 28), which may well overlap with previous phases, can be considered part of the process of the dissatisfaction and resolution stages under these conditions of highly charged interpersonal problems that are difficult to work out or resolve. Breakthrough "is the label for the relative absence of resistance and depression, and is accompanied by, or leads into, activity that accomplishes the goals of the network members" (p. 36); this is similar to the production stage. Finally, exhaustion-elation is similar to the termination stage.

Summary of Naturalistic Group Developmental Stage Studies

It would be redundant at this point to review in any detail this section on group developmental stages in various naturalistic groups, or the degree to which these are consistent with the proposed GDSs. Perhaps it is adequate to say that this review has disclosed a high degree of consistency of GDSs in groups in various educational settings, in committees, in work teams, and in miscellaneous contexts including rebellions and revolutions.

Chapter 5

GDS THEORY AND UNDERLYING PROCESSES

The first four chapters described GDSs and showed the range over which these stages occur. But not all groups undertaking a new experience and evidencing GDSs go through the five-stage sequence from orientation to termination. In this chapter the sequences that are found will be recapitulated, conditions that enhance the development of GDSs will be discussed, and an attempt will be made to go beyond the descriptive data to an examination of the processes underlying these stages.

GROUP AND GENERAL DEVELOPMENTAL STAGE THEORY

When a person enters a new experience under conditions I will soon elaborate, certain feelings and reactions are so predictable, as seen in the last chapter, that it does not seem difficult to accept a group or general developmental stage (GDS) theory. This GDS theory states that under the conditions of a new experience, as well as a sufficient number of other conditions such as the nature of the task and temporal boundaries, the participants in the experience will go through a sequence of feelings and reactions characterized as group or general developmental stages. These GDSs are usually orientation, dissatisfaction, resolution, production, and termination. When several individuals simultaneously go through the new experience as a group, the overall group will pass through these stages. In fact, these stages are easier to observe in such groups, and may well occur there with more consistency.

The more the conditions of the new experience approach those that maximize the development of GDSs, the more likely it is that these will occur, and the more easily they will be observed. Conversely, the less the underlying conditions of the experience approach those that maximize the development of GDSs, the less likely it is that they will occur and the less obvious they will be if they do occur. When conditions seem suitable for the development of GDSs and they do not seem to occur, a more careful examination should show either that GDSs are present, but perhaps partly obscured, that they are not very intense, that they have taken the form of one of the resistive variations, or that conditions are not really appropriate —for example, there has been a lack of interest in the task from the beginning and the membership may be too unstable.

The significant regular GDS variations are the absence or relative absence of a resolution stage when the dissatisfaction stage is not very pronounced or the overall experience is fairly short, and the relative absence of a termination stage when the overall experience is fairly short or lacks much personal involvement, or both. Any extended experience will usually lead to enough personal involvement to create some degree of a termination stage.

The other important variations occur when there is a negative orientation stage, generally when participation is at least somewhat involuntary. Under these conditions, depending on such factors as the length of the experience, the degree of the initial resistance, the difficulty of the task, and the particular participants, the negative orientation stage and the positive orientation and dissatisfaction stages will blur together, and these latter two stages may not be observable.

When a group has a negative orientation stage, an eventual production stage depends first on an observable resolution stage, although the resolution stage may be more spread out than usual. Although the reviewed studies support a dichotomy between positive and negative orientation stages, it is likely that in practice there is a continuum of beginnings.

Individuals or groups may abort the sequential process or become arrested in development almost anywhere along the way, but this is more likely during an unpleasant stage such as negative orientation or dissatisfaction. Whether aborted GDS sequences usually have a termination stage is uncertain, but it may well be that such sequences will often show such a stage, although it may be short. Since they come at the end of the experience, termination stage behaviors are highly visible and include behavior quite different from other GDS behaviors, for example, saying good-bye and reviewing the experience.

An individual, or individuals, might stop an experience during the dissatisfaction stage by saying, "This whole business stinks. Good-bye!," but this brief statement includes a review and evaluation of the experience and a farewell—termination stage behaviors. Alternatively, if group members merely cease showing up for the experience there will be little termination stage behavior to observe other than the lack of participation.

At this point you may be saying, "What *are* the group developmental stages anyway! Is there a set pattern or isn't there?" When a group experience is successful and does not abort or become arrested at the dissatisfaction stage—and this is the usual sequence as reported in many papers in the previous chapter—then the full series from the orientation stage to the termination stage can be seen. Under the various other conditions of completed development—the nonabortive variations—there will be orientation, dissatisfaction, and production stages, or, if there is a negative orientation stage, then at least this, sometimes a separate dissatisfaction stage, and then resolution and production stages. In addition, under most conditions there will be some sort of termination stage. These various GDS sequences are illustrated in Table 5.1.

ACTUAL AND CONCEPTUAL GROUPS: A REMINDER

Before proceeding in more detail with a psychological analysis of GDSs, a reminder of the way the word *group* is used may be in order. *Group* is used in the usual sense of a collection of individuals with some shared purpose, or what has been called an *actual group,* but it is also used to describe a looser collection or class of individuals, each with his or her individual but similar task, or what has been called a *conceptual group.*

Group has been used to describe both actual and conceptual groups partly for convenience, because the developmental stage phenomena are similar for both types of groups. Besides, actual and conceptual groups are in many ways on a continuum: Actual groups have a leader and group members who are physically present at the time of the group meetings, whereas conceptual groups have a leader and group members who are together intrapsychically to varying degrees (see Freud, 1921). For example, the individual law or medical student may think of the dean of the school or dean of students or, less specifically, "the faculty" or "the school" as the group leader and other students are thought of as part of the student group with whom one competes, and so on. In addition, in actual groups the similar intermeeting intrapsychic existence of the group leader, members, task, and so on, preserves group continuity and contributes to the group development and developmental stages.

The above examples of conceptual groups of law or medical students in their usual school contexts of lecture rooms will still allow for some observations of member-to-member and member-to-leader phenomena, and these examples are still

Table 5.1. The regular GDS sequences, and resistive and abortive developmental variations

	Negative Orientation Stage	(Positive) Orientation Stage	Dissatisfaction Stage	Resolution Stage	Production Stage	Termination Stage
Regular development						
Full sequence		XX	XX	XX	XX	XX
Short sequence (a)		XX	XX		XX	XX
Short sequence (b)		XX	XX		XX	X
Resistive development						
Resistive sequence (a)	XX		O or X	XX	XX	X or XX
Resistive sequence (b)	XX		XX	XX	XX	XX
Resistive sequence (c)	XX	XX	XX	XX	XX	XX
Abortive development						
Abortive sequence (a)		XX	XX	X		?
Abortive sequence (b)		XX	XX			?
Abortive sequence (c)	XX	X	XX			?

close to actual groups. The examples can be moved further along the continuum away from actual groups. Consider instead a group composed of new schoolteachers or executives with new promotions, each in a separate setting. For these conceptual groups the "leaders" and "co-members" will be different for each member of the conceptual group. For example, each new teacher is apt to think of his or her own principal as the group leader, and not particularly think of other group members unless, for instance, there are additional new teachers at that particular school. In such conceptual groups there will be little member-to-member behavior to observe, but primarily specific-member-to-specific-leader phenomena, and the GDS data for an observer will be primarily the observations of the isolated, single, conceptual group member.

The conceptual group will take form, from an observer's point of view, as the observer gathers data about several single members over a period of time, perhaps several school years, or over the course of observing several new executives move into similar positions, or while observing such conceptual group members in actual groups, such as new teachers at teachers' conventions, or new executives in executive training sessions.

Similarly, the isolated member will likely consider her or his experience from the point of view of an isolated individual and not as a member of a group, and though the isolated member might wonder how other individuals are managing in like circumstances, there will usually not be a great deal of direct interaction with such other individuals unless explicit attempts are made to do so. Of course, there will be direct interaction with the individual's "leader"—the principal or the executive's superior—but these persons are not usually viewed as the leader of a group of new teachers or new executives.

This review and discussion of actual and conceptual groups is intended to show the range of settings that can be considered, while accepting that GDS phenomena will occur more easily and consistently and be more observable in actual group settings.

GDSs, Groups, and Regression

GDSs depend considerably on an adequate personal and usually interpersonal focus in the group. There will not be much hope developed or frustration experienced with highly impersonal and easily definable tasks that stimulate primarily the more conscious thought processes for their fairly easy accomplishment. Interpersonal aspects will not be a significant part of an experience if the experience is very brief, and if the relationships remain superficial and do not stimulate or elicit deeper, less conscious interpersonal fantasies and feelings. Similarly, there will not be much of a termination stage if the task is not much of a personal challenge or if there is little depth to the interpersonal relationships developed during the experience.

It is not easy to characterize settings that are particularly conducive to the development of GDSs, but settings that call forth and stimulate the less conscious thinking processes, the less conscious fantasies, and deeper-lying affects and impulses do seem to be more conducive. Of course, even artificial problem-solving groups can be made more conducive to the development of GDSs by making the problem more personal and/or interpersonal, for example, by making it competitive, making the experience long enough, or dealing with an affectively charged problem.

In actual groups these less conscious characteristics are very much an inherent part of the setting. These characteristics do vary with the type of group, and with the specific group (details will be discussed soon), but immediately on stepping into an actual group we behave less maturely or as less developed people. We set aside some of our critical, reality-assessing ego and superego (conscience) faculties. Our more primitive impulses and urges come to the fore. We do not try as hard to think in a rational way or to control our impulses and behavior. Instead we let part of such rational thinking and controlling fall to the group leader when there is one, or to other group members, or both. And this happens with little specific planning or conscious thought about it, or often with little explicit questioning of oneself about who is responsible for one's behavior in this setting, or what it means, or how it will be made reasonable.

Before proceeding further in discussing this "natural" behavior, we should look at some additional examples of how pervasive it can be. In actual groups especially, many even apparently rather emotionally neutral areas of functioning can be in abeyance, for example, the ego's temporal and spatial orienting functions. We regularly see people in actual groups who need to be told specifically and repeatedly the time to end a coffee break in the context of the group experience, and when or where a meeting will be. Gross confusion often results from any change in time or location. Members will show up at the wrong time, the wrong place, or both, and they can have what seems like inordinate difficulty getting this temporal and spatial information accurate.

Such less conscious, more unconscious behavior also occurs in conceptual groups, but usually less forcefully and as less of an inherent part of such settings. The specifics will vary with the conceptual group in question. (The subject of actual-conceptual group comparisons will be returned to several times in this chapter.)

Group contexts, and especially actual groups, require that some of these regressive phenomena occur because on entering such an experience we enter a setting in which we are not the controlling, responsible party. We have ceded this function primarily to the leader, or to the group as a whole, and any individual member has only partial responsibility. It cannot be otherwise. And even if the leader has a fairly clear idea of the task, it is not usual that a particular member does, so he or she must depend on the leader for this information. Also, the skills to do the task or the applying of skills to this particular task is likely to require the help of the leader, or other participants, or both. Then in settings where other group members are important, especially in actual groups, the other members tend to be strangers. You have to sit back and examine and evaluate them, and wait to see how they evaluate you. This is even more true of evaluating the leader or leaders, and seeing how you are received and evaluated by them.

In addition, this partial abandonment of one's individual, conscious level of functioning helps in the development of a group consciousness—the sense of *group*. This can aid in the formation of group cohesion, but the group consciousness will often contain not only mentally attractive people or components, but also repulsive or hated ones—for example, a scapegoat—and this may hinder cohesion. Speculations on some of the individual developmental origins of this group consciousness along the lines of M.S. Mahler's work (1968) can be found in Colman (1975).

In groups, then, and especially in actual groups, we behave in a psychologically less developed or more regressed way; groups can be said to have a "regressive pull" on the participants. It might be argued that in some ways in such groups we behave as more developed persons since we give up individual, more self-centered goals for higher level, "common good," goals. Furthermore, in groups we may function in more developed ways by thinking more creatively via our less conscious thought processes, for example, in "brainstorming." Although the end result in groups may sometimes be of a higher level, it comes about in part through some regression in and abandonment of individual development. And the end result does not come without some risk to the individual's well-being—but more on this shortly.

By stimulating the development of more affect, enhancing and stimulating fantasies, and encouraging symbolic thought processes, the regression in groups makes a significant contribution to GDS phenomena. It will help understanding of these GDS phenomena if characteristics of this regression are examined more carefully.

This regression can be considered according to whether it is healthy or pathological, what brings it about, and its metapsychological type. Beginning with the last of these, there are various ways to consider the metapsychological types of regression (Freud, 1900; Scheidlinger, 1968); an adequate way for our purposes is to consider *developmental regression* and *topographical regression.*

Developmental regression refers to the reversion to earlier developmental levels, in general from more mature adult behavior to more immature, more adolescent or childlike behavior. This is most noticeable with regression to oral stage behaviors, such as highly dependent behavior, but as will be seen, this developmental regression also applies to other psychoanalytic developmental levels. *Topographical regression* is regression from more conscious and reasoned (secondary process) functioning to more unconscious, less reasoned (primary process) functioning, with a greater emphasis on fantasizing and on primitive methods of intellection, for example, concrete and symbolic reasoning.

These two types of regression are related in complex ways; in simplest terms they often parallel each other, with greater degrees of developmental regression associated with greater degrees of topographical regression. Such regression does not usually mean pathology; it is part of natural functioning in groups contributed to by the very nature of the situation.

This leads to another contrast in this subject of regression, that between healthy and pathological regression. Regression in milder and reversible degrees is part of healthy functioning in most of the contexts in which it occurs, including in actual and conceptual groups. For instance, a certain amount of developmental regression allows appropriate dependency and trust for adequate functioning in groups, and controllable amounts of topographical regression allows for the creative use of unconscious thought processes. Such regression is what can be called "regression in the service of the ego" (Kris, 1952), and it contributes to healthy human functioning.

But if this developmental or topographical regression is not easily reversible, or if it is severe, we are in the realm of psychopathology. For example, if the developmental regression in the group becomes so strong that it persists outside the group —for example, in repeated phone calls to the leader asking what the member should do about matters that he or she can and should resolve—then this regression is excessive. Or, if the production of unconscious fantasies via topographical regression cannot easily be stopped or regulated by the more conscious faculties of the ego—for instance, if images of retaliation from the leader symbolically represented in monsters are not adequately judged on a reality basis—then we are in the realm of pathological regression.

People differ in their ability to handle healthy regression, or conversely, they differ in propensities to pathological regression. These propensities vary somewhat with time and circumstances, but generally people who are psychologically less healthy have less ability to handle regression and more of a propensity to be pathologically affected by it, so that regression becomes disruptive. This disruption can progress to the point of severe psychological problems, such as a depressive or schizophrenic illness.

Negligible propensity to pathological regression probably makes a negligible contribution to the development of GDSs. A larger but still relatively small propensity to pathological regression likely facilitates the development of GDSs because of the contribution of such regression to the development and expression of affectively charged fantasies and hopes about the group task, other members, the leader (transference), and so on. At the other extreme, a high propensity to pathological regression will generally be so disruptive and painful to the individual that it will usually be resisted, or if it occurs it may well contribute to the member's premature withdrawal from the group (see Yalom & Lieberman, 1971).

When a member undergoes severe pathological regression, this behavior may be a significant contributing factor to other members' withdrawal, or to the dissolution of the group. This may happen when the pathologically regressed member's behavior takes on a strong paranoid, threatening, and hostile demeanor, or when the member is painfully depressed and the other members' identification with the depressed person makes their own participation intolerable.

An additional aspect of the relationship between pathological regression and healthy regression "in the service of the ego" is that a significant amount of one type of regression often precludes a significant amount of the other type. For example, a person who is severely pathologically regressing is apt to struggle against healthy regression "in the service of the ego," because the amount of anxiety and psychic disruption from the former is usually too painful and there will be diligent attempts to protect oneself against additional ego disruption and psychic pain.

The final functioning of a particular person in a specific group will partly be the result of the many factors that contribute to regression, so it is difficult to generalize. A person with a strong inclination to healthy regression who is willing to regress may find the group not especially conducive to his or her purposes. Conversely, a person with a strong inclination to pathological regression who is trying to avoid such regression may find that in a specific group he or she is not able to do so.

It has already been mentioned that regression occurs in group settings partly because that is the nature of such settings, and because this regression is required for functioning in groups. Such a setting may also contribute to regression because the experience is stressful, and possibly very much so. Examples of stresses in actual groups derive from uncertainty about one's ability to accomplish the task and difficulties in gaining the necessary skills for it, uncertainty about one's reception by the leader and other group members, varying degrees of feared or actual attack from the leader and other members, and similar factors. In addition, the regression that does occur in the group can be stressful, especially if one's conscious ego controls are tenuous.

There are analogous examples of stress in conceptual

groups, although in these settings other group members may be a less important source of stress, but there are exceptions. For instance, in a first-year law or medical school class in which one might fail unless successful in competition against one's classmates, it is obvious that other members are an important source of stress.

Do these regressive phenomena occur in all actual groups? The answer is yes, but we may have to look diligently and skillfully under certain conditions to see them. They will be minimal under conditions that are more clearly ego- and task-oriented, and maximal under conditions that allow or encourage more abeyance of the ego and more tolerance of less conscious phenomena. Examples of groups on the minimum side are Bales' one-session problem-solving groups and other groups that meet for a single session to complete a distinct task. Usual examples of groups on the maximum side are training groups and therapy groups, but there are also some naturalistic groups that approach the maximum, especially learning groups with tasks that have a strong personal pull, such as groups of student nurses in a psychiatric affiliation (Lacoursiere, 1974) and groups of oncology workers (Wise, 1977).

Does such regression affect conceptual groups? A practical answer is that in the conceptual groups that interest us here, regression does occur, although compared to actual groups there is usually not as much "regressive pull" and the regression is less obvious. The amount and nature of the regression will depend on the type of conceptual group and on the specific group in question. To illustrate, each conceptual group medical or law student carries the group leader or leaders (the school dean or dean of students, and likely particular teachers) within her or him, and in some sense each is a member of a group led by them. Members of such conceptual groups enter a new experience (the conceptual group) on which they are somewhat dependent (developmental regression) and about whose task, other members, and so on they generally lack clear ideas, so that various fantasies develop about these things (topographical regression). Conceptual groups high in regression will be those composed of participants in individual psychotherapy and other psychiatric treatment, and a conceptual group usually low in regression will be one of new factory workers.

GROUP CONDITIONS ENHANCING GDSs

Having discussed general regressive effects of groups, we will now examine some of the more specific conditions that facilitate the development of GDSs. Most of these conditions enhance the psychological nature of the group, for example, by encouraging the development and expression of fantasies, allowing less defensiveness, and encouraging dependency—all factors that enhance GDS phenomena and make them more observable.

Many of these various conditions (Table 5.2) can be viewed as continua that minimize or maximize GDS phenomena. These should be viewed in terms of practical working limits, because if some of these conditions are pushed too far, there will soon no longer be a group. At most there will remain a group in some state of disorganization. For example, the group should not be so open that members come and go at each meeting, and the task cannot be so vaguely specified that no member knows what to do.

Only a few of these conditions have been studied from the perspective of their effect on group developmental stages, most of them having been addressed from the more limited perspective of their effect on group development in general, for example, their effect on group cohesion or group productivity. Nonetheless, the expected effects on GDSs can usually be discerned or speculated on, and they should not be inconsistent with the effects on group development in general. Most of these conditions interact with each other, and in practice they can rarely be considered in isolation. In addition, external conditions cannot be ignored, although they have received little attention for their effect on group developmental stages. Such conditions will be briefly discussed at the end of this section.

It must be understood that the conditions that maximize GDSs are not necessarily the conditions that lead to optimum GDSs or optimum work on the task. These maximum conditions are conditions under which the GDSs described here are most likely to develop and be seen. Conditions under which GDSs are maximum are not likely to be optimum conditions. For example, the orientation stage can be made highly visible by starting with deprived individuals and fostering high expectations; then if these expectations are poorly satisfied and inter-member rivalry is encouraged, there will be a marked dissatisfaction stage.

The actual optimum GDSs will vary at least with the type of group, with the specific group, and with how one defines optimum. This might be defined according to the work on the task, but it could also be defined according to maximizing participant satisfaction or other criteria. The emphasis here, which will be particularly addressed in a subsequent chapter on applications, will be largely on enhancing the work on the task, but some degree of attention to participant satisfaction will also help this.

The first two conditions in Table 5.2, *pathological regression* and *regression "in the service of the ego"* were introduced above. To repeat, a low propensity to pathological regression probably makes a positive contribution to GDS phenomena. A high propensity to pathological regression likely inhibits the development and expression of fantasies, feelings, and so on that contribute to GDS phenomena; alternatively, such a high propensity may lead to the development and expression of such overwhelming fantasies or such strong feelings that group development is disrupted, at least for the individuals involved, and sometimes for the whole group. On the other hand, a high capacity for regression "in the service of the ego" probably facilitates GDS phenomena, and a low capacity likely inhibits such phenomena.

Table 5.2. **Group conditions that minimize or maximize the formation of GDSs**

Minimize	Conditions	Maximize
	Member	
High propensity	Pathological regression	Low propensity
Low capacity	Regression "in the service of the ego"	High capacity
Same	Sexual composition	Mixed
Homogeneous	Racial composition	Heterogeneous
?	Personality and social	?
Unstable	Membership stability	Stable
Open	Membership openness	Closed
Involuntary, coerced	Participation	Voluntary
	Task	
Easy	Difficulty	Hard
Clear	Clarity	Ambiguous
Impersonal	Psychological dimension	Personal
Not regarding basic needs	Basic needs (see Maslow, 1962)	Regarding basic needs
	Leader	
Same as members	Sex	Different from members
Same as members	Race	Different from members
Less skilled	Skill	More skilled
Does not instill, encourage	Trust/confidence	Instills, encourages
Not leader-centered	Interpretations/comments	Leader-centered (encourages transference
Authoritarian, high structure	Type and structure	Democratic, little structure
	Temporal and Spatial	
Indefinite	Temporal boundaries	Definite
Shorter	Length of group meetings	Longer
Shorter	Length of group life cycle	Longer
Varying	Meeting place	Same
	Group Type	
Problem-solving	Type	Training, therapy

The *sexual and racial composition* of the *group members* and the sex and race of the *leader(s)* are uncertain areas. Winter (1974), in an interesting paper dealing primarily with interracial dynamics, also includes information on the effects of a female trainer on a sexually and racially mixed training group. The sexual composition, along with the racial mixture, appeared to increase the regressive effects on the group, and, by implication, could increase certain aspects of GDSs.

In a training group study by Lundgren (1971), one of the two all-white groups had a black trainer, and there were unconfirmed impressions that this may have contributed to the group's impaired development because of reluctance to talk about racial issues. Conversely, a study of 11 leaderless groups during each of eight sessions in the context of an educational course (Philp & Dunphy, 1958–1959, discussed above with naturalistic groups) found that varying the male-to-female member ratio did not affect the group developmental stages they studied.

These issues of the sexual and racial composition of groups could partly be a function of the degree to which the task allows male-female or racial factors to affect the group's development; this would be less with impersonal, discrete tasks, and more with personal, less clearly defined tasks such as those in training and therapy groups. Such a sexual and racial mixture in the members, or between the members and leader, enhances the unconscious fantasies in the group, at least in our culture. This will often enhance the development of GDS phenomena, but under some conditions it may disrupt or inhibit the group's development (see also Gibbard & Hartman, 1973).

How do members' *personality and social characteristics* contribute to GDSs? Which characteristics particularly enhance or impede GDSs? Does homogeneity in these regards enhance GDSs? There is only a small amount of data on these questions from a group developmental stage perspective, whereas there is a large body of data and accumulated group wisdom on characteristics that enhance or interfere with the narrower perspective of group development in general.

Important characteristics are those that generally facilitate or impede group development, and these cannot be ignored. For example, a problem-solving, training, or therapy group that is highly heterogeneous intellectually might have serious difficulties with its general development, whereas socioeconomic heterogeneity would have a less significant effect.

A brief sampling of these characteristics affecting group developmental stage phenomena will be presented. We have already seen that GDSs develop in groups of individuals that are homogeneous in being above average intellectually and socioeconomically (executives in learning groups, legal interns, and so on), and in patient groups fairly homogeneous in regard to psychiatric diagnosis.

In problem-solving groups without assigned leaders, Heinicke and Bales (1953) found that groups in which members agreed more on the leadership status of members could more easily resolve dissatisfaction stage behaviors and move on to the production stage, and were more satisfied with their group experience. Groups whose members agreed less on their leadership status did poorer in these regards. Status is not quite so simple when other variables are introduced.

Lundgren (1973) studied the members in two training groups, one group led by more inactive, nondirective trainers, the other by relatively active, directive trainers. In the less actively led group the higher status members were more appropriately involved, productive, and satisfied with their experience, whereas in the more actively led group, higher status members tended to be more negative toward the trainer and the experience and less appropriately involved in its task.

Another study on member characteristics and their relationship to the group's development comes from Bugen (1977), who studied eight training groups composed of members with differing degrees of need for inclusion ("belonging") as measured on the Schutz' (1958) Fundamental Interpersonal Relations Orientation-Behavior (FIRO-B) scales. Four levels of inclusion need were differentiated, and the two groups with low to moderate inclusion needs surpassed the other groups in the development of cohesion, generally resolution stage behavior. Groups composed of members with higher or lower needs for inclusion both had lower levels of cohesion.

A conclusion from this brief discussion of the subject of members' personality and social characteristics is that we can expect observable GDSs from any reasonable collection of such characteristics, as long as the group is not so heterogeneous that it cannot be kept together.

Next come the related conditions of *membership stability* and *membership openness.* Keeping the same members, or maintaining *membership stability,* increases group development in general and the development of GDSs in particular. Holding down *membership openness,* that is, the addition of new members once the group begins, also facilitates group development in general and GDS development in particular.

The opposite extremes would be groups in which new members were repeatedly added and old members frequently dropped throughout the groups' life cycles. This can happen in psychotherapy groups that continue for many months to a few years (see Hill & Gruner, 1973). This state of flux, along with the very long histories of some such groups, can make their GDSs more difficult to observe, especially after the orientation and dissatisfaction stages.

The type of member *participation*—voluntary or involuntary—was explained when we discussed groups that start with a negative orientation stage. Groups with voluntary participation will allow more positive expectations to develop at first, and subsequently there is often more contrast between the beginning of the group (orientation) and its next stage (dissatisfaction). Conversely, groups with coerced participation will more often begin with a negative orientation stage, which will usually blend more imperceptibly into the dissatisfaction stage so that these two stages are difficult to discern separately. (A positive orientation stage will occasionally be observable between these two stages.)

There are several related characteristics about the task conditions that enhance the psychological and regressive atmosphere of groups and that facilitate GDSs. These have been mentioned before, but will be summarized here.

The greater the *difficulty* of the task, the more members must struggle to get involved with it. Also, the less *clarity* a task has, the more members must struggle to get involved in defining the task. It is not that the task should be made deliberately ambiguous, but that tasks that are by their nature ambiguous or difficult to define—for example, "learning about groups"—require more involvement. These conditions of task difficulty and ambiguity both facilitate GDS phenomena. Similarly, the more personal the *psychological dimension* of the task and the more the task touches on *basic needs,* the more likely it is that GDS phenomena will be facilitated.

The minimum ends of the continua for these characteristics would be an easily completed, clear, impersonal task covering some unimportant area, such as a work group that does not particularly need the money but has been hired to mow a large lawn. Such a group would usually show minimal GDSs.

The characteristics of the leader also affect GDSs. The leader's sex and race have already been mentioned. A *more skilled* leader can facilitate the GDS process to help the group along and may thus make the overall process more observable. With a *less skilled* leader there is a greater chance of abortive development. Similarly, a leader who instills *trust and confidence* probably facilitates GDSs, as opposed to a leader who does not instill such trust and confidence so that the members are more reluctant to reveal themselves, to lower defenses, and to get involved.

In training and therapy groups, leader-centered *interpretations and comments* will enhance the group's regression and may enhance members' expectations from the leader (transference), whereas non-leader-centered interpretations and comments will have no such effects. If this goes so far that the members' reactions to the leader are largely ignored, GDSs will be impeded, unless the members take over the leader's function.

The degree and type of *structure* provided for the group by the leader are among the more complex of these conditions. The effects of these characteristics of the leader and their influence on GDSs have been assessed in a variety of ways, including measures of group satisfaction with the experience, group cohesion, task-relevant skill acquisition, and productivity. Such measures are, of course, not only a function of the type of leadership, but also a reflection of the nature of the participants, the type of task, and probably the overall skill of the leader.

Among the difficulties in examining studies on the structure the leader provides are that what one author may call a highly structured setting is actually a lower degree of structure compared to yet higher structure, and if the degree of structure is pushed too far in either direction for the sake of experimental study it will become an artificial extreme rarely seen in practice. It is obvious that on the minimum end of the structure continuum, adequate structure must be provided so that the experience proceeds; if members do not know why they are there, what they should do, or when the meeting stops, the experience will soon deteriorate and stop.

An appropriate beginning for this discussion is the classic work of Lewin, Lippitt, and White (1939, and see White and Lippitt, 1960). They studied autocratic, democratic, and laissez-faire leadership styles in six clubs of boys who worked on craft projects. These are perhaps best considered laboratory problem-solving groups since they were artificially set up primarily for study. The leaders and type of leadership changed several times during the study, and for this and other reasons GDSs cannot be easily discerned. Yet for our purposes the following results can be noted: Members in the autocratic groups produced somewhat more craft work, were less satisfied, and showed either more direct aggression or over-repressed agression that manifested itself when the autocratic leader was not present. Members in the democratically led groups showed more originality in their work, had higher motivation to work on their own, preferred the democratic leaders, and exhibited a level of aggression that was neither excessive nor over-repressed.

In general these findings have held up under a considerable range of conditions and have made a major contribution to the subsequent study of leadership behavior. An example of this work is a more recent naturalistic study congruent with the classic work. Although giving only minimal GDS data, Mac-Donald (1967) studied Job Corps training participants in natu-ralistic groups in their dormitory and training settings over a 10-week period. Three types of staff leadership could be identi-fied, corresponding to authoritarian, laissez-faire, and demo-cratic types. They measured class attendance records and rule infractions, and found that although authoritarian leadership achieved better ratings at first, such leadership led to the worst ratings in the last five-week period. Conversely, democratic leadership, which had poorer ratings at first, had the best final ratings. The laissez-faire leadership resulted in intermediate ratings, but actually seemed to have little effect on the members over time, as other group members began to have more influ-ence than the leader. They also examined dormitory cleanli-ness, but found no significant differences. (The study is also notable for using unobtrusive measures for assessing groups.)

Some of the limits of generalization of the work by Lewin and associates come from a brief problem-solving group study (Rosenbaum & Rosenbaum, 1971) in which the tasks were performed under stressful or nonstressful conditions. The tasks involved mechanical manipulation or paper-and-pencil work calling for a low degree of ego involvement. Performance was best under authoritarian leadership in the stressful condition, and under democratic leadership in the nonstressful condition. These results are consistent with Anderson's (1959) review of authoritarian or teacher-centered versus democratic or learner-centered leadership style studies in educational settings. He concluded that although democratic leadership is generally associated with higher morale, this may not be true if there is much anxiety over grades (much stress), and under these conditions more authoritarian leadership may lead to higher performance (grades) and morale.

More recent studies of the style of leadership are more apt to look at the degree or type of structure provided by the leader; a highly structured group would be considered similar to an autocratic or authoritarian group. On the other extreme, less structure might be considered laissez-faire leadership, but if it is too little there will be no group.

An example of research on the degree of structure provided is a problem-solving group study (Tompkins, 1972) that manipulated structured leadership with the group's stage of development. The group's task was to make decisions about two case studies. The results suggested that the task was best accomplished when there was structured leadership early in the group's development.

Additional information on this subject comes from a series of studies of encounter and training groups that evaluated the effects of structure on certain aspects of group development and, by extension, GDSs. In their study of a number of encounter groups led by leaders with various theoretical persuasions, Lieberman et al. (1973) found that leaders who were strongly oriented toward group management, along with laissez-faire and impersonal leaders, had less success in helping participants achieve beneficial results. Leaders who were more caring, or attributed meaning to the individual's or group's experience, were more helpful.

Crews and Melnick (1976) studied the effects of initial, delayed, or no structured human relations exercises on six encounter groups, each meeting for a total of 24 hours. They found that the structure they used, when used initially, enhanced early self-disclosure and also a type of anxiety that facilitated group participation early in group development. But the effects of this initial structure dissipated during the course

of the groups and did not affect group cohesion. Delayed structure may have enhanced the work level later in the groups' life
cycles.

A study with six training groups used structured human
relations exercises throughout the experience in three groups,
but not in the other three (Levin & Kurtz, 1974). Participants
in the structured groups reported greater group unity and ego
involvement, and more self-perceived personality change in
their groups than participants in the nonstructured groups. It
was felt that the structure in this study not only allowed but to
some extent required participation from all members and therefore directly facilitated involvement, whereas in the nonstructured groups the more hesitant members participated less and
also benefited less.

Bednar and Battersby (1976) studied the effects of three
pregroup messages on early group development in eight two-
hour training groups with undergraduate psychology students.
These messages focused on goal clarity, persuasive explana-
tions, or general or specific instructions about behavior. Pregroup messages with specific instructions about behavior were
associated with higher group cohesion, better attitudes about
the group experience, and better quality work on the task.

Additional complex issues raised by the leader's structure
are found in a study of two training groups composed of middle-level management personnel (Lundgren, 1971). In one
group the two leaders were inactive and nondirective. Early in
this group's life cycle these traits were associated with considerable negativism and apparent interference with the group, but
later they seemed to enhance cohesiveness and work on the
task. In the second group the two leaders were more active and
directive. At first there were more favorable member attitudes,
but the group subsequently showed less cohesiveness and a
lower quality of work on the task.

Differences between the leaders other than leadership
styles may have contributed to these results. As mentioned
earlier, one of the leaders in the second group was black,

whereas everyone else was white, and this may have inhibited the second group. Both of these groups apparently began with a negative orientation stage, but this may not have been contributed to by the leader's style.

These findings on leader structure were also related to member status, as was seen in Lundgren's (1973) study, which involved the same groups. Recall that members of higher status were more satisfied and more appropriately involved in the nondirective group, and more negative and less appropriately involved in the directive group.

Some of the implications of Lundgren's (1971) work are drawn out in two related studies by Ivancevich (1974, discussed earlier in the review of naturalistic groups) and Ivancevich & McMahon (1976). The participants in these studies were eight groups of management personnel who took part in cognitive content-loaded learning groups dealing with such topics as management styles, motivation, group concepts, and organizational change. Characteristics of leadership other than the structure variable were controlled by using the same leader for both the structured, more directive groups, and the less structured, less directive, more freewheeling discussion groups. Under these conditions and with these types of participants, the groups with structured leadership showed better group cohesion, more open communication, and a better attitude toward the leader than the groups with less structured leadership. Also, structured leadership tended to promote less intermember conflict and more group work on the task.

Interestingly, one of these studies (1976) compared first-line managers, sales managers, and engineering supervisors, and found that sales managers did more work on the task under less structured leadership. The authors commented that the less structured group conditions were closer to the conditions under which sales managers usually work, and when the structure was higher they sat back and did less. This underscores the important question of participant characteristics in such studies.

This study also examined subsequent satisfaction and performance when the workers were back on the job and found some advantages to the structured leadership, but this advantage decayed over time. If the need to use the cognitive data from the group experience is considered as a type of stress on the participants, then this study showing the advantages of structured over nonstructured leadership under conditions of stress is consistent with the work of Rosenbaum and Rosenbaum (1971) and Anderson (1959).

There are many other aspects of leadership structure, for example, several studies have looked at group development as a function of the type of feedback provided. Since none of the studies examined on this subject had a broad focus of their effect on group development, they are not discussed here. Also, for GDS purposes, the discussion already provided serves as adequate background.

The studies on leadership structure lead to no simple conclusions about the effects on GDSs, but to a need to consider the type of structure, when it is used, the nature of the task, whether it is performed under stressful conditions, and characteristics of the members. Early structure in problem-solving (Tompkins, 1972), encounter (Crews & Melnick, 1976), and training groups (Bednar & Battersby, 1976) led to a better beginning in the group, especially if there was direct application of the structure to the task. This better beginning reflects the help the group was given with its orientation stage, which will be discussed in more detail in the next chapter.

Structure throughout the course of the group led to generally better results—as measured by such things as performance, satisfaction, and group cohesion—when the task was not very personal or psychological (Ivancevich, 1974; Ivancevich & McMahon, 1976), especially if there was some performance stress imposed on the participants (Anderson, 1959; Rosenbaum & Rosenbaum, 1971; Ivancevich, 1974; Ivancevich & McMahon, 1976).

With more personal, psychological, social tasks, such as those in encounter and training groups, a high degree of structure throughout the experience is apt to interfere with favorable group work on the task (production stage) and member benefit from the experience (Lieberman et al., 1973; Lundgren, 1971). But two studies in encounter-growth groups show that delayed or continuing human relations exercises with emphasis on the development of group skills may enhance work on the task (Crews & Melnick, 1976; Levin & Kurtz, 1974). Such exercises can, of course, be conducted in an autocratic, rigidly structured manner, and might then well lose their favorable effects. (Additional general discussion of this subject of group structure can be found in Kerr & Schriescheim [1974].)

The temporal and spatial conditions of group meetings also affect the psychological atmosphere and GDSs. Definite *temporal boundaries* governing the starting and ending times of meetings are necessary for adequate group development of any kind, and subsequently for development of GDSs. This applies to the temporal boundaries of the overall experience, but especially to the beginning. A definite beginning boundary facilitates the development and identification of the initial GDS stages, particularly orientation and dissatisfaction. A definite ending boundary is less crucial, but such a boundary helps force and condense termination stage behaviors.

In most types of groups, but especially in training and therapy groups, definite temporal and spatial boundaries help reinforce the authority of the leader and the dependency of the members, and thus contribute to group regression. It also takes a sufficient *length of group meeting* and *length of group life cycle* for an adequate group atmosphere and GDSs. If the group meetings and length of the group's life cycle are too short, the group experience and the GDSs will be negligible. Meeting regularly in the same *meeting place* would also be expected to enhance the group atmosphere and GDSs; at the other extreme, regularly changing the meeting place is generally so disruptive that it would interfere with the group's development and with GDSs.

How do these various conditions apply to the *types of*

groups reviewed earlier—problem-solving groups, training groups, and others? The artificial, problem-solving groups would be expected to go through the least conspicuous GDSs because of a number of conditions, especially their short life cycles, and their impersonal, usually fairly concrete tasks. If these conditions were changed by lengthening the group life cycles and making the task more personal and ego-involving, more conspicuous GDSs would be expected. This often happens in real-life problem-solving groups, such as committees, which were discussed here with naturalistic groups. Nevertheless, it is clear that artificial problem-solving groups do go through GDSs.

At the other extreme, training groups are often the easiest place to see GDSs. The task is highly personal and ego-involving and not easy to clarify or accomplish, the group lasts long enough, and membership is usually closed and stable. (Training group programs that involve small and large group meetings and intergroup exercises obscure GDSs and make them more difficult to observe.) Psychotherapy groups are usually also at the maximum extreme in exhibiting GDSs, for reasons similar to those that apply with training groups, and a number of psychotherapy group studies demonstrating GDSs are included herein. On the other hand, when the psychotherapy group lasts an excessively long time, for example, a few years, other factors affecting the members and group may obscure the fairly simple five-stage GDSs. Such factors can be fluctuations in the group's work on the task during production because of long-term fatigue factors, or changes in members' goals, or changes in membership.

Encounter groups would be expected to fall near the training and psychotherapy group end of this continuum, and naturalistic groups somewhere between, depending especially on such things as the length of their histories and their tasks. Highly personal, ego-involving tasks would fall closer to the maximum end; such groups include nursing students during a psychiatric affiliation, or people learning how to work with patients with cancer.

These various conditions must be taken into account even when the group under consideration is a conceptual group, such as a group of psychiatric residents, usually meaning the psychiatric residents in a particular training program, or the group of individuals with terminal illness, or the group of door-to-door vacuum cleaner salesmen, and so on. Although there are few data that bear directly on the subject, if we allow for appropriate changes in the settings, most of the conditions that minimize and maximize the development of GDSs in actual groups would also be expected to apply to conceptual groups.

Characteristics of the task and leader would be expected to have similar effects (see Table 5.2), as would appropriate temporal boundaries governing the start and end of the conceptual group experience and its overall length. The characteristics of members in conceptual groups might also have effects similar to those discussed for actual groups, again allowing for changes in the settings. For example, a conceptual group made up of the sales crew working out of a particular office would be expected to show differences in the degree of GDSs according to whether the membership was stable, whether it had the same or different sexual and racial composition, whether it was made up of people with a high capacity for regression "in the service of the ego," and so on.

In conceptual groups GDSs are usually harder to observe because conditions are less intense and because one usually cannot see the additive effects of GDS phenomena in several people at the same time and place. But intensity and an additive effect are sometimes approached, for example, by the registrar or dean of students at a medical or law school where the students can be seen frequently in the classes and corridors of the school,* or similarly, by the managers of sales crews.

Within these limits, examples on the minimum ends of these various continua for conceptual groups probably include

*It is interesting that 21% of the deans and 26% of the associate and assistant deans of law schools reported student morale as one of their major problems (Abramson & Moss, 1977).

groups of salaried employees, salesmen, and groups of law and medical students. At the maximum ends of these continua are groups of people in individual psychotherapy or medical treatment, and perhaps people in managerial positions. Among the most important continua here are the degree to which the task personally touches the participants, which can be very high in psychiatric treatment or organizational management, but might also be high in sales people working on a commission when their earnings are crucial to their sense of self-esteem and, more importantly, to the procurement of food and shelter (see Maslow's hierarchy of needs, 1962). Conversely, patients going through the motions of psychotherapy to satisfy legal or other external requirements may well show less conspicuous GDSs.

EXTERNAL CONDITIONS AFFECTING GDSs

The preceding discussion focused on conditions within the group that enhance or impede the formation of GDSs. There are also a number of conditions outside the experience that may have an affect on the GDSs, although they are usually less important and their effects less direct. The effect of these conditions on GDSs has received a minimum of attention because of their generally lesser importance. But a brief discussion of some of these conditions will help alert the reader to them; they are especially important to consider when applying this material.

If participants in an experience feel in some way in tolerable competition with others in a similar experience, this feeling will usually contribute to more diligent work on the task, and in actual groups it will contribute to greater cohesion. If the competition was considered unfair or overwhelming, the participants might be discouraged. Examples of these circumstances are work groups on competitive projects, and athletic teams.

If in the orientation stage an experience is judged by participants and perhaps others to be better than other similar experiences, this belief might well raise hopes higher than otherwise.

If this experience is a second choice or is judged second-rate, it will probably lower expectations. In the dissatisfaction stage, if not before, some of the disappointment from being in such a second-choice experience would be expected to surface, at least partly, in a reaction against the leader and the experience: "If I had gotten into the group [job, school, basketball team] I really wanted, things would be much better." "No wonder we're having such a hard time, this boss [coach, leader] isn't nearly as good as the boss [coach, leader] of the other work group [team, learning group]."

During resolution, if other comparable group or other experience alternatives seem readily available to the participants, there may be less desire to work out the problems of the dissatisfaction stage and to proceed to the production stage. If dissatisfaction and resolution are particularly difficult, and alternative experiences seem to be available, these may well be unrealistically seen as an easier place to accomplish one's goals.

During the production stage the task or product that is being worked on will be evaluated by the participants partly according to how people outside the experience view it. If a task or product is highly valued, perseverance will be enhanced; if either is devalued, perseverance will be hindered. The Watergate years had a discouraging effect on lawyers, and for a while more new law school graduates went into areas like poverty and civil rights work. Similarly, recent criticism of the FBI and CIA cannot help but make diligent work by their members more difficult. Students in colleges of education or other college programs where the job market is tight undoubtedly find it more difficult to persevere in their studies.

These considerations on how others view the task will also have important influences on the termination stage. If one is terminating an experience that is generally viewed by outsiders as positive, it will be easier to be proud of one's accomplishments than if the experience is thought to be questionable in worth. And if one is ending an experience with high hopes for the future, such as a good job after college, the termination will be more pleasant than if the future holds less promise.

An entirely different factor is what group participants do when they are not actually participating in the group. Are they in more than one dissatisfaction stage experience at once? Or more than one termination stage experience at once? Or is this orientation stage being interfered with by another experience's dissatisfaction stage? All of these experiences will interact with each other to varying degrees. (This subject will be returned to later.)

UNDERSTANDING GDSs

How do these GDSs occur? Why do they come in this sequence instead of some other one? What is there about people that results in these stages? Such questions will now be addressed, with an eye kept on the pitfalls involved.

One of these pitfalls is that attempts to understand these phenomena are speculations removed from the original, largely actual group data base. This is an acceptable danger if the resulting examination is heuristic and helps make the data more comprehensible, so that it might then be easier to apply in practical situations. Another danger in attempting to explain material from highly diverse sources, for example, an artificial problem-solving group, a psychotherapy group, or people moving, is that the discussion will be so general that it will almost be trite.

Both of these risks—speculation too far removed from the data, and generalization that may approach superficiality—appear worth taking rather than avoiding the subject altogether, even in a book of this nature. This discussion will also serve to supplement the descriptive overview of GDSs presented in Chapter 1.

Readers interested in more theoretical, psychological understanding of this subject would benefit from perusing the references in Table 5.3 and its footnotes. Greater theoretical depth will be especially relevant to settings with more pronounced regression and GDSs (psychotherapy and training groups, and certain learning groups), but will seem less relevant to the full, broad range of contexts in which GDSs can be found. More detailed theorizing would be too specialized for a book of this nature with wide data coverage and a broad audience in mind.

The Internal Consistency of GDSs

There is a series of internal consistencies, or "internal tendencies" (Bales & Strodtbeck, 1951), to the group developmental stage process that seems almost too self-evident to mention. To begin with, before any significant, extended, human activity—I will sidestep the question of nonhuman activity—can be carried out, one must first have some idea of what the activity is. Except for special circumstances, such as accidents, one first needs to know what to do and not to do (orientation) before going on to such other things as complaining that it's too hard or impossible to do, or that this is not what one wants (dissatisfaction), or before one can usually complete the task or activity (production), or review what has been accomplished and feel happy about accomplishing it or sad that the task is over (termination).

To start at the other end of the process, the experience can hardly end with asking what the task will be about and hoping that it will be enjoyable (orientation). Nor, except under conditions of an abortive sequence, can the experience end with dissatisfaction stage behaviors, and even here at least rudiments of a termination stage may well occur. By the same token, in the middle of an experience one cannot review everything that will actually have been accomplished when the experience is over and have a good feeling from having accomplished it, though of course it is possible, and often reasonable, to have anticipatory thoughts and feelings about these matters.

Clearly, under the usual circumstances that apply to a new experience, the GDS sequence is the only "reasonable" way things can unfold. Bales and Strodtbeck (1951) have suggested, in discussing their work on the orientation, evaluation, and control stages of problem-solving groups (see the earlier section where their work was discussed), that their sequence may reflect the way the human mind handles problems, and that one might think of new experiences as problems.

Harvey, Hunt, and Schroder (1961) and Schroder and Harvey (1963) propose a sequence of stages of concept development from the more concrete to the more abstract, which is analogous to the development of GDSs and which they apply to group developmental stages. Their stages (with corresponding GDSs) are (1) unilateral dependence on the external conditions (orientation), (2) negative independence from external constraints (dissatisfaction), (3) conditional dependence and mutuality with the environment or stimulus situation (resolution), and (4) interdependence with external conditions on an abstract level allowing application to other situations (production). Transitions between these stages are also discussed, and the most important of these is a rather negative one between stages one and two which seems to be an additional part of dissatisfaction. Concepts do not have a usual termination, and no stage analogous to termination is discussed.

Individual Developmental and Psychological Speculations on GDSs

Now we shall look at more specific psychological factors in each of the group developmental stages to see what understanding can be achieved. This survey will primarily involve material on individual development and psychological functioning. Before proceeding with the discussion of each stage, the reader may wish to examine the tabular presentation of the primary material on which this discussion is based (Table 5.3) and the related footnotes.

ORIENTATION STAGE. The process begins with an individual, or individuals, coming into an experience looking with some eagerness for something not already possessed—money, health, knowledge, or whatever. Although it will be a desired experience, it is almost invariably approached with some mixed feelings. There is a price to pay for every experience in the work required, risks taken, or someone or something left behind. The negative side of this ambivalence may be only minimally obvious during orientation, but it will be more explicit later in the dissatisfaction stage.

The initial expectations for something good may be quite high, and for this and other reasons perceptions of the leaders, goals, and other participants are distorted. This distortion can be caused, for example, by overidealizing, by splitting, with the previous experience seen as excessively bad and the current one as excessively good, and perhaps also by denying what has been lost to join this group and the risks now being taken. The more one "needs" the current experience, the more distortion there is likely to be. The "need" might have arisen from frustration with or a considerable sense of loss from the last experience, or from other sources.

Some of the sense of expectation and hope may not be obvious on the surface because the person will not consciously let her or his hopes get too high for a variety of reasons, including prior disappointments. Often under these conditions the less conscious desires (unconscious fantasies) are all the more out of reasonable bounds. But of course fantasies have a way of being unreasonable anyway.

Among other psychological phenomena in the orientation stage are usually a certain amount of apprehension and anxiety —such as anxiety about injury to self-esteem for not being acceptable or not being able to perform—and often on a deeper level, fear of physical injury. In a group of seriously ill schizophrenic patients, this latter fear may be explicitly and apprehensively stated in the first meeting, sometimes as a fear of castration. Of course there is some degree of anxiety throughout the group experience, but it has different characteristics and

Table 5.3. Individual developmental

Author and Year	Source	Orientation
1. Freud, S., 1940; Blos, 1962	Individual psychosexual development [1]	Oral
2. Erikson, 1963	Individual psychosexual development [2]	Oral-sensory (trust vs. mistrust)
3. Klein, M., 1948 (also see Jaques, 1955)	Early psychological development [3]	?Manic defense, omnipotence; ?Depressive position
4. Bion, 1961	Psychological basic assumptions (BA) in groups [4]	BA dependency, BA pairing
5. Freud, S., 1940; Freud, A., 1946; Bibring, 1953; Appelbaum, 1963; and many others	Psychological defenses and other mechanisms [5]	Idealization and over-idealization, denial, good-bad splitting, identification, omnipotence, incorporation, emphasis on the positive side of ambivalence

Dissatisfaction	Resolution	Production	Termination
Anal, Phallic with oedipal complex	Latency, Puberty-adolescence (genital)	Adulthood (continued genital)	
Muscular-anal (autonomy vs. shame and doubt), Locomotor-genital (initiative vs. guilt)	Latency (industry vs. inferiority), Puberty and adolescence (ego identity vs. role diffusion), Young adult (intimacy vs. isolation)	Adulthood (generativity vs. stagnation)	Maturity (ego integrity vs. despair)
Paranoid-schizoid position			?Depressive position
BA fight-flight	Early work group (some BA dependency with identification with group leader and goals)	Work group	BA fight-flight, BA dependency, BA pairing (with hope for future)
Shift to the negative side of ambivalence. Anger — acting out, projection, reaction to frustration (Dollard and Miller, 1939), protection of self-esteem, displacement of anger from leader to	Ego begins to regain ascendancy — rationalization, intellectualization, early identification, reaction-formation, suppression, sublimation	Ego regains ascendancy — continued mechanisms from resolution; stronger identification (with leader, group goals, etc.), more sublimation, and so on	Mechanisms to avoid object loss and narcissistic injury because of failure to attain ideal — denial, devaluation, omnipotence, splitting. Loss and narcissistic injury lead to aggression turned inward, sadness

Table 5.3. Individual developmental

Author and Year	Source	Orientation
6. Hartman & Gibbard, 1974, drawing on the work of Dunphy, 1966, 1968; Mills, 1964; Slater, 1966; and others	Intrapsychic develop-mental phenomena manifested in groups; importance of bounda-ries. [6]	
	(A) Oedipal, whole-object level	Whole person (individ-ual) comes into group and regresses; develops oedipal, partly sexual attraction to "female" aspects of group as a whole, and to female leader and members when present
	(B) Pre- oedipal, part-object level	Greater degree of regression in indivi-duated person leads to symbiotic ties with

Dissatisfaction	Resolution	Production	Termination
members and vice versa. Depression — threat or harm to self-esteem (narcissistic injury), shattered hopes and fantasies, ego-ideal failure.			and grief; when these are well-handled result is working through with realistic assessment
Oedipal complex with revolt against "male" aspects of group — leader, authority demands, perhaps other male members	Discomfort over the revolt (fear of retaliation, anxiety over loss of structure), leads to resolution of oedipal complex with guilt and internalization of leader's and group's goals, and to more mature interaction between members	Leads to work group	
Anger and rebellion against symbiotic group, in part via	Resolution via more individua-tion helps growth from the	Leads to a productive work group with shifting but	Separation from symbiotic group (mother)

Table 5.3. Individual developmental

Author and Year	Source	Orientation
		nurturing, maternal aspects of group, especially the group as a whole; stimulates most primitive fears, anxieties, and defenses — fear of loss of self/ object boundaries, and so on

Further, and sometimes somewhat different elaborations of some of the ideas in the above table can be found in various sources.

[1]Sutherland (1951) has similarly applied the classic Freudian psychosexual developmental stages to the learning process of psychiatric residents and other students in psychiatric settings, and Pedigo and Singer (1977) have done so for training groups, as has King (1975) in a brief, more popularized presentation. Bennis (1968), focusing primarily also on training groups, makes a slightly different comparison. He sees group developmental stages as corresponding to the psychoanalytic oral, anal, and genital stages. His genital stage has characteristics of both the usual phallic and genital stages, which formerly he otherwise omits. Of these writers, only Pedigo and Singer (1977) comment on termination, but they do not relate it to psychoanalytic developmental theory. Powles (1959) applied psychoanalytic developmental theory to the development of a therapy group of disturbed adolescents who progressed to a genital stage (production?), then regressed. The group development was confounded in that the membership, and to a lesser extent the task, changed during the group's history. Saravay's work (1978; see also 1975) is consonant with the above, with elaboration of the structural personality aspects of these individual developmental stages (ego, superego, and so on); see also Horwitz's (1978) comments on this work.

[2]Similar use of Erikson's ideas can be found in Dolgoff (1975), who also extends group developmental stage ideas to organizations (see below). Zenger (1970) makes a more simplified comparison of the full human developmental cycle with group developmental stages in training groups, but he neglects termination. His stages are infant, child (both orientation), adolescence (dissatisfaction), young adult (resolution), and adult (production). Tucker (1973) made an interesting attempt in sensitivity training groups to measure the correspondence between individual development and group developmental stages along the lines discussed here. The hypotheses investigated stated that for an individual to achieve a group developmental stage he or she would have had to have achieved that stage of individual development. These are difficult hypotheses to study, but Tucker found some corroboration for "more developed" individuals, but not for "less developed" individuals who tended to have a progressively more positive outlook in the group without a stage of dissatisfaction.

Dissatisfaction	Resolution	Production	Termination
primitive mechanisms such as projection of anger and fear onto the group leader and situation, splitting, and so on: "This is a 'bad' group and I won't get involved."	dependent, symbiotic postion of wanting to be cared for; toleration of some regression in group so that the group can function	sufficiently comfortable equilibrium between engulfing group as a whole and individuated members	

[3]The ideas of Klein are difficult to apply to group developmental stages, but such application can be found in Jaques (1955). However, Klein's work has been important to the work of Bion, and Hartman and Gibbard, in the above chart.

[4]Bion (1961) himself does not believe that his "basic assumption" groups go through a developmental sequence. Nonetheless, it does appear that certain of these basic assumptions are more predominant areas of group concern in certain GDSs, though they are also present at other times. Others have so viewed Bion's ideas, for example, Slater (1966); Hare (1973, see also his footnote 3 regarding Slater); and Babad and Amir (1978), who present empirical support from three T groups for a sequential view of Bion's work, although it differs somewhat from that presented here.

[5]Appelbaum (1963) used the psychoanalytic concepts of the pleasure and reality principles to give an overview of general group processes, particularly as they apply to training groups. This is similar to some of what is discussed here in terms of the ascendancy of the ego (reality principle) over more unconscious impulses and urges (pleasure principle). The descriptive hypothesis that frustration in the pursuit of one's goals leads to aggression (Dollard et al., 1939) seems applicable to the GDS dissatisfaction stage; Davies (1969) and Feierabend et al. (1969) used these ideas in an attempt to understand revolutions and rebellions (discussed earlier). "Frustration itself is defined as the thwarting or interference with the attainment of goals, aspirations, or expectations. On the basis of frustration-aggression theory, it is postulated that frustration induced by the social system creates the social strain and discontent that in turn are the indispensible preconditions to violence" (Feierabend et al., 1969, p. 499). They apply these concepts to social groups when the frustration is "simultaneously experienced by [many] members of social aggregates" (Feierabend et al., 1969, p. 499). Further description of the psychological mechanisms in termination is provided in the work of Husband & Scheunemann (1972), and Kubler-Ross (1969), discussed later in this chapter.

[6]The ideas of Hartman and Gibbard on psychological processes underlying group developmental stages are presented in briefest outline (see Hartman, Gibbard & Mann, 1974, pp. 83–93; and Hartman & Gibbard, 1974, pp. 154–176, in the same reference; their ideas draw considerably on the work of Bion, 1961; Freud, 1921; Jaques, 1955;

severity at different times. Several writers (for example, Bion, 1961; and Hartman & Gibbard, 1974) have emphasized that the anxiety during the group experience can become severe and psychotic-like, and this is most likely in groups that maximize GDS phenomena.

There are strong dependency aspects to the orientation stage as the individual and the group look to the situation and its leader for satisfaction of needs: "The leader will do something to help me, psychologically and/or physically feed me; the teacher will make me smarter; the manager will make me richer." Sometimes this grows into over-dependency as the participants seem to function as if the leader had all the responsibility for satisfying their needs and they had none.

Bion (1961) has examined various less conscious concerns under which the group seems to operate, calling these "basic assumptions." Relevant here is the basic assumption of dependency wherein there is a sense that the group is together "in order to be sustained by a leader on whom it depends for nourishment, material and spiritual, and protection" (p. 147). The basic assumption of pairing with its "air of hopeful expectation" (p. 151) also seems to be operating in the orientation

---

M. Klein, 1948, 1963; Scheidlinger, 1968; Slater, 1966; and others). These concepts are too complex for a thorough discussion here. They emphasize that changes in group structure and functioning occur to protect members from severe (psychotic-like) anxiety and other disruptive changes, and that these changes in group structure and functioning occur in a pendular way, with a shifting equilibrium between the group and the individual. This occurs on two developmental psychological levels simultaneously. The first and more mature of these levels is a whole-object (whole person) level and is similar to the traditional psychoanalytic individual development model of progression from oral, to anal, to phallic levels, with the conflicts of the oedipal complex and its resolution leading to the genital level and greater maturity (work, production). The second, and more primitive, regressed, or immature of these levels is a part-object (part person) level that evinces more primitive anxiety and distress and the use of more primitive defenses, for example, splitting and more pathological projection. In either case there is an emphasis on the formation of group boundaries for protection against the distress, for example: "We are the (good) group/members, they are the (bad) outsiders." The (bad) outsiders can include the leader and/or certain members, or perceived bad parts of the leader and/or members, such as their anger, arbitrariness, authority, maleness, and withholding of love projected outside the group (good members).

stage. But whereas dependency looks to the immediate situation for gratification, the sense of hope in pairing looks to the future (see Boris, 1976).

In either case, satisfaction is not to be found within the members themselves in the present; rather it is achieved largely because they are loved and taken care of by the leader, or because they expect something good will come later. In some settings the amount of work on the task (Bion's work group) in orientation will also give some satisfaction. As mentioned in the footnote to Table 5.3, even though Bion does not particularly see his basic assumptions as part of a GDS sequence, it does seem that certain basic assumptions are more predominant in certain GDSs.

There are also certain relationships between the orientation stage and psychoanalytic personality theory, for example, either Freud's oral stage or what Erikson (1963) calls the oral-sensory stage with the development of trust or mistrust. With the orientation stage we do not have mere similarities, but undoubtedly aspects of the psychological origins of orientation stage behaviors. A person whose oral development was not adequate is limited in his or her ability to put trust into new experiences, to put hope and confidence into a new venture, and so forth (Benedek, 1949).

DISSATISFACTION STAGE. Eventually the realities of the experience force themselves upon the person so that there is a clash between the desires and hopes and the reality. Frustration inevitably ensues. There is no easy achievement, no pre-eminent satisfaction of unconscious needs for dependency; the task *is* work. Over-idealization of the new situation breaks down, and perhaps the loss from the activity that was left sinks in.

There are two main psychological reactions, anger and depression. These are often present simultaneously, and one may cover or be a defense against the other. The anger is partly a direct reaction to the frustrated desires and hopes (see Dollard et al., 1939), and partly a counter-reaction to malevolence projected onto the group leader, the organizer of the activity, the supervisor, teacher, or other group members: "I wouldn't be having such a hard time learning this (doing this task, etc.) if the leader wasn't so incompetent (out to get me, etc.)."

There may well be some acting out of the frustration at this time, for example, by leaving the group or organizing a protest. Much of this serves to defend against the injuries or threats of injury to self-esteem: "I'm not competent to do this." "I'm not working hard enough at this task." "My needs aren't being met because I'm not worth it." "I'll never get a case to the Supreme Court this way." "I don't know how to cure this schizophrenic patient."

There is some emphasis here on Bion's basic assumption of fight-flight, in which the anger is expressed in the fighting stance, especially via verbal attacks on the leader, group situation, or other members. Or, flight from the situation at hand can serve to protect the person from experiencing or continuing to experience feelings of discouragement and frustration; sometimes the flight is from anger projected onto the leader or other group members.

There are some relationships between the dissatisfaction stage and the psychoanalytic anal and phallic stages, in both of which growing independence and more individual assertion become manifest. Erikson's analogous terms are the muscular-anal stage and the locomotor-genital stage. In the former, successful resolution (development) leads to a sense of autonomy, and unsuccessful resolution leads to feelings of shame and doubt; in the latter the opposing characteristics are initiative and guilt. These early personality developmental stages are undoubtedly again at least partly the precursors of phenomena in the dissatisfaction stage, and the ability to resolve dissatisfaction stage difficulties is related to this early development.

RESOLUTION STAGE.   In the resolution stage more energy must gradually be directed to the task, and earlier struggles must gradually be laid aside. The more conscious ego functions of judgment, intelligent thought, and growing skills in the situation begin to predominate over the more unconscious fantasies and impulses with which one came into the experience, and which were more involved in the orientation and dissatisfaction stages. In short, the reality principle gains ascendancy over the pleasure principle.

There must be an assessment of realistic goals in this setting. The group is more solidly into a Bion work group, with less intrusion by basic assumption proclivities. There is more emphasis on the use of healthier defense mechanisms. Important is the progressive internalization (via introjection, identification, and other devices; see Kernberg, 1976, pp. 75–80) of the goals and skills of the group situation as defined by the leader. This is analogous to the psychoanalytic resolution of the oedipal complex (Freud, 1940 and elsewhere; Erikson, 1963; Hartman & Gibbard, 1974; and Gibbard & Hartman, 1973), which is marked by internalization of (identification with) the leader. Instead of fighting against the leader, members behave progressively like the leader. This helps overcome fears of retaliation, including the fear that one might be ejected from the experience (and no longer loved).

Other predominant defense mechanisms here are rationalization and intellectualization of why one's (more unrealistic) hopes cannot be satisfied and why one must accept different goals: "This schizophrenic patient's upbringing was so pathological that he can't develop enough of a relationship to make good use of psychotherapy"; "I probably could have gotten this client completely off these charges, but he wanted to get the case over with so we accepted the plea bargaining." An example of a more realistic assessment is, "I guess it's not realistic to think this group therapy will help me completely get over my uptightness with people, but I do seem to be getting more comfortable in many situations."

Other mechanisms may include sublimation, through which the energy of the anger and discontent aroused earlier might gradually be used in productive work. Or, via reaction formation, anger toward the leader might be transformed to obsequiousness, but at least that might allow enough listening to enable eventual learning from the leader or group situation so that more productive work can be done.

The continued comparison of GDSs to psychoanalytic developmental theory along the lines of Erikson (1963) and Blos (1962) becomes more tenuous. Whether the GDS roots of resolution and subsequent stages stem from these personal developmental origins is not as obvious as with earlier GDSs. But resolution is analogous to the psychoanalytic stages of latency, puberty, and adolescence, with a lessening of earlier fantasies and mechanisms, and growth toward maturity (productivity). In Erikson's terms, we have latency (with problems of industry versus inferiority), puberty and adolescence (ego identity versus role diffusion), and young adulthood (with intimacy versus isolation).

Part of the impetus for these changes in resolution is the discomfort of the dissatisfaction stage with its anxiety, discouragement, primitive fears of physical and psychological harm if one doesn't do what is expected, and probably also the push of basic human growth forces.

PRODUCTION STAGE. In the production stage changes begun during resolution continue; ego functions such as reasoning and judgment become more securely predominant over more unconscious impulses and fantasies. This development is aided by the increasing acquisition of skills in the task, whatever it is, which should by now have reached a decent level of mastery. The same healthier defense mechanisms are active, but perhaps there is more sublimation and creative elaboration, suppression, and reaction formation, and progressively more internalization of the goals and skills of the leader.

This does not mean that the person will not return to earlier defense mechanisms such as denial, or re-experience unrealistic hopes, or recurring frustration, but these will usually be less disruptive than before, and there will be a quicker and more comfortable return to healthier functioning. (Vaillant [1977] has described similar changes with more mature, healthier, adaptation in the middle adult years.)

This is primarily Bion's work group with less basic assumption group intrusion. It is the psychoanalytic developmental analogy of adulthood (Erikson's generativity versus stagnation). We can see here that the comparison of later GDSs with psychoanalytic developmental theory is even more one of analogy, since for people who are young adults or younger, there is a stage of production but no individual developmental stage of adulthood from which it might have its developmental roots.

TERMINATION STAGE.   The main phenomena to try to understand in the termination stage are feelings of loss and sadness, and feelings of pleasure. The feelings of loss and sadness are brought on by the prospect of losing something and someone to which and to whom one has become affectively attached. They may also be brought on by an experienced loss of self-esteem because one did not do as well as one expected in the experience, did not come to understand oneself enough, get to know others, overcome anger at the leader, or do as good a job as possible.

The sense of pleasure is related to the degree that the task was accomplished, and well accomplished, and sometimes also to the feeling of completing an experience that was good human work. Some sense of pleasure also comes from the good feelings of having made friends, having gotten to know others, having met a good teacher, and so on, and without this there would not be much of a sense of loss over these other people. Some of the positive feelings in termination also come from realistic anticipation of future gains, for example, in the next experience, perhaps partly because of what was accomplished in this experience.

The degree of positive and negative feelings during termination, and which are predominant and when, will vary with a number of factors including the individual participants, the type of experience, other participants, and the leader.

As termination is approached, the negative feelings associated with it are often initially avoided. One of the most frequent ways of doing this is by denying any loss or sadness, sometimes along with pseudoeuphoria. The avoidance of the negative feelings may be aided by concentrating on the gains from the experience or gains hoped for in the future from a new experience. Final group meetings may be filled with nervous laughter, or the sadness may be avoided through absence. One may hear, "[There's nothing to miss here because] my next job will offer me so much," or "It's such a good feeling to get this group therapy over with." Occasionally anger will cover the sense of loss or failed accomplishments: "I'm glad to get out of this crappy school!" "I never had a decent client during my whole internship." "She was so demanding I don't know why I went out with her for so long in the first place!"

Some of the difficulty in accepting that the experience is ending is reflected in frequent talking about a reunion, when actually such reunions are often unrealistic and rarely occur. Such talk is part of the normal range of denial in most participants in meaningful group experiences. This is not to say that the reunions that do come about are not very meaningful. Of course they can be. But sometimes they are based partly on a denial of the termination of a significant experience.

If termination does not go successfully, this denial, avoidance, or anger may continue to the end of the experience, perhaps facilitated by more distorting psychological mechanisms, such as even more devaluation of the experience and the friends and leader one is losing, and perhaps feelings of omnipotence: "No one taught me anything I didn't know," "None of these people were worth making friends with." Or we might again find the splitting mechanism discussed in orientation, except here the bad part of the split (bad object) is the current experience and the good part (good object) is the experience to come, and the group member fails to make a sufficiently realistic assessment of either situation.

The ability to handle the loss associated with termination is related to the soundness of one's infantile separation from the mother. But of course there is no easy one-to-one correspondence (Kauff, 1977, and many others; for example, Bowlby, 1952, and M.S. Mahler, 1968). Subsequent separations are also undoubtedly important, such as the loss of a parent at a young age.

If the feelings of loss associated with the termination stage are handled well, the denial and avoidance will only be temporary, and one will acknowledge the feelings of sadness and grief. Then one can work through the meaning of the sadness and grief—the loss of friends, a good experience, perhaps an opportunity not optimally used, and so on.

When the loss is strongly felt—such as in group or individual psychotherapy, a good training group, or psychiatric residency—but is adequately handled, there will be further work of evaluation and integration (reconstruction) and healthy internalization of aspects of the leader, and often of other participants. This further work will include a realistic appraisal of what one has gained, the friends one is losing, hopes for new realistic goals and friends, ways to continue appropriate parts of the relationship in the future, and so on. These final steps may not occur, or they may not until long after the experience is over: "It took me months to realize how much I was missing my school friends and what I had gained from them!"

The stress of the termination stage may lead to regressive behavior to earlier GDSs as a way to handle termination feelings, for example, a return to the dependency of the orientation stage, or to the anger of the dissatisfaction stage. At times this may include the repeating of prior activities or the re-examining of topics as if they had not been handled before. This or other means may be used to attempt to show the leader that the group experience must continue.

This discussion has described a series of substages of the more difficult aspects of termination, starting with denial and avoidance, moving to acceptance with acknowledgment of sadness and grief, working this through, and then finally evaluating the experience and integrating (reconstructing) growth aspects. The process can become arrested along the way, most often at denial. The sequence does not, of course, occur as systematically as described; in practice there is much oscillating back and forth between substages.

There are times when the positive feelings of termination are as dominant as or more dominant than the negative feelings, without particularly being a means to avoid these negative feelings. This is apt to be true when the task has been particularly difficult or dangerous, or has required much work, and has been well done. Often such tasks require a cooperative effort that pulls participants together. While feelings of loss are also a part of such groups (for example, civil defense teams and combat platoons), the loss may not be experienced until later, after the group is disbanded. At other times the work required will lead to considerable fatigue so that the sense of elation at a job well done hardly gets expressed, or gets expressed later after recovery from the fatigue.

Bion's ideas can easily be seen in the above discussion. His basic assumption fight-flight group is reflected in the denial, and his basic assumption dependency group, frustrated in its desire to be cared for, contributes to regressive behavior. The pairing group can also be active in looking to the future for something good (since it did not occur here), or in various other forms of denial and avoidance: "We'll produce our own leader . . . who won't leave us . . . will help us better . . . etc." The pairing group may well exhibit pseudoeuphoria in its grosser denial. Insofar as the termination experience is well handled, the group will function as a Bion work group.

Within the limitations previously mentioned about comparisons of GDS theory and psychoanalytic developmental theory, termination is like Erikson's final developmental stage of maturity, with ego integrity on the healthier side and despair on the less healthy side.

The discussion of the loss felt on termination drew on the work of Husband and Scheunemann (1972) and Garland et al. (1965), and there are some similarities between these writings and those of Kubler-Ross (1969) on dying patients. These studies provide a more detailed breakdown of the phenomena occurring during termination when it is a prolonged and profound loss experience. Death is the ultimate termination and can bring forth more complex behaviors than lesser terminations, such as termination from a training group.

In a particular setting the complexities of termination will depend not only on the setting, but also on such other factors as the individuals involved and the leader. For example, under certain conditions termination from individual or group psychotherapy, or from a job one has had for years, can be as complex as or more complex than the termination of death with a person who welcomes it because of long-standing illness or old age.

Table 5.4 compares the works of these authors. These studies complement each other; for example, Kubler-Ross elaborates the change from denial to depression via anger and bargaining. The work of Garland et al. (1965) was included in the table, but it required some modification since they identify more substages which are seen in a less definite progression. (In an empirical study of 16 primarily adolescent counseling groups, B. F. Lewis [1978] largely confirmed the termination behaviors of the Garland model.)

NEGATIVE ORIENTATION STAGE. How is the negative orientation stage to be understood—a GDS sequence that begins with more resistance and anger than the usual positive orientation stage? How is this resistance and anger to be understood? Part of it is undoubtedly a reaction to fear experienced on various levels, ranging from not knowing what the experience will be and/or what will be expected, to deeper-lying fears of physical and

Table 5.4. Elaboration of the termination experience

Studies						
Husband & Scheunemann (1972, learning groups)	Denial and avoidance			Grief and sadness	Working through; Detachment	Reconstruction
Garland et al. (1965, social work therapy groups)	Denial	Nihilistic flight; Regression	"We still need the club"		Positive flight; Re-enactment	Positive flight; Review; Evaluation
Kubler-Ross (1969, dying patients)	Shock then Denial	Anger	Bargaining	Depression and grief	Acceptance .. to	.. Decathexis
Mechanisms	Denial, rationalization, intellectualization, splitting	Protection of self-esteem via anger, attack; projection of inner parts onto external world		Loss of self-esteem, loss of good object	Reconciling losses/gains, good/bad objects	Ego functions of intellection, judgment; abandoning of psychological attachments

psychological injury or even annihilation by the leader, other members, or forces outside the experience. Part of this fear of annihilation is apprehension over the breakdown of self-other boundaries and engulfment by the (symbiotic) group. The anger also leads to projection, so that part of what is feared is the fury or maliciousness of the reluctant member projected onto the leader and other members.

Remember that many of the groups beginning with a negative orientation stage were therapy groups composed of seriously disturbed or acting-out participants. When attempts are made to stop the disturbed behavior of these participants, they are forced to face their own pathology more directly—their inner fears, destructiveness, and inordinate dependency needs. This may well be more disturbing than the experience itself, and hence they offer strong resistance. For some of these participants the resistance will be against the intolerable acknowledgment that there is a need for help or change, or even learning, which will imply that there is some deficit in the first place. At times the resistance may be passive-aggressive: "No one is going to force me . . . to submit to them . . . reveal myself . . . etc."

Bion's fight-flight basic assumption group is easily recognized in this negative orientation stage. Psychoanalytic personality developmental roots are also easily seen. Among these are the struggles with oral stage dependency problems and resistance to dependency, some on rather primitive levels, such as fears of symbiotic engulfment and M. Klein's (1948) paranoid-schizoid position. And the roots of passive-aggressive resistance can be located in the anal stage.

If the member or group is to develop beyond the negative orientation stage, then further progression along the lines discussed above must take place. This stage usually blends into the dissatisfaction stage, which may not be separately distinguishable, and then development progresses to the resolution stage and so on.

A Note on Individual Differences and GDSs

The above speculations are directed primarily to participants in general, in an attempt to look at what psychologically lies behind or contributes to the course of GDSs. It is also possible to ask more about individuals than has so far been considered, and to examine more specifically the psychodynamics of various individuals. This subject will not here be given the major examination it deserves, but a few comments will be made.

Some individuals are perpetually ready to begin new experiences, to start a new orientation stage, whereas others seem to have such great inertia that they rarely eagerly become involved in anything new. And some people can take the falling morale of dissatisfaction and handle it easily through resolution to production, whereas others have great difficulty: Once demoralized, which may happen easily, they have much trouble recovering. Then, during production, some individuals can continue to maintain a steady and long production stage without much difficulty, whereas others easily begin to drift to lower and lower levels of work on the task, to lower morale, and perhaps to other dissatisfaction stage behaviors. And some individuals handle termination without too much difficulty, whereas others easily become overwhelmed and may become depressed and have trouble recovering. A few individuals get depressed whenever successful completion of an experience is imminent—they feel a paradoxical fear of success.

To say that these are the extremes of the more versus the less mentally healthy person may be part of the explanation, but it would be a grossly oversimplified explanation. Some of the perpetual optimists who eagerly get into new experiences at times seem to lack much human depth. And some of the people who have little difficulty with termination may never have been really personally involved in the first place. Further elaboration of these issues would take us into the realm of individual psychology and psychopathology and will not be pursued here.

Chapter 6

THE USE OF GDS THEORY

Is all of this material largely an interesting academic exercise? Can anything practical be done with this information? The answers to these questions are undoubtedly already clear.

This chapter will discuss the use of GDS theory. Although some of it may seem too much like a cookbook, I hope that the recipes provided, if they don't satisfy the reader's appetite, will at least stimulate him or her to look elsewhere and to experiment with one's own culinary ingenuity.

Before proceeding with applications, we will look at whether a particular setting, namely classrooms, might be a place where GDS material can be used. This will help the reader in thinking of the range of use of GDS theory, although a reminder may be unnecessary in view of the broad range of settings from which the data originate in the first place.

Is a Classroom a Setting For GDS Use?

Is a classroom an actual group setting, or at least a conceptual group setting? And are classrooms places where there occur group developmental stage phenomena like those proposed here? When the classroom under consideration is primarily a discussion-focused, or so-called learning-group-focused setting, it is easy to see that it is an actual group with a leader, set temporal boundaries, a closed membership with interaction between members, and so on. As we saw earlier, there are several examples of such classroom settings with developmental processes consistent with the proposed GDSs (for example, Lacoursiere, 1974; Mann et al., 1970; and many others; see Table 4.12).

What about other classroom settings? Classrooms can be considered on a continuum from the above examples, which are highly group-process oriented and regularly show GDSs, to classrooms that have a more formal lecture format, with rather impersonal topics of study (such as arithmetic, calculus, biochemistry, and contract law), and perhaps additionally, are taught by several lecturers. Yet even at this end of the classroom continuum, there is some degree of group process, and probably GDSs, although they are not apt to be as conspicuous.

In addition, anywhere along this continuum there may be an overlapping conceptual group with a GDS sequence. For example, the law, medical, or other college student in a class that may not particularly embody an actual group process orientation or have obvious GDSs, is also part of a conceptual group in which GDS phenomena may be conspicuous—for example, the conceptual group of medical or law students due to graduate in a particular year. (For additional material on the usual classroom as a group, see Bany & Johnson, 1964; Schmuck & Schmuck, 1971; and Trow et al., 1950. The Bany and Johnson book contains many practical suggestions for addressing a variety of group phenomena in the classroom; although group developmental stages are not addressed, some of their material is applicable to such phenomena.)

A classroom may then be a setting for GDSs, and under certain circumstances, a place to apply GDS ideas. It is obvious that a standard classroom is not meant to be a "learning group" as we have used that term, let alone a training group or therapy group. Yet comments can easily be made in any classroom about orientation, dissatisfaction, and termination phenomena that are appropriate to such a setting.

Many a good teacher does this automatically without specific thoughts about the group developmental stage sequence. For example, by adequately orienting the class to its goals at the start of the course, by making these goals realistic, by teaching the required skills to reach these goals, by discussing during the course how the class is progressing (during the dissatisfaction stage and at other times), and by evaluating near the end of the class what they have accomplished, what they have not accomplished, how the students react to it, and so forth (termination). Conversely, if the initial goals for a classroom were highly unrealistic no matter how much the students wanted them, if skills for achieving them were poorly taught, and if the students were told they were doing poorly, it would soon be a seriously disorganized class, and a class desperately in need of GDS help.

THE APPLICATION OF GDS THEORY

In discussing the application of GDS theory, both actual and conceptual group settings will be considered, but the emphasis will be on actual groups in which GDS theory is most easily used. Material from the previous chapter is also relevant in applying GDS theory, and should be kept in mind. This is especially true for external conditions affecting GDSs and for conditions enhancing the formation of GDSs, particularly conditions of leader structure.

The use of GDS material requires a setting where GDSs occur, where the leader can observe them, where they in some way probably interfere with members accomplishing the task, and where the leader has the skills to work with the GDSs in that setting. In earlier chapters we examined many settings in which these phenomena occurred and were significant enough to be observed by a skilled leader. The settings examined included training, therapy, and encounter groups, and various naturalistic settings of both actual and conceptual groups.

Examples of naturalistic settings are health treatment teams (Modlin & Faris, 1956), law and medical students (see Rothman & Marx, 1974), people moving (Mitchell, 1975), larger sociopolitical contexts (Davies, 1969; Feierabend et al., 1969), and, as was just noted, sometimes classrooms. The reader can probably provide other examples from personal experience. Conversely, in many artificial problem-solving groups, especially short-term groups whose problem entails a low degree of personal involvement, there will be less conspicuous GDSs.

The need for GDSs to be significant enough to be worked with implies that the leader has adequately formulated ideas about group or general developmental stages. (Occasionally this knowledge will reside with the leader's supervisor, who will then help the leader acquire it.) Without such knowledge one is not apt to observe what is happening, nor to have ideas about where the group or individual should be or might get to.

This brings us to the related question of gathering data to be able to assess where the group or individual has been and is now—information that is usually relevant to both social-emotional and task areas. There is also a need to assess reasonable expectations for the group or individual. The data will generally come from the leader's usual observations—all verbal and nonverbal behavior relevant to the experience, and the work product when there is one. Data can also come from more sophisticated observations, as discussed in the chapter on research. This might include making data forms to ask about social-emotional and task areas or inquiring directly about the members' GDS.

Even with an appropriate setting and a way to observe these stages accurately, they should nonetheless usually be troublesome, and usually in a way that interferes with the task before working with the GDSs. (The exception here is when one wants to teach about GDSs.) If the GDSs are observable and do not seriously interfere with the task, it is probably a credit to some degree of leadership that already focuses on GDS matters, perhaps without being actually aware of it.

Group developmental stages like those presented here are undoubtedly used by experienced group leaders in many contexts; the numerous group workers in training and therapy groups who have developed such concepts surely use them in their work. On the other hand, explicit reports on the use of group developmental stage concepts throughout or in the course of group work are limited in number. But a few such reports are available. For psychotherapy and counseling groups, see Crocker & Wroblewski (1975), Gazda (1975), Hill (1974), and C. A. Mahler (1969); also see Whittaker (1970) and Yalom (1975); for training groups see Culbert (1970, 1972) and Charrier (1974, pp. 142–145); and for naturalistic groups see Engs (1976), W. W. Menninger (1964), and Lacoursiere (1974, 1980). Kaplan (1974) makes some preliminary comments about applying group developmental stages in an organizational setting, apparently without actually doing so; also see the analogous ideas of Dolgoff (1975). A subsequent section will discuss organizational applications.

Given a setting in which to use GDS theory, the next step is *how* to use this material. This will first be considered for the overall experience, and then each stage will be discussed. Often the leader can use GDS ideas by incorporating appropriate GDS-directed comments into his or her usual statements, blending these unobtrusively into the general framework being used. For example, early in a psychotherapy or training group, if there are problems with orientation—as so often happens—the leader might comment, "There seems to be some difficulty in deciding why we are here." This is little different from what the leader might say without such GDSs, in mind, but it is said, along with other statements during orientation and other stages, with some focus on helping the group with its GDSs. In group counseling settings where physical activities are appropriate, these activities can be chosen with GDSs in mind, for example, using games or activities with a goal-directed focus during the orientation and/or dissatisfaction stages (see Crocker & Wroblewski, 1975).

In settings where the members' and groups' personal behavior is not explicitly on the agenda, such as some learning groups and many other naturalistic groups, GDS theory can be used in even more indirect ways. In learning groups with case material (legal interns, medical or nursing students), the case material can be discussed not only with a focus on the particular client or patient, but also with a focus on the group's developmental stage at that time, sometimes by considering the case material as a metaphor.

Examples follow of the indirect use of case material for GDS purposes. The first is from the orientation stage of a legal intern learning group. It shows the use of guided discussion while keeping GDS theory in mind (slightly modified from Lacoursiere, 1980).

> In the initial meeting of a group, two or three clients were discussed who were not as eager as the interns in pursuing the legal situation that brought them to the clinic. One of these clients was a woman who had filed for divorce but did not seem to be actively cooperating with the intern in pursuing it. The intern wanted to push the divorce "for her own good." We discussed how to assess what clients wanted and some of the reasons people file for divorce. We also noted that in Kansas one-third of all filings for divorce are subsequently dismissed without divorce. The discussion helped the interns temper their enthusiasm and more realistically assess the situation. (As might

have been anticipated, we learned in the next meeting that the client had returned to her husband, and so the legal case was closed.)

The above material presented by the interns from the large number of cases they had can also be seen as a metaphor for the interns themselves. There are clients (law students) who are not sure what they want or how to get it (orientation stage concerns). How much such a metaphor is pursued will depend on the setting, the degree of GDS work required, and so on. The next example is from another legal intern group in the dissatisfaction stage; it demonstrates the use of guided discussion (Lacoursiere, 1980).

> After a brief review of the prior meeting, an intern asked what to do with clients who lie or cover up. This problem was frustrating many of the interns. We talked about helping clients separate their attorneys from the judicial system, and the need to confront prevaricating clients as early as possible and ways to do this (e.g., "I don't think a judge or jury will ever buy that story . . ."). By the end of the hour their sense of frustration was lessened. They had learned that this was a problem shared with other interns, and they had increased their skills in dealing with such clients.

The next example is from the dissatisfaction stage of a group of student nurses during a psychiatric training experience (slightly modified from Lacoursiere, 1974). This example contains a metaphor and its use as such in the discussion.

> At the fourth of 10 meetings the students were boisterous and distracted, giving the impression that they did not want to be at the meeting. Gradually, a few of the students began to discuss a depressed male patient who had been hospitalized for many months. During a weekend visit home, it seemed to him that his family was doing better without him, so he felt he really was not needed.
> The students' participation picked up considerably while we discussed the ramifications of this case, which had metaphorical

implications for the students, who were frustrated in their learning of psychiatric nursing. I emphasized the man's feelings of not being needed and his desire to stick to what he knew best and to avoid any change, in other words, to stay in the hospital and not return home. The students were asked if that brought any thoughts to mind, and one said that that was how things were for them. She said that she found herself unnecessarily making beds and straightening patients' rooms because that is what she felt most comfortable with. (Two or three weeks earlier these frequent student nurse tasks had been strongly avoided by the students who felt that they should be "working with the patients.") Further talk about what they could reasonably do to help patients and learn psychiatric nursing made the group more comfortable.

Instead of, or in addition to, such minimally intrusive uses of GDS ideas, very explicit use can be made. In group situations with pronounced and troublesome GDSs, this can be done in an overall way at the start of the group experience. Then each stage can be discussed as the group reaches it—what constitutes it, how to work with it, and so on (see Culbert, 1970, 1972; Hill, 1974).

In other situations in which group developmental stages are less troublesome, a single discussion of GDSs can be conducted. A graph of the GDSs such as Figure 2.1 can be useful in these presentations. A good time to make such a single presentation is during the dissatisfaction stage, when the presentation will help to acknowledge the members' difficulties and will suggest that things can get better (W. W. Menninger, 1975; Lacoursiere, 1980). Subsequently, during termination for example, additional brief GDS comments can be made, about which the members will have been forewarned in the earlier discussion.

Limited only by the ingenuity of the group leader and the usefulness and degree of work required on the GDSs, various other methods can be used. For example, after a lecture on GDSs, members can be asked in which GDS they find themselves, and where their morale is relative to the neutral base line. This can be done for various settings; for example, if the members are psychiatric residents in a course learning about groups, it can be done for that course, but also for their overall psychiatric residency. Or the members might observe a group in action and note behavior related to the group's GDSs. (Details on one way of doing this with human relations exercises are presented by Charrier, 1974, pp.8–12.) Some of these methods are particularly applicable in didactic settings where the group members will themselves be working with groups, for example, when teaching group processes to future group psychotherapists or trainers.

Now we can look at each of the GDSs and offer suggestions for helping throughout the GDS experience. For the sake of clear presentation, the discussion will divide each stage into task and social-emotional areas, but of course these occur simultaneously, and often both need to be addressed at the same time. After discussion of all of the stages formulated generally enough to cover a wide range of actual and conceptual group settings, some special settings will be considered. These are personal relationships ("being in love"), organizational uses, and sociopolitical uses including Jimmy Carter's presidency.

Orientation Stage

In the orientation stage, major task problems include having realistic expectations about what can be achieved with the task, and determining whether one can acquire or has acquired the skills necessary to make satisfactory use of the experience. A variety of sources support the importance of realistic initial expectations, particularly task expectations.

In a community psychiatry treatment program where the patients had unrealistically high initial expectations, they subsequently made poor use of the treatment (Otto & Moos, 1974; also see Lazare et al., 1975). In group psychotherapy patients realistically oriented beforehand to the psychotherapy subsequently fared better in treatment (Yalom, 1975, pp. 286–300;

Yalom et al., 1967). Encounter group "casualties" were found to have higher initial expectations for growth from the experience, along with a lower level of mental health and fewer group skills (Yalom & Lieberman, 1971). People given realistic as opposed to unrealistic job previews subsequently had equal job acceptance, but more realistic job expectations, and a slightly higher job survival rate (Wanous, 1973). In a similar vein, Zwerski (1966) and Klein and Maher (1968) discussed the demoralization that can result from overselling in recruitment, and Maher and Piersol (1970) showed that when job objectives are clearer there is better job satisfaction and organizational morale. The need to be realistic during orientation has been mentioned in relation to foreign policy by Owen (1976a; and see 1976b, and Owen & Schultze, 1976), who talks about the need to avoid an "inflation of expectations" about détente. The current apathy toward the NASA program may be the result of overselling the American public on unrealistic possibilities such as life on Mars (Spivak, 1977), or gaining widespread general technological spin-offs (Hollomon, 1978).

Other very important elements in orientation are expectations regarding the social-emotional aspects of the group—will the leader like me, will other members like me, will I like them? I will return to some of this shortly.

In many contexts the delineation of what can be realistically expected from the task and social-emotional aspects of the experience can be handled by an accurate initial presentation and discussion of the expectations and goals. Such a discussion should often also mention unrealistic goals and expectations. By doing so, participants' unspoken and often unconceptualized fantasies, which are unlikely to be realistic, do not have such an opportunity to develop or continue to flourish. For example, a legal intern will not be so likely to fantasize about taking a case to the state Supreme Court during the internship, or for the experience to be catastrophic. Consideration of a wide range of goals may reveal that some are contradictory. (A form for discussing goals with legal intern learning groups is included in the appendix; it can be modified for other settings.)

At other times the new experience may entail considerable risks and perhaps contingent gains, so somewhat more sophisticated methods might be required. Such methods can be used before the formal beginning of the experience, for example, before a first therapy group meeting or before actually beginning work on a job, and under these conditions the orientation stage should be considered to include this initial activity. (Recall the first chapter discussion of the temporal limits of each stage.)

One method that helps put expectations in perspective is a simple balance sheet on which the anticipated gains and losses are listed in two columns to allow a more careful assessment of the situation. (A balance sheet form is included in the appendix.) Another method is goal attainment scaling: Each goal is listed, and the most favorable and unfavorable outcomes thought likely are described as accurately as possible, along with the expected level of success (see, for example, Kiresuk & Garwick, 1975; and Kiresuk & Sherman, 1968, as applied to mental health work). Again, unrealistic goals and outcomes should receive consideration. (Additional discussion of the importance of goals and their use can be found in Ryan, 1973, and Doverspike, 1973; although their discussions focus on counseling groups, they are applicable to other groups as well.)

Janis and Mann (1976, 1977) suggest some additional methods which they applied especially to situations involving choices or decisions, and entering into a new experience is begun with such a decision. Although these methods can be applied to any situation, they might be especially appropriate when the decision has particularly weighty implications or requires considerable self-sacrifice, such as whether to undergo coronary bypass surgery, to go on a nuclear submarine assignment, or to become a NASA pilot.

Besides the balance sheet approach mentioned above, Janis

and Mann employ "outcome psychodrama" and "emotional inoculation." In outcome psychodrama a future scenario is plotted out to portray the likely consequences of the decision to take part in this activity. For example, if a person goes for six months on a nuclear submarine, what will it be like, what will his spouse think about it, and so on. Or, what will it be like to have a leg amputated because of cancer.

Emotional inoculation, usually done between the initial decision and its implementation, aims to convey as accurately as possible the negative effects of a particular decision so that these effects are subsequently more tolerable. (Caplan [1964, pp. 84–85] discusses the use of a similar method in potential or actual crises, giving it also the alternate name, "anticipatory guidance.")

Other social-emotional aspects of orientation include feelings toward the leader. Is the leader perceived as likable, acceptable, immediately unlikable, skilled? All of these perceptions are determined in great part by the member's experience with people in authority, including especially the member's parents (transference), and by experiences comparable to the present one. The leader can usually help with these aspects of orientation by being an appropriately accepting person.

There will be some members who react to the leader in an idiosyncratic way, for example, with a strong dislike or overidealization. These members can often be helped to overcome distortion by a realistic presentation of oneself. The leader must avoid being seduced by myriad kinds of flattery about her or his skills, kindness, magnanimity, and "genuineness," not only for the sake of truth, but because the more distorted the overidealization is in orientation, the greater the disappointment will be in the dissatisfaction stage.

Orientation also includes issues of acceptance by other members and one's acceptance of these members, both on a personal level and in relation to the skills brought into the experience or later developed and effectively used. The importance of other members in a conceptual group depends on the conceptual group context, but it can be considerable. When the conceptual group consists of classmates in a three- or four-year law or medical school program, the degree of acceptance between members will usually be more important than in an actual group working on a relatively impersonal problem during a small number of meetings. The leader will need to work with the group members to help facilitate adequate acceptance between them and to encourage appropriate member roles for the setting. The better this is done in orientation, the less chance for serious difficulties later.

More detailed discussion of helping with the social-emotional aspects of orientation, as with the stages to follow, goes beyond the limits of this presentation and into the realm of good leadership. The reader is referred to previously mentioned general sources, such as those on group dynamics and group psychotherapy.

Falck (1976) has written about another part of the orientation stage, the need to leave and sometimes mourn the old situation before one can enter into a new situation. The leader may have to help the member accomplish this. If one still carries much unfinished business from a prior job, a former teacher, and so on, it can interfere with a realistic acceptance of the new experience. This will happen especially if the new experience is largely entered to get away from a previous bad experience, such as an unsatisfactory job or marriage.

And of course during orientation, as during every other GDS, the leader must help the participant with the specific task, whatever it is—learning, understanding groups, treatment, committee work and so on. No amount of concern and attention to GDSs will make an experience satisfactory if the leader cannot help the participant complete the task.

Dissatisfaction and Resolution Stages

Adequate attention to one GDS helps with any subsequent stages and with the overall experience. If orientation is well handled in its task and social-emotional aspects that will usually help the dissatisfaction stage so it will not be too long or too disruptive. It is not that the difficulties in the dissatisfaction stage can be avoided, because the conditions contributing to dissatisfaction largely have reality only when a person is in the middle of them. No matter how well orientation is handled, the realities of the experience will not be as clear as they will be in the dissatisfaction stage. At times this transition from orientation to dissatisfaction is fairly dramatic. It has been called the "confrontation with reality" in work with Peace Corps volunteers (W. W. Menninger, 1975), and the "bursting of the Perry Mason bubble" in work with legal interns (Lacoursiere, 1980).

The stages are further interrelated in that insofar as we are helping with dissatisfaction we are in the realm of resolution stage behaviors—resolving goal and reality discrepancies, inappropriate and excessive feelings, and so on. It is too artificial to talk about helping with dissatisfaction without also talking about resolution, just as helping with orientation assists dissatisfaction, although orientation could more easily be discussed by itself.

The major social-emotional concerns of the dissatisfaction stage are frustration, anger, often discouragement about one's success in the experience, and member-to-leader and intermember rivalry and anger. The amount of consciously experienced negative feelings of various kinds and the degree of decreased morale will depend on the leader, group situation, individual members, and rapidity of change from orientation to dissatisfaction. Although social-emotional problems in the dissatisfaction stage can be serious enough to interfere with the task in any type of group, this is most likely to occur in groups with significant personal involvement, such as training and psychotherapy groups and some naturalistic groups.

Before explicit help is directed at dissatisfaction, it should usually have been interfering with the task for some time. This is because participants will generally resist acknowledging dissatisfaction stage behaviors when they first appear, and at that time in an actual group setting some members will not yet be experiencing the negative feelings of dissatisfaction. In some experiences some members of the group will show pronounced dissatisfaction stage behaviors quite early. Under these conditions the leader must acknowledge these feelings and work with them or risk the loss of members or dissolution of the group, or at least the loss of a sufficiently positive disposition to the task to insure its adequate completion.

Sometimes adequate help with dissatisfaction stage problems will be given by verbal acknowledgment of the difficulties, and this will encourage work on these problems. ("This class seems in the dumps!" "Where's the team spirit gone?" "The group seems confused about what you should be doing now.") When dissatisfaction is a pronounced stage, much work over several meetings will be required. Sometimes it will take several meetings before a member or members even consciously experience and acknowledge their difficulties.

In many contexts verbal methods will be the primary if not the only way of helping with dissatisfaction, and with some groups and members this will require considerable ability from the leader. These are skills not easily acquired and not represented by a few passing comments, but in difficult situations the leader will have to rely on considerable training and experience in working with that type of group.

Methods that can be used to help with the social-emotional concerns of dissatisfaction include modifications of many of the methods discussed above for the orientation stage. These can include examining achievements, which in itself can help members realize that in spite of how frustrated they might feel they are accomplishing something. This is a time to discuss again the goals and expectations and to clarify which are realistic. The discussion should include such social expectations as members' roles in the group and other aspects of the relationships between members. This discussion will allow an assessment of which realistic goals must still be pursued diligently to be achieved.

When the group is well into the dissatisfaction stage, it

may be appropriate to make a presentation on GDSs, if this hasn't already been done. This acknowledges the members' current difficulties and gives them hope that things will get better. In human relations settings, exercises on anger and relationships between members can be done at this time—for example, an exercise to encourage trust to help group cohesion, such as having one member safely lead another blindfolded member.

Frank (1974) sees the process of psychotherapy largely as "the restoration of morale," which can involve helping patients through the demoralization of a prolonged dissatisfaction stage or through demoralization that develops later in the production stage. The ways he suggests to help patients are basically the components of good psychotherapy, but they include an opportunity for cognitive and experiential learning, and inspiring a realistic sense of expectation that the patient can feel better. The group leader provides similar opportunities to the members by offering hope, sometimes by personal example (fostering identification and internalization as discussed above), and by facilitating learning.

The main task problems in the dissatisfaction stage are adequately specifying the nature of the task, increasing learning of skills for the task, and applying these skills. The adequate and accurate specification of the nature of the task is interrelated with what was said above about clarifying members' goals. But one must be careful not to define the task in terms of members' goals when that is not appropriate and when the task will not or is not meant to fit into particular members' goals. For example, a main goal of group psychotherapy is not to find new friends in the group, and a main goal of a nonpersonal growth-style training group (such as a Tavistock group) is not personal therapy. Imprecision in these regards will prolong the dissatisfaction stage or delay its onset, and when it occurs it will probably be more marked.

The methods for the continued imparting of the skills for the task will vary with the type of experience. This will usually include many of the methods of good teaching, such as organized presentations and demonstrations, role modeling (identification), and so forth. When the necessary skills are fairly easily learned, as they are in some work settings, the skills will be adequately acquired early in the experience (in orientation, and perhaps also dissatisfaction). But in other settings (complex work settings such as managerial jobs, training, therapy and learning groups), skill acquisition and teaching will have to continue throughout the experience.

There is a need not only to impart and acquire the skills, but also to apply them to the situation at hand, and this again may be moderately easy or very difficult. Certain work skills are easily applied, but other skills are applied only with varying degrees of difficulty, for example, lawyering skills applied to clients, medical skills to patients, psychotherapeutic knowledge to oneself, and group dynamic understanding to a group.

Adequate application of the material of this section usually helps participants through the dissatisfaction stage and the resolution stage, but passage through the resolution stage depends largely on appropriate handling of the dissatisfaction stage. This is not to imply that the resolution stage will necessarily proceed automatically, because in more intensive and prolonged experiences it will usually take considerable time and considerable work on the leader's part. Of course there are times when the conditions will not lead to a satisfactory transition through the GDSs. These are many, but the most common are the members' refusal to accept or change to realistic goals, the failure of members in actual groups to get along with each other, the inability or refusal of members to acquire the required skills for the task, the failure of the leader to impart the necessary skills, and the failure of the leader to help the members through the GDS sequence. The GDS sequence can also be derailed when the nature of the experience changes. Possible reasons for this change include outright abandonment of all goals because they cease to be relevant, a change of goals throughout the experience, and loss of the leader.

Negative Orientation Stage

A negative orientation stage at the beginning of the experience, which is associated with some degree of coerced participation, can be overcome by applying the methods discussed for the orientation stage, or for the dissatisfaction and resolution stages. This can include, for example, examining the coercive circumstances and looking at what would have happened if the member had not given in to the coercion. Work with this stage will usually require an acknowledgment and discussion of the ambivalent, maybe highly ambivalent, participation in the experience. Successful work by the leader on this stage will generally blend into work on the dissatisfaction and resolution stages, and proceed as above.

Under some of these conditions the member or group will be fairly easily won over, for example, when the highly resistant therapy group member begins to appreciate the help, or when the reluctant training group member finds the experience interesting or useful (see the morale curve based on the data of Mann et al., 1967). Sometimes in a negative orientation stage with marked resistance, the chance of a successful experience leading to adequate production and termination will depend on individual factors and on the type and strength of external coercion. For example, some alcoholic patients in treatment as a condition of parole will do fairly well, but others will abort the treatment process even though it may mean that they will have to return to the penitentiary instead of being released after completing treatment. It was seen in the Zurcher (1969) data that most community groups with the chance of "free" federal monies gave up before completing a grant application for such funds. In practice many experiences beginning with a negative orientation stage will proceed to production, as was seen with a number of studies in Table 4.9.

Production Stage

The attention to group members described above should bring development to the production stage if all has gone well, unless the goals become irrelevant, the leader is lost, or some other disruptive factor supervenes. On the task side of production there is the need to keep skills at an appropriate level, with additional training if required, along with the need to maintain a sufficient level of application of skills to the task. In addition, during the course of many experiences new goals may be added and steps will have to be taken to address these goals. For example, additional or modified skills may have to be developed and applied. The leader will also have to keep the focus directed on the task and not allow social-emotional interests to dominate, unless that *is* the task, as it is in a social group. An excessive social focus can easily sidetrack a therapy or training group whose members may progressively focus on the social aspects of the experience rather than on the task. Similarly, work groups may be disrupted by an excessive social focus. Some socialization in work groups helps the task, but beyond that it is apt to interfere.

The main social-emotional aspects of the production stage are usually the growing positive feelings among the participants, the growing independence of the participants from the leader, and sometimes fatigue with the task. At this time the leader must try to maintain appropriate relationships between members, sometimes by encouraging cohesive aspects and trying to resolve disruptive ones. On the other hand, as stated above, social relationships cannot be allowed to become so important that they interfere with the task. Growing independence also needs to be encouraged by the leader, but not usually to the point where there is no continuing leadership. At this time the leader has to guard against his or her own sense of discomfort and loss as members grow appropriately more independent. (I will return to the leader later.)

Throughout production expectations must be kept reasonable and balanced with what is feasible. This may require repeated reassessment and modification of goals. (If the earlier goals are abandoned completely, we will usually have a new experience, and if the goals are all achieved, we will have termination of the experience.) If the task is fairly easy, such as selling a new item that is well received, or defeating inferior athletic teams, the leader may have a difficult time keeping the expectations from becoming unreasonable, and the group may risk marked problems when the goals cease to be achieved.

The failure to attain some of one's goals, the fatigue, the loss of excitement in the experience, and other factors such as the addition of new goals unrelated to the current experience may contribute to downward fluctuations in morale during production, and sometimes to serious demoralization. This state of demoralization is usually not as low or as angry as it was in the earlier dissatisfaction stage, but it can contribute significantly to member distress and to the failure of long-term persistence.

These negative aspects of production can be resolved through appropriate attention to members' needs for rest (vacations), goal reassessment as discussed in the section on dissatisfaction, and at times a decision that it is time to terminate the experience because optimum benefits have been realized. This approaches the area of "staff burnout," a subject that will be addressed later.

Termination Stage

This leads to the end of the GDS sequence, the termination stage. The main task concerns at this time are to complete the task as well as possible and to evaluate what has been accomplished. This task portion of termination can be aided by helping the members complete the work, which may require additional skills in task completion, and sometimes in termination itself when this is an important part of the task, such as in training, therapy, and certain learning groups. A review of the overall experience will contribute to task completion by allowing an assessment of what has been accomplished and what yet needs to be done.

This task completion and review of the experience are also part of the social-emotional acknowledgment of where the group is, in other words, acknowledgment that it is time to terminate. Social-emotional concerns of termination include the sense of loss and sadness with saying good-bye to other members of the group and to the experience itself, some sense of disappointment if goals were not adequately accomplished, and some sense of pride if they were.

The leader will often need to help the members acknowledge both these positive and negative feelings about termination. Both are usually there, but one type of feeling can be covered by the other, that is, sadness can cover appropriate pride, or pleasure at completing the task can cover the feelings of loss. It is usually this latter feeling that is more difficult to acknowledge, especially if it is pronounced.

Participants can usually be helped through these termination stage difficulties by verbal methods appropriate to the context: "We're coming to the end of another school year; what do you think about that?" "What's it like now that your jail term is ending?" "There seems to be a lot of joking since it's been made clear we will soon be stopping the group." "There's a lot of talk about death as the group is coming to an end."

Appropriate termination work will often need to be pursued diligently throughout the length of the termination stage. It will sometimes be helpful to talk about and prepare for the next experience to come—postgraduation, post-therapy, the use of knowledge from a training group, and so on.

In settings where termination is a major and very important part of the experience, as in psychotherapy and training groups, and in learning groups like those that deal with death or termination in some other form (see Husband & Scheunemann, 1972), this stage may take considerable work and time. Attention may have to be directed to several of its possible substages, such as denial, anger, depression and grief, acceptance, reconstruction, and decathexis (Husband & Scheunemann, 1972; Kubler-Ross, 1969; and see above). In some settings that do not involve actual groups, it may be feasible to set up an actual group to address termination; such a "termination group" has been used with psychiatric residents in the Menninger School of Psychiatry. When the termination stage is not adequately handled, the unfinished business may interfere with the next experience, and with the new orientation stage. This brings us full circle, to where one GDS sequence overlaps with the next—but more on this later.

SPECIAL APPLICATIONS OF GDSs

There are some special areas where GDS ideas can be applied. These include personal relationships ("being in love"), and organizational and sociopolitical settings. This is by no means an exhaustive list of possible special settings, but it will show some additional areas where GDSs may be useful. The reader can make other applications that seem appropriate. (The appendix includes self-help suggestions for applying GDS material to the reader's personal life.)

Is "Being in Love" a GDS Sequence?

The process in love relationships bears more than a slight resemblance to a GDS sequence. Love often starts with an overenthusiastic, overwhelming, "love at first sight" stage where the loved one is overidealized and the relationship is viewed as meeting innumerable personal needs (orientation).

This somewhat symbiotic stage eventually leads to a confrontation with reality in which one sees that the partner is real and has faults, and is not some ideal person who meets all needs. It also becomes clear that many of one's needs do not exactly coincide with those of the loved one, who is now becoming a more ambivalently loved one. Only if this (dissatisfaction) stage with its bickering and anger is handled with satisfactory individuation and an adequate meeting of more realistic individual needs (during resolution) will the relationship continue (to production). Otherwise, the (GDS) sequence is apt to be aborted with an abrupt and premature termination.

If the relationship does reach a mutual working stage with more realistic expectations of each other and satisfactory meeting of mutual needs (production), then the hard and long-term work of a relationship really begins with growing underlying stability and more manageable fluctuations in feelings for each other. Subsequently, a termination stage comes only when the relationship ends in death, divorce, or separation.

This is clearly an oversimplified view of complex human relationships, yet it seems to apply to many love relationships. Insofar as GDSs do apply to these relationships, GDS ideas can sometimes be used by an individual to examine his or her relationship, to determine the current stage of the relationship, and to examine expectations. This is also a framework that can be usefully applied in marriage enrichment and marriage counseling groups. (Day [1967] makes brief reference to this comparison of group developmental stages and love relationships, and Krain [1973, 1975] has done a preliminary empirical study. He failed to substantiate a GDS sequence, but as he points out, his sampling methods may well have filtered out such data.)

Organizational Applications

There are several places in the business or organizational world that adequately meet the conditions of GDS theory. Brief examples have been mentioned several times, such as the sales manager and his staff, but here other applications will be considered, including some of broader scope.

One example is a change in management in an organizational division that has the effect of creating a new "group" under the new "leader." These GDS effects will usually be most obvious in those more directly and immediately affected by the new leader, as opposed to those several steps down the hierarchical ladder, where changes may be harder to observe. And these effects will likely be more marked when the new leader is brought in from outside that area of the organization. A frequent enough current example of this situation comes when new companies are acquired by conglomerates, and there is a change not only in ownership, but also in management on several levels. The bringing in of such outsiders contributes more to the development of fantasies, hopes, expectations, apprehensions, and so on, than when people who are known are promoted from within.

The magnitude of the GDSs produced by this change in leadership will also depend on several other factors, only some of which will be touched on. We can start with the new leader, and whether the person is likable, if he or she comes from a respected or hated competitor, whether prior policies and procedures are largely continued or many changes are made, and so on. There are also several factors related to the leader who was replaced, and if that person was strongly liked or disliked there will be some unfinished business to deal with. If the former leader was well liked, orientation with the new leader may have little positive to it, and the dissatisfaction stage may occur quickly and be profound. If the former leader was disliked, everything may not come up roses either, because the positive expectations in orientation from the new leader may be very unrealistic. Most GDS difficulties from a change of leader will be in the orientation and dissatisfaction stages, and once resolution is well under way the crisis of change will be largely resolved.

It would be possible to discuss the later stages of production and termination, but these follow naturally enough from what has already been said. However, perhaps it is not superfluous to point out that when termination comes, it would be well to handle it as much as possible in the presence of the current leader rather than to leave it to the next leader who will have plenty to do starting out with orientation—his or her personal orientation stage in the job, and that of the group. (Although he does not have a GDS focus, Golembiewski [1965] provides a good discussion of actual groups within organizations.)

When a new organization begins fairly intact, with a largely stable management, a moderately stable group of employees, and a set task, the conditions for GDS application to the organization as a whole may be adequately met. Examples might be anything from new, small businesses to the beginning of new, professional athletic franchises or the purchasing of old ones by new investors, sometimes with the geographical movement of the franchise. Under these conditions one would expect to see an initial orientation, then dissatisfaction, and if these stages are adequately handled, resolution and production. Under some conditions termination phenomena would also be seen, for example, with the death or retirement of the owner, or with the too rapid demise of the sports franchise. (Some new athletic organizations meet their demise during the dissatisfaction stage, aborting the GDS sequence. (See Nader & Gruenstein [1978].)

Dolgoff (1975) and Kaplan (1974) have speculated about the application of group developmental stage ideas to growing organizations. Their major thrust has been on trying to get a better understanding of the development of such growing organizations. The degree of extrapolation required to apply GDS ideas to growing organizations is greater than that required above, where the size, goals, and tasks of the organization were more stable. The development of a growing organization is different from this and may not meet the criteria required for the development of GDSs as discussed previously (top management may be an exception). Important differences are that growing organizations involve a changing group that is increasing in size, their time boundaries are less fixed and often without as clear a starting point, and except for those highly involved in management and ownership, the task is only minimally or moderately a personal one, and it may change considerably with time. Also, in a growing organization it is usually more difficult for the board of directors, chief executive officer, or other group leaders to have fairly clear ideas about where and when the organizational growth should culminate, and about how to get it there.

All of this contrasts at the other extreme with the development of GDSs in a training or psychotherapy group with an experienced leader who has realistic expectations of where the group should end up, and approximately when. Such groups also have moderately specific goals as the group develops, and they start and end with a fairly stable membership. Still, this does not mean that a growing organization as a whole cannot be an appropriate place to apply GDS theory, but such a growing organization will be a more difficult place in which to see and apply GDS theory than a fairly stable, less actively growing organization. (Discussions of the development of growing organizations and non-group developmental stage models thereof can be found in Dale [1952], Starbuck [1965], and Udy [1965].)

GDS THEORY AND ORGANIZATIONAL CHANGE.   It may be helpful to compare and contrast GDSs and the area of change. This is a broad area of practice and study whose focus is on change of some significant degree. Included within its scope are changes in structure and function in a variety of settings, including organizations. It is this organizational change area which perhaps most distinguishes the change area from other bodies of knowledge, and this is the area that will be considered here. (Only the briefest summary of this work will be presented; the interested reader is referred to the literature, for example, Baldridge et al., 1975; Bennis et al., 1969; and Burke, 1977.)

Organizational change seeks to effect lasting changes in the organization—addressing a problem area in order to correct it, however that will be done, implementing a new treatment program or new manufacturing method, introducing a major educational innovation, introducing a new leader, revamping the leadership structure, and so on. Sometimes the only clear item at the start will be that there are problems that need correction, but there may not be much certainty about the nature of these problems or how to correct them. Maybe it is not even clear who should investigate the problems or be involved in the corrective process.

At times the change that has to be introduced will be very specific, for example, a change mandated by law or more efficient manufacturing methods, and under these conditions the task is to implement the change or carry out the change process. Sometimes the changes themselves are changing so that it is difficult to delineate the process: Looking into problems or beginning changes leads to certain additional problems or changes, for example, in personnel, and these require other changes.

It will usually take some degree of individual change before organizational change can occur, but the individual change, which may occur in actual group settings, may or may not show a GDS sequence. This will depend on the occurrence, or lack thereof, of the various conditions that contribute to GDSs. In an organizational change these will include the extent to which participants in the change are fairly constant, the extent to which a distinct change process can be delineated as opposed to a series of changes overlapping each other, the extent to which temporal boundaries are clear, and the extent to which the task is personally meaningful and important to the participants.

Examples of actual groups within an organizational change process that could show GDSs are a steering committee with fairly stable membership set up to implement specific changes, and the executive body responsible for correcting a problem with a distinct program of innovations. Similarly, as discussed above, the change of leader in a division of an organization creates GDS conditions in the employee group immediately led by this leader. In complex organizational change situations there are often so many significant changes in structure, function, and participants going on simultaneously or overlapping each other, that GDSs are not easy to see or are only visible to a well-trained observer, sometimes in fragmentary form.

The reason for looking for GDSs in all these situations is a highly pragmatic one; to address them in order to make the GDS process more manageable and thus to facilitate completion of the task. (It is a little ironic that actual groups showing GDS sequences specifically set up to bring about changes in individuals to facilitate organizational changes may or may not be effective in doing this; training groups set up for such purposes often have not had impressive results [Bowers, 1973].)

Sociopolitical Applications

One area in which GDS ideas can be applied is the sociopolitical arena. Several sociopolitical reports that seem consistent with the GDS concepts have already been mentioned. These include material on revolutions and rebellions (Davies, 1969; Feierabend et al., 1969), on the space program (Holloman, 1978; Spivak, 1977), and on détente negotiations (Owen, 1976a). They all discuss difficulties that can be encountered in the dissatisfaction stage when original expectations exceed subsequent satisfactions. In these examples we have expectations for basic human needs for work, education, dignity, and so on, and when these hopes are kindled and not fulfilled we have rebellions and revolutions. The expectations of finding life on other planets and great technological spin-offs were encouraged by the space program, and when they were not met, apathy about the program developed. If expectations for rapid, large arms reductions are not met, there will be apathy, frustration, and discouragement over the idea of détente, or worse, an escalation of the arms race.

Applications of GDS concepts to these areas seem to follow easily enough from what has already been said, so this point will not be labored. Much relies on establishing realistic expectations and keeping them realistic, and then trying diligently to satisfy these hopes. This is not as simple as it may sound, because frequently political leaders deliberately fire expectations to accomplish something they want at the time—to get elected, to appropriate money for space research, to decrease the defense budget, or whatever. Sometimes hopes may be raised rather callously for short-term gains, but at other times they are exaggerated by excessive enthusiasm over the matter in question, which is inadequately checked by reality or relevant experience. Carter's presidency may be an example of such a GDS sequence.

CARTER'S PRESIDENCY: A GDS MANIFESTATION?   Does Jimmy Carter's presidency manifest GDSs? Carter won the nomination, and then was elected president, predominantly on the basis of many promises to improve matters in the country, and on the basis of his apparent honesty and determination in these promises. He even wrote an autobiography entitled *Why Not the Best?* (Carter, 1975). However, he had little experience with national politics against which he or the public might judge his promises or ability to deliver. But after the Nixon years, tainted by the Watergate scandal, the country was ripe for a newcomer from outside the Washington political arena. All this in the orientation stage set expectations and hopes very high, and the feelings in the country were that Carter would achieve his promised goals. Confidence in the new President was high, and he seemed self-confident; his photographs at this time were all broad smiles!

But quickly things changed; there was a "confrontation with reality." President Carter faced the political life of Washington, the House, and the Senate. He had problems with his own staff and appointees, such as with Bert Lance. Promises were much easier to make than to keep, no matter how much determination and honesty one had, no matter how much one wanted to be "the best." Confidence in the President fell drastically, and he seemed to lose his earlier self-confidence. The pictures now showed fewer smiles, and they often revealed a worried look. Mr. Carter and his Presidency were in the throes of the dissatisfaction stage. (Some acknowledgment that Carter's popularity tumbled because he had raised hopes too high is found in a UPI report of Hamilton Jordan's analysis of the Presidency in the *Topeka Daily Capital,* April 13, 1978, p. 11.)

There were then struggles in the early resolution stage with various examinations reported in the public media of promises achieved, not achieved, achievable, and not achievable. Also, by late 1978 President Carter and his staff were progressively learning how to work in the world of Washington politics, though not without significant additional problems, such as getting along with Speaker of the House O'Neill, and disagreements with Senator Kennedy on national health legislation. Mr. Carter then brought off the dramatic Camp David agreement between Israeli Prime Minister Begin and Egyptian President Sadat, and his popularity rose. In late 1978 Congress passed significant amounts of the President's legislation. Who would have expected that a few months before?

At the mid-point of the Presidency perhaps the resolution stage was well along and the production stage not far behind. But at times we appeared to be heading into an abortive GDS sequence ending without achieving a good production stage; the handling of problems in Iran and Afghanistan helped avoid this.

As the term nears its end and the termination stage approaches, the President will need to consolidate his accomplishments and review them with the electorate (the group). If they are not substantial, and in some way commensurate with the initial and revised promises and goals, and our expectations, there is unlikely to be a second term and another GDS sequence for President Carter.

OTHER INSTANCES OF LOW MORALE IN GDS EXPERIENCES

We have already seen that low morale occurs primarily in the stages of negative orientation, dissatisfaction, and termination, at least when loss and disappointment are important parts of termination. Low morale can affect GDS experiences under circumstances other than those already emphasized, and we will discuss some of these now.

There are some experiences in which low morale is not noticeable until the end of the experience, for a variety of reasons. Academic semesters and years are sometimes like this. In these situations morale in the dissatisfaction stage may not have gotten very low, so near the end of the experience in termination the decline in morale is more striking. This is a time when the task is largely completed for that semester or year, so there can be a letdown in energy and enthusiasm. Also, there are often examinations to face which are not viewed eagerly and which sap energy.

At other times the fall in morale with the ending of the experience is part of the dissatisfaction stage, often combined with some termination stage phenomena, such as feelings of loss. In these cases, such as the demise of a social club or small business, the experience ends as a result of failure to work through (resolve) dissatisfaction stage difficulties. That is, realistic and achievable goals were not properly pursued. Whether an experience that is stopping is doing so after a full GDS sequence or with the dissatisfaction stage can usually be determined by examining whether the goals of the experience were clear enough and whether they were accomplished.

There still remain experiences in which dissatisfaction stage phenomena appear to have been adequately handled, there are no temporal factors forcing termination, the task continues to be ostensibly adequately accomplished in the production stage, and yet the morale of the individual or group is going progressively downhill. Situations in which the task demands much from the participants often fall into this category.

Examples are researchers who must continuously apply for grants to have their work funded, and workers in certain areas in the health field, such as late-stage cancer work, hospital psychiatry, and the alcoholism and drug abuse fields. In these latter contexts this demoralization under the pressure of the task has been characterized as "staff burnout," and includes, besides low morale, various psychological symptoms such as depression and irritability, and at times physical symptoms, often with a psychosomatic flavor, such as headaches and peptic ulcers (Freudenberger, 1975; Pines & Maslach, 1978).

In these circumstances it seems that the task demands more of the participants than they can continue to give, and leads to psychological and physical fatigue: Research funds are limited and only some topnotch grant proposals are funded; patients and clients are very demanding and often poorly able to manage without much help. This is not to say that the fall in morale in these settings can be solely attributed to the task demands, because some of it undoubtedly stems from some failure at realistic goal setting, for example, whether a researcher can continue to be funded from grants, or whether a mental health worker can attain more than certain changes in most patients and clients by an approach that can do little about the broader context of these problems.

MORALE IN WORK SETTINGS

This book has been concerned with morale primarily as it occurs in the course of the developmental stages of actual groups and various other experiences. There are other ways to consider morale, as we saw earlier, and many contexts in which such morale has been studied, such as in the armed forces and work settings. (A great many work settings have been studied; see Argyle, 1972; Benoit-Guilbot, 1968; and Dubin, 1968.)

It might be argued that in these contexts the morale is part of a GDS sequence and should be so viewed. Although this is sometimes true, at other times at this stage of knowledge this would be a premature conclusion. Eventually the GDS and non-GDS areas that consider morale may interrelate more closely to the benefit of both areas, but for the present, until more is known about GDSs, it appears more expedient to view some of these settings where morale has been studied independently as non-GDS areas, and accordingly to consider the morale largely separate from GDS phenomena. Work settings are one setting in which there are extensive non-GDS data on morale, and some of this material was discussed earlier, but it will now be considered in the context of helping employees with their morale.

Some of the reasons to attend to morale in work settings are because of its effects on such things as absenteeism, labor turnover, productivity, and probably labor sabotage. Viewing employee morale in its narrow sense of job satisfaction, Argyle (1972, pp. 238–241) reviewed some of its correlations. The correlations with unexcused absences are typically approximately -0.30, and with labor turnover -0.20 to -0.30. Correlations between such morale and productivity for manual workers, salesmen, and insurance agents are in the area of 0.15, and it is possible that this correlation is higher for highly skilled workers or for those more highly involved with their work. Conversely, a brief review of the literature did not convince A. R. Martin (1969) that there was a clear positive correlation between morale measured as job satisfaction and productivity; the final results in this area are yet to come.

In work settings morale can be defined more broadly than job satisfaction to include employees' eagerness to do the work, their appreciation of the company, and so on. Defining morale in this broader way, Table 6.1 lists a number of the conditions in work settings that have been found to contribute to employee morale. This summary draws particularly on the work of Argyle (1972), Baehr and Renck (1958), Deutsch (1968), and Mahoney (1956). Although some of these conditions clearly relate to GDS material (such as characteristics of the leader,

Table 6.1. Conditions in work settings that affect employee morale

Company Conditions

Size — Smaller companies are generally better.

Managers — Morale is better when managers are better trained and more skillful.

Management — Participatory management is generally better.

Status — The higher the status of the company and its product, the better the morale.

Miscellaneous — Personnel policies; relationships with employee organizations such as union.

Supervisory Conditions

Personnel — Personable supervisors are better.

Supervision Method — A participatory method is generally better.

Work Conditions

Group Size — Smaller groups are generally better, but the optimum size varies.

Cohesiveness — More cohesive groups fare better.

Interaction — Morale is better if there is an opportunity for interaction with other group members.

Group Status — Morale is better if the group status is higher compared with other groups.

Individual Status — Individual morale is better for those with higher status in the group.

Group Developmental Stage — Morale varies with the stage; it is lower in dissatisfaction and negative orientation, for example, when an employee is pushed into a job or position.

Individual Conditions

Sex — Women often have better morale.

Age — Younger employees often have lower morale, but the limits here are unclear.

Intelligence — Intelligence must match the job for good morale.

Psychological — The more emotionally disturbed employees often have lower morale; occasionally higher work morale compensates for such personal problems.

Nonwork Status — If status outside work is higher, morale is often higher.

Orientation to Work — If the task is liked morale is better.

Material Rewards — The better the pay and fringe benefits, the better the morale.

work group cohesion and size and degree of interaction, and the GDS of the work group), most of these conditions have not been adequately considered or studied from a GDS perspective and may or may not have significant GDS relevance (for example, the company conditions and such individual conditions as the age and sex of adult employees).

Even though the work setting and GDS morale are being viewed somewhat separately, it is clear that if one is trying to help more clearly work-related morale (for example, through the quality of supervisors and material rewards) but ignores obvious GDS morale, then there may well be continuing difficulties with morale. This could happen, for example, if there were frequent changes of one quality supervisor (leader) for another, or if workers' (group members') expectations were ignored and if there were no reasonable chances for them to fulfill their expectations.

This brief presentation of non-GDS related morale in work settings is but an introduction to this area. The reader with a greater responsibility for and interest in employee morale is referred to current work in industrial psychology and sociology, and in management principles, perhaps beginning with Argyle (1972). Also, the important conditions affecting employee morale and how they do so are to some extent contingent on the task and context in which it is performed, among other variables. See the "contingency theory," as explained, for example, by Negandi (1973).

A NOTE ON GDSs AND THE LEADER

The group leader would be expected to go through a developmental sequence during the experience similar to the members' GDSs. In addition, there will be interaction between the leader's and members' GDSs. This means that the leader's reactions will reflect what is personally brought into the experience, as well as the members' GDSs (leader countertransference). (The members' behaviors similarly include components of reaction to the leader's behavior.) To do adequate GDS work, the leader will have to attend to these various personal reactions.

During orientation the leader must be cautious not to oversell the task-related aspects of the experience because of personal needs—for example, the need to be successful or appreciated. Nor should the leader oversell or otherwise distort herself or himself; leaders should be realistic about their leadership and other task skills. During dissatisfaction the anger and disappointment of the members must be realistically assessed and not taken personally inappropriately, even when directed at the leader. The leader must be able to tolerate the members' dissatisfactions without attempting to cover them up or deny them, and without trying to meet all expectations no matter how unrealistic; growth often comes through struggle.

This is not to deny that problems with leadership, such as imparting skills, may not occur. When these problems occur the leader must accept that things may not be going as they should and that some changes have to be made, such as leading a different way or trying other avenues to impart the skills. The working out of dissatisfaction difficulties will get the leader through the resolution stage, but easy solutions to leadership problems and other problems should not be particularly expected. The appropriate handling of the dissatisfaction and resolution stages usually means that the leader will not end up as revered as he or she was in orientation, and this must be expected and accepted.

During the production stage the leader must not harbor grudges from earlier group member anger, nor become too complacent with gains. The task may become fatiguing or boring, and new expectations and new skill imparting may be necessary. And, as the task approaches completion, the leader must not try to keep the experience going because it is comfortable, or gratifying, or to avoid the next experience with its new member or members and new problems.

In the termination stage leaders must be able to tolerate the termination and use their feelings to help members, for example, using feelings of sadness to help members with their sadness. Leaders who work repeatedly with actual groups or are involved with other intensive repeated experiences with people often find that termination is the most difficult stage for them. Under these conditions a tendency can develop to insulate oneself against the sad feelings of the termination stage, but if this is overdone the members' struggles with termination will be largely ignored, and this may reinforce their denial.

Much more could be said about the leaders' feelings and reactions during GDSs, but again this falls in the realm of the general psychological literature, for example, that on countertransference in groups. The interested reader is referred, for example, to Mullan and Rosenbaum (1978).

DOES THE USE OF GDS MATERIAL HELP?

Is there evidence that the application of GDS theory is helpful? Can we show that it makes the experience more satisfying for the participants or that it enhances work on the task? It is obvious that a thorough disregard for GDS matters—for example, the expectations of participants, the purpose of the experience, and the development of necessary skills—could easily lead to chaos. Such chaos could be engineered by the leader who proceeded precisely contrary to GDS guidelines, for example, by discussing termination at the start of the experience, by setting contradictory and unachievable goals, and by aggravating the frustrations of the dissatisfaction stage. Such a scheme would be highly artificial and unreasonable, but it does raise the question of the usefulness of GDS theory under more reasonable circumstances. If a leader with average skills adds a GDS focus to his or her work, will that improve leadership? Without evidence from a careful test of such a question, what data are available?

Some references on the usefulness of GDS-relevant material were discussed above in relation to the orientation stage. These references included reports that psychiatric patients with more realistic initial expectations fared better in treatment (Lazare et al., 1975; Otto & Moos, 1974; Yalom, 1975; Yalom et al., 1967; Yalom & Lieberman, 1971). Similarly, employees more realistically recruited later did better on the job (Klein & Maher, 1968; Maher & Piersol, 1970; Wanous, 1973; Zwerski, 1966).

On the other hand, some research attempting to isolate the effects of pregroup or initial group activities on the group experience was not successful. Two such studies of skill-focused activities before the formal group began will be summarized. This will show some of the variables research must consider in determining the effectiveness of using a GDS approach.

Bugen (1977) found that no significant cohesion effects resulted from a "general orientation" or a "cohesion-focused orientation" instruction message in eight "growth" groups. Comparing his study with other work, he felt his orientation message may have been too weak, and possibly he missed whatever effects there were by waiting too long to look for them. In addition, the groups were composed homogeneously on the basis of need for inclusion (belonging), and this may already have had a strong effect on cohesion that the orientation message could not further enhance.

Wogan et al. (1977) tried to determine the effects of four types of pregroup experimental manipulation in nine psychotherapy groups. Two of these conditions were control conditions. One of the active experimental conditions was the use of audiotaped cognitive-experiential instructions, which included interaction skill exercises which the participants practiced. The other active experimental condition was a series of experimenter-led human relations exercises. Little significant effect could be attributed to these four pretreatment conditions. Whatever the effects of pretreatment were, they may have been measured too indirectly to be detected. The main differences found were thought to be due to the different group leaders, a condition that was not controlled across groups.

Although hardly an unbiased test of the usefulness of this material, the people who use a group developmental stage approach in their work must find it helpful (for example, Charrier, 1974; Crocker & Wroblewski, 1975; Culbert, 1970, 1972; Engs, 1976; Gazda, 1975; Hill, 1974; Lacoursiere, 1974, 1980; C. A. Mahler, 1969; W. W. Menninger, 1964; Yalom, 1975). My GDS-focused learning group work with legal interns is rated as helpful by the interns, as is a specific presentation during the experience on GDSs. Similarly, executives and other professionals who take part in the Menninger Foundation seminars "toward understanding human behavior" say that they are helped by a presentation on group developmental stages (the morale curve).

Chapter 7

GDS RELATIONSHIPS AND FINAL COMMENTS

This last chapter will discuss a number of subjects either previously alluded to, such as GDS sequences following one another, or taken up here for the first time, such as the relationship of GDSs to other phenomena, for example, crises. This discussion will delineate some of the possible ramifications of GDS theory and place it within a broader perspective.

GDS THEORY AND REACTIONS TO CRISIS, STRESS, AND DYING

In recent decades important turning points or crises in life and the reactions and adjustments to them have been the focus of a number of studies (for example, Caplan, 1964; Tyhurst, 1958; and references in these works). The crisis may be primarily favorable, such as marriage or receiving a major award or promotion, or primarily unfavorable or traumatic, such as divorce or being fired at work. It is especially these latter crises that have been studied and interest us here. To call these unfavorable crises does not mean that their final outcome will be unfavorable, because such crises may ultimately be positive growth experiences.

Holmes and Rahe (1967) developed a rating scale for a number of life events requiring readjustment, and about half of these events can be considered unfavorable crises. The others either are favorable life events, or lack the impact of a crisis; some of the events listed may or may not have the impact of a crisis. Table 7.1 lists examples of these unfavorable crises and their ratings. Holmes and Rahe ranked 43 events and assigned values to these events based on the degree of readjustment required by the event.

Among their events that I have omitted are (7) marriage, with a value of 50; (9) marital reconciliation, with a value of 45; (18) change to a different line of work, with a value of 36; (25) outstanding personal achievement, with a value of 25; (27) begin or end school, with a value of 26; and (43) minor violations of the law, with a value of 11. Additional crises that are not included in the Holmes and Rahe work and that have more of a social or community impact include natural disasters and wartime events.

Unfavorable crises are faced with a rather characteristic sequence of reactions. This sequence, as summarized in the work of Caplan (1964), is consistent with the ideas of several other workers in this field. What happens precisely in a particular crisis will depend on several factors, including the internal and external resources of the person involved, the strength and significance (disruption potential) of the crisis, and how easy or difficult it is to revert to a more usual state of affairs or to use the crisis as an opportunity for growth. When an immediate and enduring response is required and the crisis is intense and not easily overcome, we have the following four-part sequence. (A similar but generally less pronounced sequence can occur in favorable crises.)

Table 7.1.   Some crises and their relative disruption potential

Holmes and Rahe's Ranking	Crisis	Readjustment Value (Relative Disruption Potential)
1	Death of spouse	100
2	Divorce	73
3	Marital separation	65
4	Jail term	63
5	Death of close family member	63
6	Personal injury or illness	53
8	Fired at work	47
10	Retirement	45
11	Change in health of family member	44
13	Sex difficulties	39
14	Gain of new family member	39
16	Change in financial state (crisis ?)	38
17	Death of close friend	37
20	Mortgage over $10,000 (crisis ?)	31
21	Foreclosure of mortgage or loan	30
23	Son or daughter leaving home	29
28	Change in living conditions	25
30	Trouble with boss	23
32	Change in residence	20

Adapted from Holmes and Rahe, 1967; see text. Reprinted with permission from the *Journal of Psychosomatic Research*, The social readjustment rating scale, 11:213-218, copyright 1967, Pergamon Press, Inc.

1. *Impact or shock* lasting minutes to hours when the crisis begins. Short-term emergency reactions and attempts to handle the situation are mobilized.

2. *Recoil and increasing turmoil* as the former emergency adjustments fail. There may be a flood of various emotions, such as anger, guilt, anxiety, and depression. By this time it becomes clear that one's usual problem-solving methods are ineffectual.

3. *Mobilization of new resources,* both internal and external, as the crisis persists without an adequate resolution. There may be a different way to see the crisis and a greater willingness now to relinquish solutions previ-

ously unworkable and to abandon unrealistic goals in these circumstances. For many situations this may involve a redefinition of one's relationship to others. This is a time of major reconstruction.

4. *Continuation of the reconstruction* begun in part 3 of the sequence with an integration with the rest of the person when the crisis is successfully handled. When the crisis is not successfully handled, there is a failure of reconstruction and integration, and major personal *disorganization* may well result.

Now what does this have to do with GDS theory and the material of this book? Some relationships are probably already obvious. When it is a crisis affecting a number of people, such as a natural disaster or the loss of many jobs because of a plant closing, we witness a group going through an experience. But unlike most of the group experiences already discussed, this experience begins primarily or exclusively negatively. That is, such crises begin an experience that starts with something similar to a negative orientation stage, except that in these crises the beginning is often more abrupt or severe than in GDS sequences that have a negative orientation stage.

As Table 7.1 shows, crises can be viewed on a continuum of severity and abruptness of impact, and when so viewed the severity and abruptness in crises overlap with the beginnings of GDS sequences that have a negative orientation stage. For example, the work of Masterson (1972) and Rinsley (1974) on severely disturbed adolescents reacting and adjusting to their treatment experience can be viewed as the reactions of these adolescents to the crisis of their (no longer avoidable) severe illness and its treatment, including hospitalization. In other words, the sequence of reactions to a crisis and negative orientation GDSs can be thought of as differing primarily in degrees of severity and abruptness in how they start.

Although the cited examples with a negative orientation stage were primarily situations of considerable growth potential (coerced treatment and some training and learning groups), many crises can also be viewed as opportunities for growth. The sequences of crisis theory and GDS theory are compared below:

Crisis Theory		GDS Theory	
Impact or shock (usually more abrupt and traumatic beginning)		Negative orientation	
Recoil and increasing turmoil		Dissatisfaction	
Mobilization of new resources and Reconstruction	Mobilization fails and Disorganization	Resolution then Production	Resolution fails Abortive sequence

The GDS-type termination stage will often not be visible in crises because crises do not usually terminate with a feeling that a favorable experience has been completed or with a sense of loss for the crisis itself. A loss such as death or divorce may initiate the crisis, but one does not long for the loss to occur again, or to continue, the way one might want a favorable group experience to continue. Also, there will usually not be a clear ending to the crisis; instead it will generally end by blending into a person's overall experience, or often by merging with the beginning of a new experience that starts with a positive orientation stage. For example, the divorce crisis may blend into a new relationship or remarriage, or a job loss crisis may blend into a new job.

In a related area of study a crisis is viewed as a stress or "stressor" (Selye, 1976). Selye has produced a large volume of work in this area (1956, 1974, 1976), but there are many other contributors with the same focus, for example, Dohrenwend and Dohrenwend (1974), Gunderson and Rahe (1974), and Holmes and Rahe (1967).

Selye emphasized the physiological and pathophysiological reactions to stress and articulated the nonspecific *general adaptation syndrome* of response to stress. This begins with an *alarm reaction* as the person (or animal, in many studies) is confronted with the stress or crisis. In this first stage the person has a nonspecific over-reaction to the situation involving over-activity of general bodily defenses and lowered resistance at this time to additional stress.

If the person is not overwhelmed, adaptation occurs in a *stage of resistance* in which the earlier levels of bodily over-reactivity decrease, and physiological handling of the stressful situation improves. There are limits to the person's ability to maintain this adaptation, and if the situation continues at a highly stressful level without being adequately resolved or handled, a *stage of exhaustion* ensues with a breakdown of bodily defenses, and disease or eventual death.

The general adaptation syndrome can be viewed as a re-statement—from the perspective of primarily physiological adaptation—of what was said above about crisis theory and negative orientation GDS theory. Although the discussion of crises and this presentation of the general adaptation syndrome emphasize somewhat abrupt and severe or traumatic beginnings, this need not always be so. A situation can cause severe stress because of the long duration of a stressor or the accumulation of several lesser stressors in close temporal proximity. The general adaptation syndrome, crisis theory, and negative orientation GDS theory are compared below:

General Adaptation Syndrome	Crisis Theory	Negative Orientation GDS Theory
Alarm reaction (includes the impact and initial over-reaction and attempts at adaptation)	Impact or shock	Negative orientation
	Recoil and increasing turmoil	Dissatisfaction

Stage of resistance	Mobilization of new resources	Resolution
(Failure leads to) Stage of exhaustion	(Failure leads to) Disorganization	(Failure leads to) Abortive sequence

A considerable amount of work has tried to discern the development of illnesses in the context of reactions to crises or stressors (for example, Dohrenwend & Dohrenwend, 1974; Gunderson & Rahe, 1974; and Selye, 1976). The types of illnesses found are somatic or psychosomatic, such as myocardial infarction and hypertension, and psychological, such as depression and chronic anxiety. Such studies have not usually reevaluated the same people after they had been exposed to a crisis or stress to see when in the reaction sequence to this crisis or stress illnesses did or did not occur. Rather, most of this work looks for increases in illness after crisis or stress without clearly placing this illness within some stage of the reaction sequence to the crisis or stress. Therefore, when we go from the stages of reaction to crisis or stress, to physical and psychological illnesses, we are becoming increasingly speculative, not about the development of such illnesses, but about the temporal relationship of the development of such illnesses to particular stages in these reactions.

Having said that, can we determine if there is an increased incidence of illness during the overall GDS sequence or during some particular stage or stages? The usual more stressful parts of the GDS sequence—negative orientation, dissatisfaction, and sometimes production and termination—are often not stressful enough or prolonged enough to make contributions to illness easily discernible, but they may do so. Under the GDS conditions discussed earlier in the book, the stress or crisis could often be avoided by leaving the experience, or it was fairly weak compared to many crises or stresses, but this is not always true. These various situations make up a continuum of contributions to physical and psychological illness, varying from abrupt and severe crisis or stress on one end, to milder degrees towards the other end, for example, in training groups, encounter groups, and learning groups. This is not to say that these latter groups cannot be highly stressful, since training groups and encounter groups can precipitate severe psychiatric reactions (see, for example, the work of Yalom & Leiberman [1971]), and patients in psychotherapy groups sometimes get worse instead of better. We saw from the Holmes and Rahe work that GDS experiences such as moving one's residence can be distressing (Holmes & Rahe, 1967; Mitchell, 1975).

The work of Kubler-Ross (1969) on patients' reactions to their terminal illness was looked at earlier as an elaboration of the GDS termination experience for the ultimate termination, death. In the light of what has been said here, her work can instead be viewed as consistent with crisis theory and negative orientation GDS experiences for the crisis of terminal illness and death. The stages she has enumerated are *shock and denial, bargaining, depression and grief, acceptance,* and *decathexis.*

The first stage of *shock and denial* is similar to the negative orientation stage and the impact or shock phase of crisis theory. The experience of facing death often has an initially overwhelming impact; it is an experience from which there is no nontragic resolution when viewed from the perspective of most goals in life. The initial denial and the subsequent *bargaining* stage are parts of the struggle to avoid, then to face obliquely, this ultimate experience. This stage can be viewed as an exaggerated, special dissatisfaction stage, and as the recoil and turmoil phase of crisis theory.

Only when one begins to face the realities of the situation, approaching death, do we enter the GDS resolution stage. And when dying, resolution involves beginning to face the ultimate loss, so this third stage is one of *depression and grief;* in crisis theory this is the mobilization of new resources. Once dying is no longer avoided but is adequately faced, there can be an *acceptance* stage where whatever good there is in the dying experience can be acknowledged and accepted, and the task of dying can hold potential for growth. This is similar to the GDS production stage or the crisis theory reconstruction stage. As death becomes imminent, the final stage of *decathexis* is reached, the ultimate good-bye, similar to the GDS termination stage, but as stated above, without a usual clear parallel in most crisis theory situations. (I will return to these comparisons presently.)

A NOTE ON GDSs AND GENERAL SYSTEMS THEORY

There is an area of study called general systems theory that looks for common ground between living systems and branches of science (see, for example, Bertalanffy, 1974). General systems theory has popularized a number of concepts and terms such as feedback, boundary, input, and output, and these ideas can be applied to groups (Miller, 1971). I will not try to articulate in any detailed way how GDS theory and general systems theory interrelate, but I will underscore how GDS material is consistent with a broadly focused approach. Two particular items will be pointed out—the range of groups to which GDS theory has application, and the isomorphism between the GDS sequence and other sequences.

The GDS sequence and its variations apply to a very broad range of groups, both actual and conceptual. The actual group examples include artificial, small, problem-solving groups, all the way through to encounter groups, training groups, therapy groups, and a variety of naturalistic groups including learning groups. The concepts that apply to actual groups can also be extrapolated to sociopolitical bodies, for example, in rebellions. Many other group types were also mentioned, for example, the conceptual group of people hospitalized for psychiatric treatment, or the people reacting to new jobs or new promotions, although with some of these examples there were few hard data to cite. Group and general developmental stages (GDSs), then, are found not only under a narrow set of circumstances, but in groups and individuals in a broad range of settings adequately meeting certain conditions such as temporal boundaries and type of task.

In addition, there is isomorphism between the sequences of GDSs, negative orientation GDSs, crisis theory, the general adaptation syndrome, and the reaction to death and dying. These sequences are not the same, but there is considerable similarity, and there are systematic changes in the sequences according to how much the experience begins with a favorable, desired beginning, to a coerced, less desired beginning, and finally to an unavoidable, usually undesired beginning, the knowledge that one is dying. This isomorphism is easier to see when shown tabularly, as in Table 7.2.

These comparisons between GDS theory, crisis theory, the general adaptation syndrome, and the death and dying experience have been made to show relationships of GDS theory. GDS theory does not, of course, elucidate the detail and sensitivity that is obtained from the study of reactions to death and dying or to other crises and stresses, and serious students must study the situations that concern them. These comparisons are meant to stimulate thoughts and comparisons on issues of broader perspective, such as the similarity of our reactions to many experiences in life.

SIMULTANEOUS AND CYCLICAL GDSs AND ADULT DEVELOPMENT

The emphasis throughout this book has been on single sequences of GDSs—involving either an individual in one experience only, or an actual group or the individual members of an actual group in that GDS experience only. From the practical point of view of identifying and working with GDSs, such an approach is usually appropriate. But this will not always be so, since at times GDS phenomena from another GDS experience may interact significantly with GDS phenomena in a current experience.

Table 7.2.   Isomorphism in GDSs and other sequential reactions

Sequence	Type of beginning	Start	....................Stages....................			.........End
GDS	Favorable, desired; avoidable, anticipated, not abrupt.	(Positive) Orientation	Dissatisfaction	Resolution	Production	Termination
-GDS*	Coerced; may be avoidable; not usually severely negative.	Negative Orientation	Dissatisfaction	Resolution	Production	Termination
Crisis	Coerced; not easily avoided; severe, often abrupt.	Impact, Shock	Recoil, Increasing turmoil	Mobilization of Resources	Reconstruction (If fails, Disorganization)	(Usually gradual ending)
General Adaptation Syndrome	Coerced; not easily avoided if at all; severe, often abrupt.	Alarm Reaction		Stage of Resistance	(If fails, Stage of Exhaustion)	(Usually ends gradually, can lead to disease and death)
Death, Dying	Coerced; not avoidable; severe, often abrupt.	Shock, Denial	Bargaining	Grief and Depression	Acceptance	Decathexis and Death

*-GDS: A GDS sequence beginning with a negative orientation stage.

For example, the dissatisfaction stage in a job may be seriously aggravated because the individual is having dissatisfaction stage or termination stage difficulties in a nonwork area, such as a personal relationship. The legal intern and student nurse learning groups I have worked with have more difficulty with their termination stage if they happen to be graduating at that time, that is, if they are also facing the termination stage from law school or nursing education.

Important GDS sequences may also follow each other in a cyclical manner. Common examples are one job following another, one personal relationship following another, or one psychotherapeutic experience following another, such as when patients are transferred to another therapist or from individual to group therapy or the reverse. We have already seen how unfinished business from one experience, or an inadequately handled termination stage, may interfere with and influence the next experience's orientation stage. Similarly, anticipation of the next orientation stage influences the current termination stage.

None of this implies that unpleasant GDS effects in one experience will be avoided if a person is in a highly positive stage of some other GDS experience. Any meaningful experience one is in has a high degree of GDS independence from other experiences, and only other very potent GDS experiences are apt to override an experience altogether.

It is probably also true that other negative GDS effects are more important in this regard than other positive effects. For example, good feelings in orientation might be overwhelmed by another experience's very difficult termination stage, but an experience's even moderate dissatisfaction stage will not likely be covered up except by the most highly positive of other GDS experiences, for example, perhaps the orientation stage of a new marriage or new parenthood.

This discussion offers a bridge to material on adult development, which will now be briefly discussed.

GDSs and Adult Passages, Seasons, and Transformations

In recent years a number of related books on adult development have variously emphasized stages and crises in this development. The best known of these, *Passages,* by Gail Sheehy (1976), is conceptually related to two other books, *The Seasons of a Man's Life* (Levinson et al., 1978) and *Transformations* (Gould, 1978). In a similar mode, but with less emphasis on stages, is *Adaptation to Life* (Vaillant, 1977). What is the relationship between GDSs and this adult development? Is there any relationship?

Our primary focuses are very different. These authors emphasize individual adult character or personality development through whatever vicissitudes it takes, usually with certain predictable sequences. My primary focus is on a group or individual going through a specific experience and looking for whatever developmental stages can be found related to this experience. Most of the time, therefore, our focuses are separate, but at certain times they may well be expected to overlap, although the hard data for this are yet to be collected. If there is a GDS sequence for a major area of life, such as marriage or a particular job, this will interact with and influence adult developmental changes, and conversely, adult developmental changes will interact with and influence GDS phenomena.

If during a more disruptive adult period (a "passage," "transformation," or "transition") a person seeks a new job, it may well be that the person will have higher expectations (in the orientation stage) from that job, and may hope that it will provide not only income and work satisfaction, but also deeper human gratification for some of the personality disruption.

Such an "inflation of expectations" makes a pronounced dissatisfaction stage all the more likely, and the resolution stage usually more difficult. Or, some of the usual fluctuation in morale during a long production stage will be more difficult to manage during a more unsteady adult developmental period. Likewise, the termination stage from a job will be handled less effectively during a time in life that is being viewed as a largely unsuccessful period. On the other hand, if this termination stage occurred after a time in life that was viewed successfully, and if one were looking eagerly to the next adult developmental level, then the job termination stage would also have a better chance of being viewed positively, for example, as the culmination of a job well done and a step into a promotion, or into well-deserved and prepared for retirement.

GDSs in other areas of life could also be examined for examples. It is not completely idle speculation to wonder if various growth, encounter, and perhaps training groups are more likely entered at times when adult development is in a more disruptive, unsteady state. Again this would exaggerate expectations in the orientation stage and probably contribute to more difficulties in the dissatisfaction stage. The examples of interaction between adult development and GDSs could be expanded endlessly, but I will leave this to your imagination.

One additional comment before leaving this section: Earlier, Erikson's (1963) developmental sequence over the life cycle was used to draw comparisons with GDSs and to attempt to add some understanding to them. Other developmental sequences might have been used, such as Levinson's (1978), but Erikson's are better known and more congruent with the other theoretical speculations on GDSs.

Final Comments

A number of additional areas could be investigated. Among such items are those on individual characteristics. For example, who are the people especially prone to join a variety of new experiences, and what happens to such "high joiners" during the experience? What types of people are prone to drop out of experiences? Among other items of interest are questions about whether some psychiatric treatment "innovations" are really attempts to deal with staff group demoralization, either in the dissatisfaction stage or in a difficult production stage, for example, with chronic relapsing patients such as alcoholic or schizophrenic patients. And what of the developmental sequence—or sequences—for members of the proliferation of religious cults? Are there any GDS surprises? At this writing, post-Jonestown, this is an area of much interest, and data to answer these questions will soon be readily available. Besides work on all of these issues, it would be especially instructive to have a body of research addressing the question of whether or not the use of GDS material, or similar concepts, increases productivity and participant satisfaction.

Well, it's good to leave some work for the future. It's been a good experience. I leave it with pleasant sorrow. Good-bye.

APPENDIX

PERSONAL GDS USE

If you, the reader, are like me, you look for whatever personal applications you can find in the material you read. Although this is not meant to be a self-help book in the usual sense of that term, personal use of this material is quite feasible, and I want to make some suggestions for doing so.

This material can probably be applied most easily to actual groups that you may be in, such as a committee or work group. Some readers may not be in actual groups to which this material can be applied appropriately, but we are all in many conceptual groups, some of which are better suited to GDS applications than others. One such area you can consider is your job, or your schooling if you are a student. Think of the overall experience in GDS terms. Begin by specifying the conceptual group to consider, the leader or leaders, when the experience started, and when it is expected to end. Identify the stage you are in now. This exercise is most useful if you are in or about to begin the orientation stage, but it can also be helpful in other stages, especially dissatisfaction.

Whatever stage you are in now, go back mentally to the orientation stage of the experience you are examining in GDS terms. Specify as well as possible, preferably on paper, each of your goals for the experience, including social-emotional goals of a personal, intermember, and member-to-leader nature, and task or work goals, and the skills required to be able to complete the task and achieve the goals. If a goal is considered, jot it down, up to a reasonable number of goals. Then for each goal specify the worst possible and best possible outcomes, being sure at this time not to restrain your fantasies unnecessarily in regard to such outcomes, or in regard to goals. (A format for doing this follows this section.)

If you find that the number of goals is unmanageable, the most important of each of various types of goals may be adequate, that is, task goals, and goals of a personal, intermember, and member-to-leader nature. But also include unrealistic goals or some of these later, since failure in accomplishing them is sure to haunt you later. It may help to specify these goals and outcomes in very concrete terms, though they can also be specified in general terms, for example, not only to become an engineer, or lawyer, but also to pass a particularly difficult course, or not only to have a job that is enjoyed, but also to earn enough money to buy certain items, to work near your home, and so on. And in terms of best and worst and expected outcomes, be as specific as citing your anticipated earned salary, and whether you hope to gain close male or female friends on the job.

You should gather whatever factual data you need to do this exercise, according to how important the goals are and how much work is required to obtain the data. At the very least your information should not be left to vague rumors. In school courses you can get some idea of the pass/fail rate, the required work, what you can expect to learn, and so forth, and in jobs, the salary scales, rates and routes of promotion, and work required.

After you have taken these steps for the orientation stage, you should do the same for the dissatisfaction stage, if you are at that stage or if you have passed it. This will help you specify appropriate goals more carefully, perhaps adding new ones, revising skill needs, and determining reasonable outcomes. Such steps, with occasional review of what you have written, additional factual information, and assessing what you have accomplished so far on your goals, should get you through to resolution and production. Don't ignore any accomplishments you may not have been expecting.

In the dissatisfaction, resolution, and production stages, you may find that even though the experience seems boring or frustrating or demoralizing, when your accomplishments are actually examined they are much more significant than you would have thought. Such a realization can help bolster your morale. With longer GDS sequences, repeat reviews during production may well be necessary, and you may have to update your goals and skills, and reassess your accomplishments.

Then for termination, and preferably before it is imminent, the overall achievements of the experience should be reviewed. Again you should consider not only the task achievements (skills learned, salary, etc.), but also the social-emotional achievements (friends acquired, confidence gained, etc.). Do not ignore anything gained even if you had not expected it. Then what is going to be lost by leaving the experience should be carefully considered, and you should try to gauge how you are apt to react. Are losses particularly difficult to handle? Are they manageable? What is your experience in previous similar situations? You should then consider the anticipated gains from the next experience—your next job or move, for example— being careful to make these estimates as reasonable as possible and not to distort them in either a negative or positive direction: "My new job is going to be such a treat!"

At this time, before a decision is made to leave an experience and start a new one, it may be helpful to construct a Comparison Balance Sheet and to compare the two experiences. This can be done by dividing a large sheet of paper into gain and loss columns, and then dividing the sheet in half crosswise so that gains and losses in the current experience can be compared with reasonably expected gains and losses in the next experience. Some of these can be directly compared, for example, salary and living conditions. Others are not easily compared, for example, known pleasant working conditions versus relatively unknown working conditions. It often helps to rank the gains and losses from most to least important to help in this comparison. (Such a Comparison Balance Sheet is shown at the end of this section.)

After carefully considering these various aspects of termination, it may be feasible to decide to stay in the current experience, that is, not terminate, and such an exercise can help you make the decision. At other times (job relocation, forced retirement, graduation from college), there is little reasonable choice, and the above exercise then helps to put termination and the new orientation in proper perspective, along with one's feelings and reactions to this situation.

Such a careful examination in itself usually helps considerably with termination, including helping to identify termination work that must be done; what must be done to complete the task, to whom do I need to say goodbye, how can I make the losses—personal and more impersonal—more tolerable.

Goals in the_____stage

(Complete at least for orientation, dissatisfaction, and termination.)

Goals	Worst Possible Outcome	Reasonable Expected Outcome	Best Possible Outcome
Task			
A) General			
1.			
2.			
3.			
B) Skills Required			
1.			
2.			
3.			
Social-Emotional			
A) Personal			
1.			
2.			
3.			
B) In Relation to Leader			
1.			
2.			
3.			
C) In Relation to Other Members			
1.			
2.			
3.			

Comparison Balance Sheet:

If you continue the current experience

Gains	*Losses*
	(Consider also the expected gains from the anticipated experience.)

If you take the anticipated new experience

Gains	*Losses*
	(Consider also the expected gains if you stay in the current experience.)

My Goals in the Legal Clinic

Date: _____ Name: _____

Below are listed various goals that you may or may not be hoping to accomplish while you are an intern in the legal clinic. Check the appropriate column for each goal, and add additional ones you may have. (Leave the columns on the right blank; we will return to these later in the semester.)

	This is one of my goals			Extent the goal was achieved		
	Yes	No	Un-sure	Not achieved	Average achieved	Well achieved
1. Learn the way courts work.				1 2 3 4 5		
2. Get experience in the practice of law.				1 2 3 4 5		
3. Get experience in working with clients.				1 2 3 4 5		
4. Avoid exams.				1 2 3 4 5		
5. Get some trial experience.				1 2 3 4 5		
6. Be able to put clinical experience on resume.				1 2 3 4 5		
7. Get a case that goes to the appellate court.				1 2 3 4 5		
8. Gain confidence in working with clients.				1 2 3 4 5		
9. Gain confidence in the practice of law.				1 2 3 4 5		
10. Learn the ethical practice of law.				1 2 3 4 5		
11. Provide a service to clients.				1 2 3 4 5		
12. Avoid the drudgery of constant law books.				1 2 3 4 5		
13. See what type of law I would like to practice.				1 2 3 4 5		
14. See if I would like to practice law.				1 2 3 4 5		
15. Get experience working with other attorneys.				1 2 3 4 5		
16. Other (list) _____				1 2 3 4 5		
17. Other (list) _____				1 2 3 4 5		
18. Other (list) _____				1 2 3 4 5		

Now take all the goals you checked *Yes*, and number them from most important (1) to least important.

REFERENCES

Abrahams, J.: Group psychotherapy: Implications for direction and supervision of mentally ill patients. In T. Muller (Ed.), *Mental health in nursing.* Washington, DC: Catholic University Press, 1949.

Abramson, L. W., Moss, G. W.: Law school deans: A self-portrait. *Journal of Legal Education,* 1977, *29,* 6–30.

Akehurst, A. C.: Post-mastectomy morale. *Lancet,* 1972, *2,* 181–182.

Alexander, L.: Morale and leadership. In I. Galdston (Ed.), *Panic and morale.* New York: International Universities Press, 1958.

Anderson, R. C.: Learning in discussions: A resume of the authoritarian-democratic studies. *Harvard Educational Review,* 1959, *29,* 201–215.

Anthony, E. J.: The generic elements in dyadic and in group psychotherapy. *International Journal of Group Psychotherapy,* 1967, *17,* 57–70.

Appelbaum, S. A.: The pleasure and reality principles in group process teaching. *British Journal of Medical Psychology,* 1963, *36,* 49–56.

Appelbaum, S. A.: *Out in inner space.* Garden City, NY: Anchor Press/Doubleday, 1979.

Argyle, M.: *The social psychology of work.* New York: Taplinger Publishing, 1972.

Arsenian, J., Semrad, E. V., Shapiro, D.: An analysis of integral functions in small groups. *International Journal of Group Psychotherapy,* 1962, *12,* 421–434.

Austin, D. M.: Goals for gang workers. *Social Work,* 1957, *2,* 43–50.

Babad, E. Y., Amir, L.: Bennis and Shepard's theory of group development: An empirical examination. *Small Group Behavior,* 1978, *9,* 477–492.

Baehr, M. E., Renck, R.: The definition and measurement of employee morale. *Administrative Science Quarterly,* 1958, *3,* 157–184.

Baldridge, J. V., Deal, T. E., Ancell, M. Z. (Eds.): *Managing change in educational organizations: Sociological perspectives, strategies, and case studies.* Berkeley: McCutchan, 1975.

Bales, R. F.: *Interaction process analysis: A method for the study of small groups.* Cambridge, MA: Addison-Wesley Press, 1950.

Bales, R. F.: Some uniformities of behavior in small groups. In G. E. Swanson, T. M. Newcomb, E. L. Hartley (Eds.), *Readings in social psychology.* New York: Henry Holt, 1952.

Bales, R. F.: *Personality and interpersonal behavior.* New York: Holt, Rinehart and Winston, 1970.

Bales, R. F., Strodtbeck, F. L.: Phases in group problem-solving. *Journal of Abnormal Social Psychology,* 1951, *46,* 485–495.

Banet, A. G.: Yin/Yang: A perspective on theories of group development. In J. W. Pfeiffer, J. E. Jones (Eds.), *The 1976 annual handbook for group facilitators.* La Jolla, CA: University Associates, 1976.

Bany, M. A., Johnson, L. V.: *Classroom group behavior: Group dynamics in education.* New York: Macmillan, 1964.

Beck, A. T.: *Depression: Clinical, experimental and theoretical aspects.* New York: Harper and Row, 1967.

Bednar, R. L., Battersby, C. P.: The effects of specific cognitive structure on early group development. *Journal of Applied Behavioral Science,* 1976, *12,* 513–522.

Benedek T.: The psychosomatic implications of the primary unit: Mother-child. *American Journal of Orthopsychiatry,* 1949, *19,* 642–654.

Bennis, W. G.: Patterns and vicissitudes in T-group development. In L. P. Bradford, J. R. Gibb, K. D. Benne (Eds.), *T-group theory and laboratory method.* New York: John Wiley and Sons, 1964.

Bennis, W. G.: Toward a genetic theory of group development. *Journal of Group Psychoanalysis and Process,* 1968, *1,* 23–35.

Bennis, W. G., Benne, K. D., Chin, R. (Eds.): *The planning of change* (2nd ed.). New York: Holt, Rinehart and Winston, 1969.

Bennis, W. G., Shepard, H. A.: A theory of group development. *Human Relations,* 1956, *9,* 415–437.

Benoit-Guilbot, O.: The sociology of work. In D. L. Sills (Ed.), *International Encyclopedia of the Social Sciences* (Vol. 7). New York: Macmillan, and The Free Press, 1968.

Berger, D. M.: The multidiscipline patient care conference: Learning in groups. *Canadian Psychiatric Association Journal,* 1976, *21,* 135–139.

Berkowitz, B.: Stages of group development in a mental health team. *Psychiatric Quarterly,* 1974, *48,* 1–11.

Bertalanffy, L., von: General system theory and psychiatry. In S. Arieti (Ed.), *American handbook of psychiatry* (Rev. ed., Vol. 1). New York: Basic Books, 1974.

Bibring, E.: The mechanism of depression. In P. Greenacre (Ed.), *Affective Disorders: Psychoanalytic contributions to their study.* New York: International Universities Press, 1953.

Binder, J. L.: A method for small group training of psychiatric ward staff. *Psychiatry,* 1976, *39,* 364–375.

Bion, W. R.: *Experiences in groups.* New York: Basic Books, 1961.

Blocker, C. E., Richardson, R. C.: Twenty-five years of morale research: A critical review. *Journal of Educational Sociology,* 1963, *36,* 200–210.

Blos, P.: *On adolescence: A psychoanalytic interpretation.* New York: The Free Press, 1962.

Bonney, W. C.: Group counselling and developmental processes. In G. M. Gazda (Ed.), *Theories and methods of group counselling in the schools.* Springfield, IL: Charles C. Thomas, 1969.

Bonney, W. C.: The maturation of groups. *Small Group Behavior,* 1974, *5,* 445–461.

Bonney, W. C.; Group counselling and developmental processes. In G. M. Gazda (Ed.), *Theories and methods of group counselling in the schools* (2nd ed.). Springfield, IL: Charles C. Thomas, 1976.

Boris, H. N.: On hope: Its nature and psychotherapy. *International Review of Psycho-Analysis,* 1976, *3,* 139–150.

Bowers, D. G.: OD techniques and their results in twenty-three organizations. *Journal of Applied Behavioral Science,* 1973, *9,* 21–43.

Bowlby, J.: *Maternal care and mental health* (2nd ed.). Geneva: World Health Organization, 1952.

Braaten, L. J.: Developmental phases of encounter groups and related intensive groups. *Interpersonal Development,* 1974–1975, *5,* 112–129.

Bradford, L. P.: Membership and the learning process. In L. P. Bradford, J. R. Gibb, K. D. Benne (Eds.), *T-group theory and laboratory method.* New York: John Wiley and Sons, 1964.

Bradford, L. P.: Group formation and development. In L. P. Bradford (Ed.), *Group development* (2nd ed.). La Jolla, CA: University Associates, 1978.

Bugen, L. A.: Composition and orientation effects on group cohesion. *Psychological Reports,* 1977, *40,* 175–181.

Burke, W. W. (Ed.): *Current issues and strategies in organization development.* New York: Human Sciences Press, 1977.

Buros, O. K. (Ed.): *The third mental measurements yearbook.* Highland Park, NJ: Gryphon Press, 1949.

Buros, O. K. (Ed.): *Personality tests and reviews.* Highland Park, NJ: Gryphon Press, 1970.

Buros, O. K. (Ed.): *The seventh mental measurements yearbook.* Highland Park, NJ: Gryphon Press, 1972.

Button, L.: *Developmental group work with adolescents.* New York: Halsted, 1974.

Caplan, G.: *Principles of preventive psychiatry.* New York: Basic Books, 1964.

Caple, R. B.: The sequential stages of group development. *Small Group Behavior,* 1978, *9,* 470–476.

Carter, J.: *Why not the best?* New York: Bantam Books, 1975.

Cartwright, D., Zander, A. (Eds.): *Group dynamics: Research and theory* (2nd ed.). Evanston, IL: Row, Peterson, 1960.

Charrier, G. O.: Cog's ladder: A model of group growth. *SAM Advanced Management Journal,* 1972, *January,* 30–37.

Charrier, G. O.: Cog's ladder: A model of group development. In J. W. Pfeiffer, J. E. Jones (Eds.), *The 1974 handbook for group facilitators.* La Jolla, CA: University Associates Publishers, 1974.

Charrier, G. O.: Cog's ladder: A process observation activity. In J. W. Pfeiffer, J. E. Jones (Eds.), *The 1974 handbook for group facilitators.* La Jolla, CA: University Associates Publishers, 1974.

Child, I.L.: Morale: A bibliographical review. *Psychological Bulletin,* 1941, *38,* 393–420.

Cohen, A. I.: Process in T-groups: Some observations. *Journal of Contemporary Psychotherapy,* 1971, *3,* 127–130.

Colman, A. D.: Group consciousness as a developmental phase. In A. D. Colman, W. H. Bexton (Eds.), *Group relations reader.* Sausalito, CA: GREX, 1975.

Comrey, A. L., Backer, T. E., Glaser, E. M.: *A sourcebook for mental health measures.* Los Angeles: Human Interaction Research Institute, 1973.

Connaughton, J. P.: A psychiatrist's observations of a school in crisis. *Hospital and Community Psychiatry,* 1971, *22,* 265–269.

Coombs, R. H.: *Mastering medicine: Professional socialization in medical school.* New York: The Free Press, 1978.

Cooper, C. L. (Ed.): *Theories of group processes.* New York: John Wiley and Sons, 1975.

Cooper, C. L., Mangham, I. L. (Eds.): *T-groups: A survey of research.* New York: John Wiley and Sons, 1971.

Crews, C. Y., Melnick, J.: Use of initial and delayed structure in facilitating group development. *Journal of Counselling Psychology,* 1976, *23,* 92–98.

Crocker, J. W., Wroblewski, M.: Using recreational games in counselling. *Personnel Guidance Journal,* 1975, *53,* 453–458.

Cronin, T. E., Thomas, N. C.: Federal advisory processes: Advice and discontent. *Science,* 1971, *171,* 771–779.

Crowfoot, J. E.: Comment on the preceding article: Comparing and developing theories of training. *Journal of Applied Behavioral Science,* 1971, *7,* 684–688.

Culbert, S. A.: Accelerating laboratory learning through a phase progression model for trainer intervention. *Journal of Applied Behavioral Science,* 1970, *6,* 21–38.

Culbert, S. A.: Accelerating participant learning. In W. G. Dyer (Ed.), *Modern theory and method in group training.* New York: Van Nostrand Reinhold, 1972.

Dale, E.: *Planning and developing the company organization structure.* AMA Research Report 20. New York: American Management Association, 1952.

Davies, J. C.: The J-curve of rising and declining satisfactions as a cause of some great revolutions and a contained rebellion. In H. D. Graham, T. R. Gurr (Eds.), *Violence in America* (Vol. 2). Washington, DC: US Government Printing Office, 1969.

Day, M.: The natural history of training groups. *International Journal of Group Psychotherapy,* 1967, *17,* 436–446.

Dell, P. F., Sheely, M. D., Pulliam, G. P., et al.: Family therapy process in a family therapy seminar. *Journal of Marriage and Family Counselling,* 1977, *April,* 43–48.

Deutsch, M.: Group behavior. In D. L. Sills (Ed.), *International encyclopedia of the social sciences* (Vol. 7). New York: Macmillan, and The Free Press, 1968.

Dinges, N. G., Weigel, R. G.: The marathon group: A review of practice and research. *Comparative Group Studies,* 1971, *November,* 339–360.

Dohrenwend, B. S., Dohrenwend, B. P. (Eds.), *Stressful life events: Their nature and effects.* New York: John Wiley and Sons, 1974.

Dolgoff, T.: Small groups and organizations: Time, task and sentient boundaries. *General Systems,* 1975, *20,* 135–141.

Dollard, J., Doob, L. W., Miller, N. E., et al.: *Frustration and aggression.* New Haven: Yale University Press, 1939.

Doverspike, J. E.: Group and individual goals: Their development and utilization. *Educational Technology,* 1973, *13,* 24–26.

Drum, D. J., Knott, J. E.: *Structured groups for facilitating development: Acquiring life skills, resolving life themes, and making life transitions.* New York: Human Sciences Press, 1977.

Dubin, R.: Workers. In D. L. Sills (Ed.), *International encyclopedia of the social sciences* (Vol. 16). New York: Macmillan, and The Free Press, 1968.

Dunphy, D. C.: Social change in self-analytic groups. In P. Stone, D. C. Dunphy, M. Smith, et al. (Eds.), *The general inquirer: A computer approach to content analysis.* Cambridge, MA: MIT Press, 1966.

Dunphy, D. C.: Phases, roles, and myths in self-analytic groups. *Applied Behavioral Science,* 1968, *4,* 195–224.

Dyer, W. G. (Ed.), *Modern theory and method in group training.* New York, Van Nostrand Reinhold, 1972.

English, H. B., English, A. C.: *A comprehensive dictionary of psychological and psychoanalytical terms.* New York: Longmans Green, 1958.

Engs, W. D.: Improving the performance of citizens committees. *Journal of Forestry,* 1976, *January,* 18–20.

Erikson, E.: *Childhood and society* (2nd ed.). New York: W. W. Norton, 1963.

Estes, R.: Determinants of differential stress levels among university students. *Journal of the American College Health Association,* 1973, *21,* 470–476.

Falck, H. S.: The old comes before the new: Reflections on coming and going. Multilith. Topeka, KS: Menninger Foundation, 1976.

Farrell, M. P.: Patterns in the development of self-analytic groups. *Journal of Applied Behavioral Science,* 1976, *12,* 523–542.

Feierabend, I. K., Feierabend, R. L., Nesvold, B.: Social change and political violence: Cross-national patterns. In H. D. Graham, T. R. Gurr (Eds.), *Violence in America* (Vol. 2). Washington, DC: US Government Printing Office, 1969.

Feron, J.: A Warsaw puzzle: Abrupt attempt to raise prices of food is regarded as an economic gamble. *New York Times,* June 29, 1976, p. 6.

Flack, F. F.: Group approaches in medical education. In H. I. Kaplan, B. J. Sadock (Eds.), *Comprehensive group psychotherapy.* Baltimore: Williams and Wilkins, 1971.

Foley, W. J., Bonney, W. C.: A developmental model for counselling groups. *Personnel Guidance Journal,* 1966, *February,* 576–580.

Foulkes, S. H., Anthony, E. J.: *Group psychotherapy: The psycho-analytic approach.* London: Penguin Books, 1957.

Franck, M.: Phases of development of a multinational training group. *Comparative Group Studies,* 1972, *3,* 3–50.

Frank, J. D.: Psychotherapy: The restoration of morale. *American Journal of Psychiatry,* 1974, *131,* 271–274.

Freud, A.: *The ego and the mechanisms of defence.* New York: International Universities Press, 1946.

Freud, S.: *The interpretation of dreams.* In J. Strachey (Ed.), *The standard edition of the complete psychological works of Sigmund Freud* (Vols. 4, 5). London: Hogarth, 1953 (originally published 1900).

Freud, S.: *Group psychology and the analysis of the ego.* In J. Strachey (Ed.), *The standard edition of the complete psychological works of Sigmund Freud* (Vol. 18). London: Hogarth, 1955 (originally published 1921).

Freud, S.: An outline of psychoanalysis. In J. Strachey (Ed.), *The standard edition of the complete psychological works of Sigmund Freud* (Vol. 23). London: Hogarth, 1964 (originally published 1940).

Freudenberger, H. J.: *The staff burnout syndrome.* Washington, DC: Drug Abuse Council, 1975.

Galdston, I. (Ed.): *Panic and morale.* New York: International Universities Press, 1958.

Gardner, J. W.: *Morale.* New York: W. W. Norton, 1978.

Garland, J. A., Frey, L. A.: Applications of stages of group development to groups in psychiatric settings. In S. Bernstein (Ed.), *Further explorations in group work.* Boston: Boston University School of Social Work, 1970.

Garland, J. A., Jones, H. E., Kolodny, R. L: A model for stages of development in social work groups. In S. Bernstein (Ed.), *Explorations in group work: Essays in theory and practice.* Boston: Boston University School of Social Work, 1965.

Gazda, G. M.: Group counselling: A developmental approach. In G. M. Gazda (Ed.), *Basic approaches to group psychotherapy and group counselling* (2nd ed.). Springfield, IL: Charles C. Thomas, 1975.

Gazda, G. M.: Group counselling: A developmental approach. In G. M. Gazda (Ed.), *Theories and methods of group counselling in the schools* (2nd ed.). Springfield, IL: Charles C. Thomas, 1976.

Gellerman, S. W.: *Motivation and productivity.* New York: American Management Association, 1963.

Gendlin, E. T., Beebe, J.: Experiential groups: Introductions for groups. In G. M. Gazda (Ed.), *Innovations to group psychotherapy.* Springfield, IL: Charles C. Thomas, 1968.

Gibb, J. R.: Climate for trust formation. In L. P. Bradford, J. R. Gibb, K. D. Benne (Eds.), *T-group theory and laboratory method.* New York: John Wiley and Sons, 1964.

Gibbard, G. S., Hartman, J. J.: The oedipal paradigm in group development: A clinical and empirical study. *Small Group Behavior,* 1973, *4,* 305–353.

Gibbard, G. S., Hartman, J. J., Mann, R. D. (Eds.), *Analysis of groups.* San Francisco: Jossey-Bass Publishers, 1974.

Gibbard, G. S., Hartman, J. J., Mann, R. D.: Group process and development. In G. S. Gibbard, J. J. Hartman, R. D. Mann (Eds.), *Analysis of groups.* San Francisco: Jossey-Bass Publishers, 1974.

Golembiewski, R. T.: Small groups and large organizations. In J. G. March (Ed.), *Handbook of organizations.* Chicago: Rand McNally, 1965.

Gould, R. L.: *Transformations: Growth and change in adult life.* New York: Simon and Schuster, 1978.

Greenwood, G. E., Soar, R. S.: Some relationships between teacher morale and teacher behavior. *Journal of Educational Psychology,* 1973, *64,* 105–108.

Guion, R. M.: The problem of terminology. *Personnel Psychology,* 1958, *11,* 59–64.

Gunderson, E. K. E., Rahe, R. H. (Eds.), *Life stress and illness.* Springfield, IL: Charles C. Thomas, 1974.

Hare, A. P.: *Handbook of small group research.* New York: The Free Press of Glencoe, 1962.

Hare, A. P.: A review of small group research for group therapists. *International Journal of Group Psychotherapy,* 1963, *13,* 476–484.

Hare, A. P.: Small group development in the relay assembly testroom. *Sociol Inquiry,* 1967, *37,* 169–182.

Hare, A. P.: Phases in the development of the Bicol Development Planning Board. In S. Wells, A. P. Hare (Eds.), *Studies in regional development.* Legazpi City, Philippines: Bicol Development Planning Board, 1968.

Hare, A. P.: Theories of group development and categories for interaction analysis. *Small Group Behavior,* 1973, *4,* 259–303.

Hare, A. P.: *Handbook of small group research* (2nd ed.). New York: The Free Press, 1976.

Hartman, J. J., Gibbard, G. S.: Anxiety, boundary evolution and social change. In G. S. Gibbard, J. J. Hartman, R. D. Mann (Eds.), *Analysis of groups.* San Francisco: Jossey-Bass Publishers, 1974.

Hartmann, H.: *Ego psychology and the problem of adaptation.* New York: International Universities Press, 1958.

Harvey, O. J., Hunt, D. E., Schroder, H. M.: *Conceptual systems and personality organization.* New York: John Wiley and Sons, 1961.

Heinicke, C., Bales, R. F.: Developmental trends in the structure of small groups. *Sociometry,* 1953, *16,* 7–38.

Hendrickson, G.: High school morale and humanistic psychology. *Journal of Humanistic Psychology,* 1973, *13,* 69–75.

Herzberg, F., Mausner, B., Snyderman, B. B.: *The motivation to work.* New York: John Wiley and Sons, 1959.

Heyns, R. W., Zander, A. F.: Observation in group behavior. In L. Festinger, D. Katz (Eds.), *Research methods in the behavioral sciences.* New York: Dryden Press, 1953.

Hill, W. F.: *HIM: Hill interaction matrix* (Rev. ed.). Los Angeles: Youth Study Center, University of Southern California, 1965.

Hill, W. F.: Systematic group development—SGD therapy. In A. Jacobs, W. W. Spradlin (Eds.), *The group as agent of change.* New York: Behavioral Publications, 1974.

Hill, W. F.: Hill interaction matrix (HIM): The conceptual framework, derived rating scales, and an updated bibliography. *Small Group Behavior,* 1977, *8,* 251–268.

Hill, W. F., Gruner, L.: A study of development in open and closed groups. *Small Group Behavior,* 1973, *4,* 355–381.

Hinsie, L. E., Campbell, R. J.: *Psychiatric dictionary* (3rd ed.). New York: Oxford University Press, 1960.

Hinsie, L. E., Campbell, R. J.: *Psychiatric Dictionary* (4th ed.). New York: Oxford University Press, 1970.

Hoch, E. L., Kaufer, G.: A process analysis of transient therapy groups. *International Journal of Group Psychotherapy,* 1955, *5,* 415–421.

Hollomon, J. H.: How to close the gap in down-to-earth technology. *Fortune,* 1978, *May 22,* 121–123.

Holmes, T. H., Rahe, R. H.: The social readjustment rating scale. *Journal of Psychosomatic Research,* 1967, *11,* 213–218.

Holt, R. R.: Personality growth in psychiatric residents. *AMA Archives of Neurology and Psychiatry,* 1959, *81,* 203–215.

Horwitz, L.: Training groups for psychiatric residents. *International Journal of Group Psychotherapy,* 1967, *17,* 421–435.

Horwitz, L.: Readers' forum. *International Journal of Group Psychotherapy,* 1978, *28,* 560.

Husband, D., Scheunemann, H. R.: The use of group process in teaching termination. *Child Welfare,* 1972, *51,* 505–513.

Ivancevich, J. M.: A study of a cognitive training program: Trainer styles and group development. *Academy Management Journal,* 1974, *17,* 428–439.

Ivancevich, J. M., McMahon, J. T.: Group development, trainer style and carry-over job satisfaction and performance. *Academy Management Journal,* 1976, *19,* 395–412.

Janis, I. L., Mann, L.: Coping with decisional conflict. *American Scientist,* 1976, *64,* 657–667.

Janis, I. L., Mann, L.: *Decision making: A psychological analysis of conflict, choice and commitment.* New York: The Free Press, 1977.

Jaques, E.: Social systems as a defence against persecutory and depressive anxiety. In M. Klein, P. Heimann, R. E. Money-Kyrle (Eds.), *New directions in psychoanalysis.* New York: Basic Books, 1955.

Johnson, J. A.: *Group therapy: A practical approach.* New York: McGraw-Hill Book Company, 1963.

Jones, J. E.: A model of group development. In J. E. Jones, J. W. Pfeiffer (Eds.), *The 1973 annual handbook for group facilitators.* Iowa City, IA: University Associates, 1973.

Jordan, N., Jensen, B. T., Terebinsky, S. J.: The development of cooperation among three-man crews in a simulated man-machine information processing system. *Journal of Social Psychology,* 1963, *59,* 175–184.

Kaplan, S. R.: Therapy groups and training groups: Similarities and differences. *International Journal of Group Psychotherapy,* 1967, *17,* 473–504.

Kaplan, S. R.: Characteristic phases of development in organizations. In D. S. Milman, G. D. Goldman (Eds.), *Group process today: Evaluation and perspective.* Springfield, IL: Charles C. Thomas, 1974.

Kaplan, S. R., Roman M.: Phases of development in an adult therapy group. *International Journal of Group Psychotherapy,* 1963, *13,* 10–26.

Katzell, R. A.: Measurement of morale. *Personnel Psychology,* 1958, *11,* 71–78.

Kauff, P. F.: The termination process: Its relationship to the separation-individuation phase of development. *International Journal of Group Psychotherapy,* 1977, *27,* 3–18.

Kernberg, O. F.: *Object-relations theory and clinical psychoanalysis.* New York: Jason Aronson, 1976.

Kerr, S., Schriesheim, C.: Consideration, initiating structure, and organizational criteria—An update of Korman's 1966 review. *Personnel Psychology,* 1974, *27,* 555–568.

King, P. D.: Life cycle in the "Tavistock" study group. *Perspectives in Psychiatric Care,* 1975, *13,* 180–184.

Kingdom, D. R.: *Matrix organization: Managing information technologies.* London: Tavistock, 1973.

Kiresuk, T. J., Garwick, G.: *Program evaluation project report 1969–73: Basic goal attainment procedures* (2nd ed.). Washington, DC: National Institute of Mental Health, 1975.

Kiresuk, T. J., Sherman, R.: Goal attainment scaling: A general method for evaluating comprehensive mental health programs. *Community Mental Health Journal,* 1968, *4,* 443–453.

Kissen, M. (Ed.): *From group dynamics to group psychoanalysis: Therapeutic applications of group dynamics understanding.* Washington, DC: Hemisphere Publishing, 1976.

Klein, E. B., Astrachan, B. M.: Learning in groups: A comparison of study groups and T-groups. *Journal of Applied Behavioral Science,* 1971, *7,* 659–683.

Klein, M.: *Contributions to psycho-analysis: 1921–1945.* London: Hogarth Press, 1948.

Klein, M.: Our adult world and its roots in infancy. In E. Jaques, B. Joseph (Eds.), *Our adult world and other essays.* New York: Basic Books, 1963.

Klein, S. M., Maher, J. R.: Education level, attitudes, and future expectations among first-level management. *Personnel Psychology*, 1968, *21*, 43–53.

Knight, D. J.: *Developmental stages in T-groups*. Doctoral dissertation. Cincinnati: University of Cincinnati, 1974.

Krain, M.: Communication as a process of dyadic organization and development. *Journal of Communications*, 1973, *23*, 392–408.

Krain, M.: Communication among premarital couples at three stages of dating. *Journal of Marriage and the Family*, 1975, *August*, 609–618.

Kris, E.: *Psychoanalytic explorations in art*. New York: International Universities Press, 1952.

Kubler-Ross, E.: *On death and dying*. New York: Macmillan, 1969.

Lacoursiere, R. B.: A group method to facilitate learning during the stages of a psychiatric affiliation. *International Journal of Group Psychotherapy*, 1974, *24*, 342–351.

Lacoursiere, R. B.: A group method in clinical legal education. *Journal of Legal Education*, 1980 (in press).

Lakin, M., Carson, R. C.: Participant perception of group process in group sensitivity training. *International Journal of Group Psychotherapy*, 1964, *14*, 116–122.

Lawton, M. P.: The Philadelphia geriatric center morale scale: A revision. *Journal of Gerontology*, 1975, *30*, 85–89.

Lazare, A., Eisenthal, S., Wasserman, L.: The customer approach to patienthood: Attending to patient requests in a walk-in clinic. *Archives of General Psychiatry*, 1975, *32*, 553–558.

Leik, R. K., Matthews, M.: A scale for developmental processes. *American Sociological Review*, 1968, *33*, 62–75.

Levin, E. M., Kurtz, R. R.: Structured and nonstructured human relations training. *Journal of Counselling Psychology*, 1974, *21*, 526–531.

Levine, N.: Emotional factors in group development. *Human Relations*, 1971, *24*, 65–89.

Levinson, D. J., Darrow, C. N., Klein, E. B., et al.: *The seasons of a man's life*. New York: Alfred A. Knopf, 1978.

Lewin, K., Lippitt, R., White, R. K.: Patterns of aggressive behavior in experimentally created "social climates." *Journal of Social Psychology*, 1939, *10*, 271–299.

Lewis, B. F.: An examination of the final phase of a group development theory. *Small Group Behavior*, 1978, *9*, 507–517.

Lewis, J. M.: The development of an inpatient adolescent service. *Adolescence*, 1970, *5*, 303–312.

Libo, L.: *Is there life after group?* Garden City, NY: Anchor Press/Doubleday, 1977.

Lieberman, M. A., Yalom, I. D., Miles, M. B.: *Encounter groups: First facts.* New York: Basic Books, 1973.

Long, T. J., Schuerger, J. M., Bosshart, D. A., et al.: Fluctuation in psychological state during two encounter group weekends. *Psychological Report,* 1971, *29,* 267–274.

Lubin, B., Zuckerman, M.: Affective and perceptual-cognitive patterns in sensitivity training groups. *Psychological Reports,* 1967, *21,* 365–376.

Lundgren, D. C.: Trainer style and patterns of group development. *Journal of Applied Behavioral Science,* 1971, *7,* 689–709.

Lundgren, D. C.: Attitudinal and behavioral correlates of emergent status in training groups. *Journal of Social Psychology,* 1973, *90,* 141–153.

Lundgren, D. C.: Developmental trends in the emergence of interpersonal issues in T-groups. *Small Group Behavior,* 1977, *8,* 179–200.

MacDonald, W. S.: Social structure and behavior modification in job corps training. *Perceptual and Motor Skills,* 1967, *24,* 142.

Maher, J. R., Piersol, D. T.: Perceived clarity of individual job objectives and of group mission as correlates of morale. *Journal of Communications,* 1970, *20,* 125–133.

Mahler, C. A.: *Group counselling in the schools.* Boston: Houghton-Mifflin, 1969.

Mahler, M. S.: *On human symbiosis and the vicissitudes of individuation. I. Infantile autism.* New York: International Universities Press, 1968.

Malmo, R. B.: Activation. In A. J. Bachrach (Ed.), *Experimental foundations of clinical psychology.* New York, Basic Books, 1962.

Mahoney, G. A.: Unidimensional scales for the measurement of morale in an industrial situation. *Human Relations,* 1956, *9,* 3–26.

Mann, R. D.: The development of the member-trainer relationship in self-analytic groups. *Human Relations,* 1966, *19,* 84–117.

Mann, R. D.: Winners, losers and the search for equality in groups. In C. L. Cooper (Ed.), *Theories of group processes.* London: John Wiley and Sons, 1975.

Mann, R. D., Arnold, S. M., Binder, J. L., et al.: *The college classroom: Conflict, change and learning.* New York: John Wiley and Sons, 1970.

Mann, R. D., Gibbard, G. S., Hartman, J. J.: *Interpersonal styles and group development: An analysis of the member-leader relationship.* New York: John Wiley and Sons, 1967.

Martin, A. R.: Morale and productivity: A review of the literature. *Public Personnel Review,* 1969, *30,* 42–45.

Martin, E. A., Hill, W. F.: Toward a theory of group development: Six phases of therapy group development. *International Journal of Group Psychotherapy,* 1957, *7,* 20–30.

Maslow, A. H.: *Toward a psychology of being.* New York: Van Nostrand, 1962.

Masterson, J. F.: *Treatment of the borderline adolescent: A developmental approach.* New York: John Wiley and Sons, 1972.

McGee, T. F., Schuman, B. N., Racusen, F.: Termination in group psychotherapy. *American Journal of Psychotherapy,* 1972, *26,* 521–532.

Meerloo, J. A. M.: Mental danger, stress and fear. II. Man and his morale. *Journal of Nervous and Mental Disease,* 1957, *125,* 357–379.

Menninger, K. A.: Civilian morale in time of war and preparation for war. *Bulletin of the Menninger Clinic,* 1941, *5,* 188–194.

Menninger, W. W.: The role of psychiatry in selection and training of peace corps volunteers for overseas duty. *Journal of the National Medical Association,* 1964, *56,* 530–533.

Menninger, W. W.: The meaning of morale: A peace corps model. In D. P. Moynihan et al. (Eds.), *Business and society in change.* New York: American Telephone and Telegraph Company, 1975.

Merton, R. K.: *Social theory and social structure* (Rev. ed.). Chicago: Free Press, 1957.

Miller, J. G.: Living systems: The group. *Behavioral Science,* 1971, *16,* 302–398.

Mills, T. M.: *Group transformation.* Englewood Cliffs, NJ: Prentice-Hall, 1964.

Mills, T. M.: *The sociology of small groups.* Englewood Cliffs, NJ: Prentice-Hall, 1967.

Mintz, E. E.: Time-extended marathon groups. *Psychotherapy Theory Research and Practice,* 1967, *42,* 65–70.

Mitchell, G. H.: Voluntary movers: A study of voluntary movement to a small southwestern community. *Journal of Behavioral Economics,* 1975, *Winter,* 87–102.

Modlin, H. C., Faris, M.: Group adaptation and integration in psychiatric team practice. *Psychiatry,* 1956, *19,* 97–103.

Morris, J. N., Sherwood, S.: A retesting and modification of the Philadelphia geriatric center morale scale. *Journal of Gerontology,* 1975, *30,* 77–84.

Morris, J. N., Wolf, R. S., Klerman, L. V.: Common themes among morale and depression scales. *Journal of Gerontology,* 1975, *30,* 209–215.

Mullan, H., Rosenbaum, M.: *Group psychotherapy: Theory and practice* (2nd ed.). New York: The Free Press, 1978.

Nader, R., Gruenstein, P.: Fans: The sorry majority. *Playboy,* 1978, *March,* 98–100; 197–204.

Negandi, A. R. (Ed.): *Modern organizational theory: Contextual, environmental, and socio-cultural variables.* Kent, OH: Kent State University Press, 1973.

Neilsen, E. H.: Applying a group development model to managing a class. In L. P. Bradford (Ed.), *Group development* (2nd ed.). La Jolla, CA: University Associates Publishers, 1978.

Northen, H.: Social group work: A tool for changing behavior of disturbed acting-out adolescents. In *Social work with groups 1958: Selected papers from the national conference on social welfare.* New York: National Association of Social Workers, 1958.

Osberg, J. W., Berliner, A. K.: The developmental stages in group therapy with hospitalized narcotic addicts. *International Journal of Group Psychotherapy,* 1956, *6,* 436–447.

Ottaway, A. K. C.: *Learning through group experience.* London: Routledge and Kegan Paul, 1966.

Otto, J., Moos, R.: Patient expectations and attendance in community treatment programs. *Community Mental Health Journal,* 1974, *10,* 9–15.

Owen, H.: Avoiding inflation of expectations about détente. *US News and World Report,* 1976(a), *December 27,* 51–52.

Owen, H.: Peace or war. In H. Owen, C. L. Schultze (Eds.), *Setting national priorities: The next ten years.* Washington, DC: The Brookings Institution, 1976(b).

Owen, H., Schultze, C. L.: Introduction. In H. Owen, C. L. Schultze (Eds.), *Setting national priorities: The next ten years.* Washington, DC: The Brookings Institution, 1976.

Page, R. C., Developmental stages of unstructured counseling groups with prisoners. *Small Group Behavior,* 1979, *10,* 271–278.

Palmer, J., McGuire, F. L.: The use of unobtrusive measures in mental health research. *Journal of Consulting and Clinical Psychology,* 1973, *40,* 431–436.

Parsons, T., Bales, R. F., Shils, E. A., *Working papers in the theory of action.* Glencoe, IL: The Free Press, 1953.

Pedigo, J. M., Singer, B.: A psychoanalytic view of group process development. Presented at the Sixth International Congress of Group Psychotherapy, Philadelphia, 1977.

Philp, H., Dunphy, D.: Developmental trends in small groups. *Sociometry,* 1958–1959, *27,* 162–174.

Pierce, R. C., Clark, M. M.: Measurement of morale in the elderly. *Aging and Human Development,* 1973, *4,* 83–101.

Pines, A., Maslach, C.: Characteristics of staff burnout in mental health settings. *Hospital and Community Psychiatry,* 1978, *29,* 233–237.

Powles, W. E.: Psychosexual maturity in a therapy group of disturbed adolescents. *International Journal of Group Psychotherapy,* 1959, *9,* 429–441.

Prasannarao, B.: Morale: A review of researches. *Indian Psychological Review,* 1969, *6,* 37–44.

Psathas, G.: Phase movement and equilibrium tendencies in interaction process in psychotherapy groups. *Sociometry,* 1960, *23,* 177–194.

Reynolds, D. K., Kalish, R. A.: The social ecology of dying: Observations of wards for the terminally ill. *Hospital and Community Psychiatry,* 1974, *25,* 147–152.

Richardson, J.: Morale in clinical medicine. *British Journal of Psychiatry,* 1972, *120,* 593–599.

Rinsley, D. B.: Residential treatment of adolescents. In S. Arieti (Ed.), *American handbook of psychiatry* (Vol. 2). New York: Basic Books, 1974.

Rinsley, D. B.: Personal communication, 1979.

Rioch, M. J.: The work of Wilfred Bion on groups. *Psychiatry,* 1970, *33,* 56–66.

Robinson, L., Seligman, R.: A scale for measuring campus morale. *Journal of Educational Measurement,* 1969, *6,* 109–110.

Rogers, C. R.: *Carl Rogers on encounter groups.* New York: Harper and Row, 1970.

Rosenbaum, L. L., Rosenbaum, W. B.: Morale and productivity consequences of group leadership style, stress, and type of task. *Journal of Applied Psychology,* 1971, *55,* 343–348.

Rosenberg, P., Fuller, M.: Dynamic analysis of the student nurse. *Group Psychotherapy,* 1957, *10,* 22–37.

Ross, M.: Morale in older people. *Journal of the American Geriatric Society,* 1962, *10,* 54–59.

Rothman, A., Marx H.: Expectations versus perceptions of a first year law class. *Journal of Legal Education,* 1974, *26,* 349–362.

Runkel, P. J., Lawrence, M., Oldfield, S., et al.: Stages of group development: An empirical test of Tuckman's hypothesis. *Journal of Applied Behavioral Science,* 1971, *7,* 180–193.

Ryan, T.: Goal-setting in group counselling. *Educational Technology,* 1973, *13,* 19–25.

Saravay, S. M.: Group psychology and the structural theory: A revised psychoanalytic model of group psychology. *Journal of the American Psychoanalytic Association,* 1975, *23,* 69–89.

Saravay, S. M.: A psychoanalytic theory of group development. *International Journal of Group Psychotherapy,* 1978, *28,* 481–507.

Sarri, R. C., Galinsky, M. J.: A conceptual framework for group development. In R. D. Vinter (Ed.), *Readings in group work practice.* Ann Arbor, MI: Campus Publishers, 1967.

Sayles, L. R.: Human relations. In D. L. Sills (Ed.), *International encyclopedia of the social sciences* (Vol. 7). New York: Macmillan, and The Free Press, 1968.

Scheidlinger, S.: The concept of regression in group psychotherapy. *International Journal of Group Psychotherapy,* 1968, *18,* 3–20.

Schmuck, R. A., Schmuck, P. A.: *Group processes in the classroom.* Dubuque, IA: W. C. Brown, 1971.

Schroder, H. M., Harvey, O. J.: Conceptual organization and group structure. In O. J. Harvey (Ed.), *Motivation and social interaction.* New York: Ronald Press, 1963.

Schutz, W. C.: *FIRO: A three-dimensional theory of interpersonal behavior.* Palo Alto, CA: Science and Behavior Books, 1958.

Schutz, W. C.: *Joy: Expanding human awareness.* New York: Grove Press, 1967.

Schutz, W. C.: *Elements of encounter: A body mind approach.* Big Sur, CA: Joy Press, 1973.

Scott, D. F., Moffett, A.: The development of early musical talent in famous composers: A biographical review. In M. Critchley, R. A. Henson (Eds.), *Music and the Brain: Studies in the neurology of music.* Springfield, IL: Charles C. Thomas, 1977.

Selltiz, C., Jahoda, M., Deutsch, M., et al.: *Research methods in social relations* (Rev.). New York: Holt-Rinehart and Winston, 1959.

Selltiz, C., Wrightsman, L. S., Cook, S. W., et al.: *Research methods in social relations* (3rd ed.). New York: Holt, Rinehart and Winston, 1976.

Selye, H.: *The stress of life.* New York: McGraw-Hill Book Company, 1956.

Selye, H.: *Stress without distress.* Philadelphia: J. B. Lippincott, 1974.

Selye, H.: *Stress in health and disease.* Boston: Butterworths, 1976.

Shambaugh, P. W., Kanter, S. S.: Spouses under stress: group meetings with spouses of patients on hemodialysis. *American Journal of Psychiatry,* 1969, *125,* 928–936.

Sheehy, G.: *Passages: Predictable crises of adult life.* New York: E. P. Dutton, 1976.

Shellow, R. S., Ward, J. L., Rubenfeld, S.: Group therapy and the institutionalized delinquent. *International Journal of Group Psychotherapy,* 1958, *8,* 265–275.

Shepard, H. A., Bennis, W. G.: A theory of training by group methods. *Human Relations,* 1956, *9,* 403–413.

Slater, P. E.: *Microcosm: Structural, psychological and religious evolution in groups.* New York: John Wiley and Sons, 1966.

Small Group Behavior, Vol. 7 (1). Beverly Hills, CA: Sage Publications, 1976.

Smith, A. J.: A developmental study of group processes. *Journal of Genetic Psychology,* 1960, *97,* 29–39.

Speck, R. V., Attneave, C. L.: *Family networks.* New York: Pantheon Books, 1973.

Spiegel, D., Yalom, I. D.: A support group for dying patients. *International Journal of Group Psychotherapy,* 1978, *28,* 233–245.

Spitz, H., Sadock, B.: Psychiatric training of graduate nursing students: Use of small interactional groups. *New York State Journal of Medicine,* 1973, *June 1,* 1334–1338.

Spivak, J.: Apathy is NASA's biggest foe. *The Wall Street Journal,* 1977, *February 25,* 12.

Standish, C. T., Semrad, E. V.: Group psychotherapy with psychotics. *Journal of Psychiatric Social Work,* 1951, *20,* 143–150.

Starbuck, W. H.: Organizational growth and development. In J. G. March (Ed.), *Handbook of organizations.* Chicago, Rand McNally, 1965.

Sterba, R.: Metapsychology of morale. *Bulletin of the Menninger Clinic,* 1943, *7,* 69–75.

Stewart, H., Poetter, M. A.: Therapeutic process with adolescents at Anneewakee. *Adolescence,* 1976, *11,* 213–216.

Stock, D.: A survey of research on T-groups. In L. P. Bradford, J. R. Gibb, K. D. Benne (Eds.), *T-group theory and laboratory method.* New York: John Wiley and Sons, 1964.

Stock, D., Lieberman, M. A.: Methodological issues in the assessment of total-group phenomena in group therapy. *International Journal of Group Psychotherapy,* 1962, *12,* 312–325.

Stock, D., Thelen, H. A.: *Emotional dynamics and group culture.* New York: National Training Laboratories, 1958.

Stone, P. J., Bales, R. F., Namenwirth, V. Z., et al.: The general inquirer. *Behavioral Science,* 1962, *7,* 484–498.

Stone, P. J., Dunphy, D. C., Smith, M. S., et al.: *The general inquirer: A computer approach to content analysis.* Cambridge, MA: MIT Press, 1966.

Sutherland, R. L.: An application of the theory of psychosexual development to the learning process. *Bulletin of the Menninger Clinic,* 1951, *15,* 91–99.

Thelen, H. A., Dickerman, W.: Stereotypes and the growth of groups. *Educational Leadership,* 1949, *6,* 309–316.

Theodorson, G. A.: Elements in the progressive development of small groups. *Social Forces,* 1953, *31,* 311–320.

Thorpe, J. J., Smith, B.: Phases in group development in the treatment of drug addicts. *International Journal of Group Psychotherapy,* 1953, *3,* 66–78.

Tindall, J. H.: *A comparative procedural descriptive analysis of the time limited and time extended encounter groups.* Doctoral dissertation. Washington, DC: American University, 1971.

Tompkins, D. S.: *Group effectiveness as a function of leadership style mode-*

rated by stage of group development. Doctoral dissertation. Columbus, OH: Ohio State University, 1972.

Trecker, H. B.: *Social group work: Principles and practice* (Rev.). New York: Associated Press, 1955.

Trow, W. C., Zander, A. E., Morse, W. C., et al.: Psychology of group behavior: The class as a group. *Journal of Educational Psychology,* 1950, *41,* 322–338.

Tucker, D. M.: Some relationships between individual and group development. *Human Development,* 1973, *16,* 249–272.

Tuckman, B. W.: Developmental sequence in small groups. *Psychological Bulletin,* 1965, *63,* 384–399.

Tuckman, B. W., Jensen, M. A. C.: Stages of small group development revisited. *Group and Organizational Studies,* 1977, *2,* 419–427.

Tyhurst, J. S.: The role of transition stages—including disasters—in mental illness. In *Symposium on preventive and social psychiatry.* Washington, DC: US Government Printing Office, 1958.

Udy, S.: Comparative analysis of organizations. In J. G. March (Ed.), *Handbook of organizations.* Chicago: Rand McNally, 1965.

United Press International: Hopes too high Carter's aides say. *Topeka Daily Capital,* 1978, *April 13,* 11.

Vaillant, G. E.: *Adaptation to life.* Boston: Little, Brown, 1977.

Viteles, M. S.: *Motivation and morale in industry.* New York: W. W. Norton, 1953.

Wanous, J. P.: Effects of a realistic job preview on job acceptance, job attitudes, and job survival. *Journal of Applied Psychology,* 1973, *58,* 327–332.

Webb, E. J., Campbell, D. T., Schwartz, R. D., et al.: *Unobtrusive measures: Nonreactive research in the social sciences.* Chicago: Rand McNally, 1966.

Weick, K. E.: Systematic observational methods. In G. Lindzey, E. Aronson (Eds.), *Handbook of social psychology* (2nd ed., Vol. 2). Reading, MA: Addison-Wesley, 1968.

Weiner, I. B.: *Principles of psychotherapy.* New York: John Wiley and Sons, 1975.

Whitaker, D. S., Lieberman, M. A.: *Psychotherapy through the group process.* New York: Atherton Press–Prentice-Hall, 1964.

Whitaker, D. S., Thelen, H. A.: Emotional dynamics and group culture. In M. Rosenbaum, M. M. Berger (Eds.), *Group psychotherapy and group function* (Rev. ed.). New York: Basic Books, 1975.

White, R., Lippitt, R.: Leader behavior and member reaction in three "social climates." In D. Cartwright, A. Zander (Eds.), *Group dynamics: Research and theory* (2nd ed.). Evanston, IL: Row Peterson, 1960.

Whitlock, G. H.: *The status of morale measurement, 1959.* USAF Personnel Laboratory Technical Report, WADD-TN-60-136, Lackland Air Force Base, TX: American Psychological Association, 1960.

Whittaker, J. K.: Models of group development: Implications for social group work practice. *Social Service Review,* 1970, *44,* 308–322.

Winter, S. K.: Interracial dynamics in self-analytic groups. In G. S. Gibbard, J. J. Hartman, R. D. Mann (Eds.), *Analysis of groups.* San Francisco: Jossey-Bass, 1974.

Winter, S. K.: Developmental stages in the roles and concerns of group co-leaders. *Small Group Behavior,* 1976, *7,* 349–362.

Wise, T.: Utilization of group process in training oncology fellows. *International Journal of Group Psychotherapy,* 1977, *27,* 105–111.

Wnuk, J. J.: Morale: An additional approach. *Personnel Journal,* 1966, *45,* 220–223.

Wogan, M., Chinsky, J. M., Schoeplein, R. N.: Stages of group development in an experimental ghetto program. *American Journal of Orthopsychiatry,* 1971, *41,* 659–671.

Wogan, M., Getter, H., Amdur, M. J., et al.: Influencing interaction and outcomes in group psychotherapy. *Small Group Behavior,* 1977, *8,* 25–46.

Wolberg, L. R.: *The technique of psychotherapy* (3rd ed.). New York: Grune and Stratton, 1977.

Yalom, I. D.: *The theory and practice of group psychotherapy.* New York: Basic Books, 1970.

Yalom, I. D.: *The theory and practice of group psychotherapy* (2nd ed.). New York: Basic Books, 1975.

Yalom, I. D., Houts, P. S., Newell, G.: Preparation of patients for group therapy: A controlled study. *Archives of General Psychiatry,* 1967, *17,* 416–427.

Yalom, I. D., Lieberman, M. A.: A study of encounter group casualties. *Archives of General Psychiatry,* 1971, *25,* 16–30.

Yalom, I. D., Moos, R.: The use of small interactional groups in the teaching of psychiatry. *International Journal of Group Psychotherapy,* 1965, *15,* 242–246.

Zenger, J. H.: A comparison of human development with psychological development in T-groups. *Training Development Journal,* 1970, *24,* 16–20.

Zinberg, N. E., Boris, H. N., Boris, M.: *Teaching social change: A group approach.* Baltimore: Johns Hopkins University Press, 1976.

Zurcher, L. A. Jr.: Stages of development in poverty program neighborhood action committees. *Journal of Applied Behavioral Science,* 1969, *15,* 223–258.

Zwerski, E. L.: The oversell: A major pitfall in college recruitment. *Personnel Journal,* 1966, *15,* 167–168.

NAME INDEX

SUBJECT INDEX